Loeb Classical Monographs
In Memory of James C. Loeb

The Transmission of the Text of Lucan in the Ninth Century

Harold C. Gotoff

Harvard University Press
Cambridge, Massachusetts
1971

© Copyright 1971 by the President and Fellows of Harvard College
All rights reserved
Distributed in Great Britain by Oxford University Press, London

The Loeb Classical Monographs are published with assistance
from the Loeb Classical Library Foundation.

Library of Congress Catalog Card Number 72-133212
SBN 674-90466-4
Printed in the United States of America

To my parents
*for whose concern, patience, and generosity
this work is but a small return*

Acknowledgments

I should like to thank the authorities of the Institut de Recherche et d'Histoire des Textes for supplying me with microfilms and photographs. I am grateful, too, to Dr. Claudio Leonardi of the Vatican Library and to Dr. K. A. de Meyier of the University Library of Leiden for dating and describing manuscripts of Lucan in their respective libraries. My especial thanks are due to Professor Bernhard Bischoff, who provided me with the dates and provenances of the ninth-century manuscripts of Lucan. I must also express my gratitude to the board of the Canady Fund at Harvard University and to the Department of the Classics at Harvard for generous grants toward the completion of this book.

If I were to mention the scholars who have at one time or another read this work, either in its original form as a doctoral dissertation or in progress toward its present state, the reader would have a right to expect a more accomplished result. I cannot omit the names of two students and colleagues, Mr. James Zetzel, for helping to assemble the appendices, and Mr. Robert Rodgers, for proofreading the entire text.

My debt to the patience and perspicacity of Mrs. Cedric Whitman, who gave editorial guidance and advice, is sincere and profound.

Finally, I should like to express my gratitude and acknowledge my debt to Professor Wendell Clausen, my teacher, colleague, and friend, whose help from the earliest stages of this study to its completion has been invaluable.

Contents

Conspectus Siglorum	xi
A Note on Abbreviations	xii
Chapter I: Introduction	1
Chapter II: The Manuscripts	11
Chapter III: The Assessment of the Manuscripts by Modern Editors	27
Chapter IV: Re-examination of M and Z	44
Chapter V: Re-examination of ABR	59
Chapter VI: Conclusion	95
Appendix I: The Added Leaves in A	99
Appendix II: The Scholia in R	102
Appendix III: On the Relationship of F to M and Z	108
Appendix IV: Readings Originating in Z^2	111
Appendix V: Readings Originating in A	137
Appendix VI: Readings Originating in A^2	143
Appendix VII: The Readings of A^v	154
Appendix VIII: Readings Originating in B	179
Appendix IX: Readings Originating in R	193
Diagram of the manuscript tradition of Lucan in the ninth century	97

Conspectus Siglorum

M	Montepessulanus H 113	ix 2/4m
Z	Parisinus bibl. publ. 10314	ix 2/4
Z²	correctiones in codice Z factae	ix 2/4m
A	Parisinus bibl. publ. "nouv. acq." 1626	ix 2/4m
A²	correctiones in codice A factae	ix m
Aᵛ	uariae lectiones in codice A scriptae	ix m
B	Bernensis 45	ix m3/4
R	Montepessulanus H 362	ix 4/4
F	Parisinus bibl. publ. 10403	ix 2/4
Y	Leidensis Vossianus Q 16	x
Q	Parisinus bibl. publ. 7900 A	ix–x
G	Bruxellensis bibl. Burgundicae 5330–5332	x
U	Leidensis Vossianus F 63	x
V	Leidensis Vossianus Q 51	x
P	Parisinus bibl. publ. 7502	x
E	Parisinus bibl. publ. 9346	xi
W	Vaticanus Reginensis 1634	xi–xii
J	Vaticanus Ottobonianus 1210 et Vaticanus Palatinus 869	xii
N	Vindobonensis 16 et Neapolitanus iv A 8, cod. rescripti frag.	iv
S	Vaticanus Palatinus 24, cod. rescripti frag.	iv–v
C	lemma codicis Bernensis 370 uel Commentorum Bernensium	ix–x
c	lectio Commentorum Bernensium a lemmate discrepans	
adn.	lectio Adnotationum super Lucanum	

Abbreviations

The superscript (^{2}) following a siglum will in general designate a corrected reading, but not one particular corrector. In the case of Z^2 and A^2, however, the correction can be limited in time.

The superscript (^{v}) will be used occasionally to show further support for a reading in the form of a variant introduced by *uel* or *aliter*. No date is assumed for the addition of such variants, except in the case of A^v, whose collation was made in the middle of the ninth century.

I have used the notations *cett.* and *rell.* indiscriminately, whether the note be in Latin or English, the former on the left side of a division of readings, the latter on the right. Each refers to all the manuscripts not cited individually.

(?) following a siglum indicates that the state of the text is such as to deny complete certainty to a presumed reading.

n.l. = *non liquet*
d. = *deest* or *desunt*
l.o. = *uersum om.*
u.o. = *uerbum om.*

Constant reference is made to single works of each of four scholars, for which I use the following abbreviations:

Hosius   C. Hosius, *M. Annaei Lucani Belli Civilis Libri Decem*, 3rd ed. (Leipzig 1913)
Housman   A. E. Housman, *M. Annaei Lucani Belli Civilis Libri Decem* (Oxford 1926)
Lejay   P. Lejay, *M. Annaei Lucani de Bello Civili Liber Primus* (Paris 1894)
Beck   F. Beck, *Untersuchungen zu den Handschriften Lucans* (Munich 1900)

*The Transmission
of the Text of Lucan
in the Ninth Century*

Chapter I
Introduction

Five complete manuscripts of Lucan written in the first hundred years of the Carolingian awakening have survived the centuries to be discovered and preserved by modern scholars. So closely interrelated are these manuscripts, however, so redundant is their evidence, that, of the five, two are disused and a third nowhere fully reported by editors. Yet, a closer examination reveals that each of these five is a source of independent information, stored in some cases in the text, in some cases between the lines and in the margins. Furthermore, when the precise relationships among the five are defined and understood, it is possible to gain a clearer picture of the way texts were copied and corrected in the ninth century. The phenomenon of related though independent manuscripts can be explained by reference to the condition of the text in antiquity and the descent of that text into the early Middle Ages. The use that modern editors have made of these manuscripts bears witness to the principles and attitudes of textual critics of the nineteenth and twentieth centuries.

So early and so full is the manuscript evidence for the text of Lucan that the editor is faced with a task not dissimilar to that of an editor of Virgil; he can select the true reading rather than conjecture it. Lucan was widely read and carefully studied in the final centuries of the Empire. Popular for its highly rhetorical style and of historical interest as an account of the Civil War, his epic became a pagan schooltext. Witness to this are the sets of ancient commentary that go by the names of the *Commenta Bernensia* and the *Adnotationes super Lucanum*. While I argue later (in Appendix II) that these may not represent two independent bodies of ancient scholia, their very presence speaks unmistakably for the interest scholars in the fifth and sixth centuries had in Lucan. He takes his place beside Terence, Virgil, Juvenal, and Persius as a favorite pagan author.[1]

The popularity of an author created a demand for manuscripts and the frequent copying of his text. Centers of scholarship would not be limited to a single manuscript, and the interest of scholars in fuller and more correct texts guaranteed a certain amount of interchange of manuscripts. When a text was read carefully, the errors and confusions of particular manuscripts came under the correcting hands of scribes and scholars. Further, manuscripts were compared with one another and again corrected and changed on the basis of that comparison. This process, the introduction of divergent readings from one text into another, is known as contamination and has serious consequences for any text it affects. The copy of a manuscript thus altered would in many important respects diverge from its predecessor once removed; and those individual characteristics that might otherwise allow scholars to isolate and distinguish strains of the tradition would be lost or distorted. In terms of the usual genetic metaphor, characteristics would not only be inherited by vertical descent but acquired as well by horizontal cross-fertilization. But the same popularity that gives rise to contamination also guarantees a widespread currency for the variants introduced into, and expelled from, manuscripts almost mechanically by successive correctors. This process and the consequent presence of a large number of alternative readings are easier to imagine than the process by which *Parin: Paris* was lost entirely from the textual tradition of Virgil at 10.705 and replaced by *Parin creat*.[2] Where one or a few manuscripts represent an author through the course of history, our knowledge of that author depends on the accuracy and fullness of the limited source. Such is the case of Catullus; and hundreds of conjectures are accepted in modern editions of that brief text. For our knowledge of Lucan we are not so limited. The tradition is contaminated, but the evidence for the text is very nearly complete.

Contaminated traditions are, after all, the rule, rather than the exception, for the texts of Latin authors. The tradition of the manuscripts of Lucretius is congenial to the orderly and consistent reconstruction described by Maas[3] to an

---

[1] This is nowhere explicitly stated. Lucan's popularity in antiquity, however, is attested. Suetonius *Lucani uita ad fin.*: *poemata eius etiam praelegi memini*. Jerome *Adv. Ruf.* 1.16: *puto quod puer legeris Aspri in Vergilium et Sallustium commentarios . . . et aliorum in alios, Plautum uidelicet, Lucretium, Flaccum, Persium, et Lucanum*. Also Martial 14.194.

[2] I assume that Bentley's emendation is almost universally accepted.

[3] P. Maas, *Textual Criticism* (transl. Barbara Flower, Oxford 1958).

Introduction

extent that few others are; but what this indicates is that Lucretius must have been at least relatively unpopular and ignored in the final centuries of the Empire.[4] Pasquali's chapter "Varianti antiche e antiche edizioni" is far more responsive to the textual tradition of classical authors than is Maas's account.[5] Most of the significant variants in contaminated traditions are ancient; frequently they are also found in the citations of grammarians or recorded by pagan scholiasts, as for example, in the *Commenta Bernensia* to Lucan 1.416: *DVCAT aliter tollat*. Already in the fragments of early manuscripts in capital script, some less good but easier readings are found in the text.

We also have, among other such pieces of evidence, the explicit word of a pagan scholar in a subscription found in a number of manuscripts of Livy, NICOMACHVS DEXTER V. C. EMENDAVI AD EXEMPLVM PARENTIS MEI CLEMENTIANI, that he corrected his book by comparing it with another manuscript. Something of the activity of pagan scholars in the correction and transmission of texts can be learned from a study of such subscriptions. The subject has been dealt with masterfully by Otto Jahn,[6] who distinguishes three kinds of statement in such notices. Some scholars, like Nicomachus Dexter above, acknowledge the use of a second manuscript; others state plainly that they made their corrections freehand, *sine antigrapho* or *mea manu solus*; the rest do not specify their source of correction. The meaning of the usual word in subscriptions for making corrections, *emendare*, has been variously explained but cannot be defined with precision. Talent as well as industry must have varied in different correctors. In some cases, only the most rudimentary changes by a rather casual reader may be meant, but Quintilian's use of the word (9.4.74) suggests that correction in other cases may have been extensive: *sed initia initiis non conuenient, ut Liuius hexametri exordio coepit:* "*Facturusne operae pretium sim*" (*nam ita edidit, estque id melius quam quo modo emendatur*). Without exception the manuscripts of Livy read *Facturusne sim operae pretium*. Somewhere between these two extremes of correction may be listed the changing of a sound but difficult passage, deliberate simplification, and the improvement of a corrupt passage which nevertheless fails to restore the words of the author. Beyond this,

---

[4] The citation from Jerome in n. 1 above indicates that Lucretius retained his popularity into the fourth century. The loss of interest in him, as indicated by his textual tradition, may not be merely coincidental with the ascendancy of Christianity.

[5] G. Pasquali, *Storia della tradizione e critica del testo* (Florence 1952).

[6] O. Jahn, "Über die Subscriptionen in den Handschriften römischer Klassiker," *Berichte über die Verhandl. der kön. sächs. Gesellsch. der Wiss. zu Leipzig, phil.- hist.* Kl. (1851) 327-372.

interlinear glosses—synonyms or explanations of words—may in future transcriptions descend into the text itself and replace the readings they were intended to elucidate. With all these hazards it becomes clear that the forthright and modest acknowledgment of subscriptions, *emendaui* or *legi et emendaui*, may be the confession of large-scale and sometimes untraceable changes in the text.

These, then, are the causes of variation in a manuscript. When such variations are preserved in the simple descent of a text through copying, they become isolated in one branch of the tradition of that text; an editor will, then, find it possible to discover most of the deviations by comparison of manuscripts exhibiting these peculiarities with other manuscripts of the work that are not descended from the same source. When, on the other hand, manuscripts were compared and corrected in antiquity, with variant readings transferred from one book to another, a certain number of the variants would in the next transcription replace the original readings. By this process manuscripts would, in a short time, lose their character, that is, the resemblance to the manuscripts from which they formally, or vertically, descend and represent, as Housman put it (p. vii), not families but factions. This is precisely what occurred in the late Empire with popular authors like Lucan. The ancient manuscripts were by and large contaminated; and medieval manuscripts copied from such books would necessarily inherit the contamination and allow no confidence that the text they contain has any claim to a pure, vertical descent from the author's time. It may even be suspected that scholars of the Empire working on classical authors gathered together available manuscripts in much the same way in which Alexandrian scholars did and that vulgate editions with interlinear variants were produced.[7] It is in any case not improbable that the earliest Carolingian manuscripts of authors popular in antiquity were copied from exemplars containing some variants and corrections.

While by this process an uncontaminated tradition would be precluded, a second result is that very little of the evidence needed to establish the text of an author so treated would be wholly lost; with an abundance of evidence the truth is more likely to be preserved amidst the variations, and the editor's task would consist more of sifting what is before him than restoring what is not. In the case of Lucan, difficulty in following the poet's diction and his use of rheto-

---

[7] In some cases it may be almost impossible to get any closer to an author than ancient scholarly editions. F. Leo, *Plautinische Forschungen* (Berlin 1912) 50ff, suggests that we might have to content ourselves with the text of Plautus as it existed in the second century A.D.

Introduction

rical devices has occasioned a greater number of changes in the text than is demanded by any inadequacy of the manuscript evidence. A. E. Housman, never one to bow before the authority of manuscripts, acknowledges as much in the preface to his edition of Lucan (p. xxvi): "The text of Lucan contains about 48,000 words; and an editor who sees cause to alter only 60 or so, 1 in 800, professes thereby that it is good." There is something perhaps slightly unsettling in so statistical an approach by a textual critic, but it has the force of demonstrating the fullness of the evidence. That this evidence was preserved in such a way that we can put little prima facie reliance on any particular manuscript that carries it was also understood by Housman (p. vii):

> The five manuscripts on which we chiefly depend ZPGUV cannot be divided and united into families or even classes. The circumstances in which Lucan's text was transmitted from his time to the scholars of the Carolingian renascence did not afford the requisite privacy and isolation. There were no sequestered valleys through which streams of tradition might flow unmixed, and the picture to be set before the mind's eye is rather the Egyptian Delta, a network of watercourses and canals. Lucan was popular; variant readings were present not only in the margin of books but in the memory of transcribers; and the line of division is between the variants themselves, not between the manuscripts which offer them. The manuscripts group themselves not in families but in factions; their dissidences and agreements are temporary and transient, like the splits and coalitions of political party; and the utmost which can be done to classify them is to note the comparative frequency of their shifting alliances.

While this assessment of the textual tradition of Lucan is in large part correct, it cannot be accepted without qualification.

Passing over the dubious assumption that transcribers consciously emended the texts they were copying, and leaving in abeyance the avowal of the first sentence that ZPGUV are the manuscripts on which we chiefly depend, we may note that Housman permits himself one confusion which deprives his contention of much of its importance. While the text of Lucan was contaminated in antiquity and while the capital manuscripts from which the extant Carolingian manuscripts descend had undergone the process of correction, it is not true that the Carolingian manuscripts are incapable of classification, only that they cannot necessarily be traced back further than to late antiquity. And while

The Text of Lucan in the Ninth Century

the manuscripts from which medieval books descend may have undergone correction, it is not necessarily true that they all suffered equally by this process. The acknowledgment that the Pithoeanus of Juvenal is superior to any other manuscript of that author does not mean that it descends from an uncontaminated ancient manuscript; on the contrary, though justly respected, it contains interpolations. Rather it descends from a manuscript that was less thoroughly vulgarized by the process that caused the much greater loss of individuality in the other medieval manuscripts of Juvenal.[8] In the case of Lucan, all five of our ninth-century manuscripts and the fragmentary remains of a sixth, MZABRF, are closely related to each other; and I suspect, though I have not studied them all, that many of the tenth- and eleventh-century manuscripts, in particular the Paris manuscripts first used by Lejay, are descended from one or another of the extant ninth-century books. I shall cite throughout this study the readings of a Leiden manuscript of the tenth century (Y), previously only partially reported, to show its often close resemblance to MZABR. QGUVP cannot be closely related to each other or to the rest, though by the time that M was copied, the mutilated exemplar of the main portion of its text was housed in the same scriptorium (at Orléans, perhaps) as a manuscript antecedent to P. Z^2, the correctors of Z whose date can now be determined as about the middle of the ninth century, had at their disposal a manuscript agreeing in some of its peculiarities with a source of G. In selecting six manuscripts on which to base his text, Housman does not reflect the lack of interrelation among the extant ninth- and tenth-century manuscripts but rather creates the appearance of a chaos in which he delighted, since for some reason he felt that it gave him a freer hand as an editor and emendator. Yet it can be plausibly argued that the kind of transmission he envisaged is, in theory at least, more restrictive to the emendator.

Hosius, on the other hand, belonged to a class of editors who, influenced as it would seem by Lachmann's *Lucretius*, tried to force upon textual traditions an order not permitted by the character of their transmission. His tendency to elevate one manuscript to the position of *codex optimus* was, however, an attempt not to shirk his duty but to have, where possible, a scientific basis for judgment and preference. While no manuscript of Lucan is so far superior to the others as to be consistently reliable, Housman's contention that no manuscript has any

---

[8] W. Clausen, *A. Persi Flacci et D. Iuni Iuuenalis Saturae* (Oxford 1959), stated the case too strongly when he said of Pithoeanus (p. xii) *casu accidit ut grammaticorum curam prope solus, quod sciamus, falleret codex ille unde Pithoeanus eiusque adfines originem duxerunt*. It is comparatively much freer of contamination.

Introduction

more intrinsic value than another is also an oversimplification. That he had to hand only Hosius' reports of the manuscripts is not a mitigating circumstance, but a self-imposed limitation. His overriding desire to make the tradition suit his purposes further detracts from his assessment of the manuscript evidence. His treatment of M is a major case in point (p. x):

> The reader had been starving this long while for news of M, which, they tell him, is "*codex optimus*" and "die führende Handschrift" and so forth; and he wonders how soon he is to hear again such honeyed words as "die Vorzüglichkeit von M, dem Hauptvertreter der"—never mind what. Well, it is M's turn now ... M is a manuscript whose text falls into three parts derived from three separate sources. Through more than seven books, I 483–IX 85, M is twin brother of Z. From IX 86 to X 546, the end of the poem, it is twin brother of P, though as P breaks off at X 107 the relationship is not demonstrable beyond that point. From I 1–482 it has no alliance with any manuscript, but stands about half-way between Z and U, which are generally opposed to one another.

This account of M's contents will be discussed and somewhat modified later. Housman's motive was to demolish Hosius' *codex optimus*; but, having rhetorically accomplished this purpose, he in no way disposes with M. Though he fails to mention it in the preface, Housman must acknowledge in his apparatus criticus a significant number of places in the text between 1.483 and 9.85 where M and Z disagree and each has the support of unrelated manuscripts. How this came about and what it might mean for the text were not concerns of Housman; but the evidence of his apparatus criticus makes it clear that the inconsistency was not unknown to him. He preferred to rail against a manuscript (p. xiii): "This sovereign codex may therefore be called a king of shreds and patches, and its devotees, believing themselves good unitarians, have been engaged in worshipping a trinity. Of all the manuscripts it is the one we could best dispense with."

This performance must be said to owe more to a flair for the dramatic and an inclination toward the polemical than to that "moral integrity and intellectual vigilance which are for them [i.e. emendators] not merely duties but necessities" (Housman, p. xxvii). In spite of its bastard origins, acutely exposed by Housman, M is an important manuscript and one indispensable for the constitution of the text. The slighting of M and the manuscripts in general was Housman's peculiar contribution to the study of the transmission of Lucan's

The Text of Lucan in the Ninth Century

text. Rather than attempt to understand the nature of the evidence, he preferred to ignore it. It would be relevant to ask an editor with such an attitude why he bothers to provide an apparatus criticus.[9]

Each in his own way, Hosius and Housman failed to give the reader what he can reasonably expect from the editor of a critical edition—a clear, comprehensive indication of the evidence for the constitution of that text and some notion of the transmission of the text in the period from which the evidence comes. Neither saw that the problem in evaluating the earliest medieval evidence is briefly this: manuscripts formally related to each other contain readings independent of each other. It was this failure to distinguish between two criteria for classifying manuscripts that confused the accounts of the tradition by all modern editors of Lucan.

On the basis of omitted lines, transpositions, and other formal criteria, like the subscription of Paulus Constantinopolitanus, the manuscripts divide in certain ways. At any given context where a variant reading is recorded, the division may be quite different. To point out this distinction and the confusion that results from a failure to notice it, I shall cite the argument of Bourgery, the editor of the Budé *Lucan*.[10] On p. xii in a footnote on Z, he says, "Généralement ZM ne font en quelque sorte qu'un manuscrit, sauf à partir de IX où les divergences sont nombreuses." But in appraising the contribution of Paulus Constantinopolitanus, whose subscription appears in MPU but not in Z, he adduces the following argument. At 4.677 where the text should read

> Autololes Numidaeque uagi semperque paratus
> inculto Gaetulus equo, tum concolor Indo
> Maurus

Bourgery has the following note: *uersum inde a* q; uagi *z in ras. sub qua* lor indo *dispici potest* semper que paratus *in ras.* m *om.* PU^1Q 678 *om.* M^1Z^1 *add.* m et ... z. Of this situation he says (p. xv, n. 1):

> ... le copiste de l'archétype de MZPU avait dû écrire *Autololes Numidaequo tum concolor Indo*. L'altération était manifeste, mais d'où vient la restitution de *que uagi* qui est dans MPU? D'une collation avec un autre manuscrit? Mais alors le copiste se serait aperçu que la lacune était plus étendue. Ne

---

[9] The form and function of an apparatus often present problems that are not faced by editors. They are peculiar to the author and the tradition, but for an excellent approach see E. J. Kenney, *P. Ouidi Nasonis Amores etc.* (Oxford 1961) p. xi and appendix.

[10] A. Bourgery, *Lucain, La Guerre Civile* (Paris 1962) 2 vols.

Introduction

peut-on pas croire qu'ici un erudit perspicace a amendé le texte sans l'aide des manuscrits ? Et qui, sinon Paul de Constantinople ? Si notre hypothèse était admise on en conclurait : 1° Que Paul a bien apporté des corrections au texte ; 2° Que Z n'appartient pas à la recension paulienne ; 3° Que M au contraire s'y rattache. Dans tous les cas, M, comme PU, représente un état du texte plus récent que Z.

Whatever else may be learned from the state of the manuscripts at 4.677–678, it cannot be that Z and M, which "ne font en quelque sorte qu'un manuscrit," belong to different recensions.[11]

The fact is that the closest formal relationships are no guarantee against the disagreement of two manuscripts in places where the tradition offers two readings. While the formal interrelationship of the five ninth-century manuscripts is undeniable, it does not preclude the possession by any of them of information not found in the others. The horizontal process of cross-reference is at work as well as vertical descent. The ninth-century manuscripts we have are examples of a continuing process of copying, correcting against other manuscripts, and recopying. What is remarkable about MZABR is that, with all the corrections, they behave in many ways as a group. Their combined testimony gives more evidence than is likely to have been included in a single ancient manuscript, no matter how extensively corrected; yet a considerable number of correct and/or ancient readings are omitted from all five. MZAB are united by more than 850 common errors. With R, some of these errors are corrected and a number of variants appear, in the chronology of the extant manuscripts, for the first time: R will be shown to have been influenced by a type of manuscript formally different from MZAB, one which contained scholia. By and large, freehand correction, even of the most obvious errors,

---

[11] The state of the text at 4.677–678 is as follows: *semperque...equo* is omitted by MQUP. It is not commented on in either set of scholia. The phrase is added by correctors in MU. In Z -*que uagi semperque paratus* is written in an erasure by Z², who added 678 at the bottom of the page. ABRYGVEWJ have 677–678 complete. Bourgery assumes from the erasure that Z had *Autolopes Numidaequo tum concolor Indo*, that he got this from his exemplar, that MUP (and presumably Q) derive from the same erroneous source but that in their case an intermediary was corrected conjecturally to *Autolopes Numidaeque uagi tum concolor Indo*. Aside from the fact that an error like the slipping of the scribe's eye from -*que* in one line to *quo* in the next is mechanical and should not be adduced to prove a relationship between manuscripts, Bourgery should not have decided on the basis of an erasure what Z read. In this case it is simpler to assume that Z originally had precisely what MQUP read and that Z² began his erasure prematurely.

cannot be proved by the Lucan manuscripts to have been practiced in the ninth century. While some obvious corruptions may have been corrected without reference to another manuscript, the number of impossible readings entered into texts by correctors indicates that they were misreading or slavishly following mistakes in other manuscripts. Thus the ninth-century manuscripts more faithfully preserve the evidence, whereas QGUVP and even R have a more comprehensible text. More often than not, when a variant appears for the first time in R, it is inferior to the reading of MZ. To compare the textual tradition of Lucan with that of Juvenal, the common traits of MZAB more closely resemble the Pithoeanus than the other, more highly contaminated manuscripts of Juvenal. In both traditions contamination is a relative force; no manuscript is wholly free of it. No manuscript of Lucan has the singular worth of the Pithoeanus. MZAB are distinguished by the tolerance of much that is corrupt, but by the relatively high exclusion of *lectiones faciliores*.

With this new evaluation of MZABR and the fragment F and a fresh consideration of the evidence they provide, a different and more detailed understanding of the *paradosis* of Lucan's poem will emerge. I believe that the editor of Lucan who uses the ninth-century manuscripts according to their merits will be able to indicate in his apparatus criticus, much more fully than has up to now been the case, the evidence on which the text of *De Bello Ciuili* rests.

Chapter II
The Manuscripts

Before tracing in any more detail the steps by which the prevailing assessment of the manuscript tradition of Lucan was reached, it will be necessary to describe the manuscripts.

Z

Parisinus bibl. publ. lat. 10314 is described by Bischoff as being "saec. ix 2/4 oder Mitte, wohl linksrheinisch, zwischen West und Ost."[1] It contains the text of Lucan on ff. 1r–139v, in single columns, with an almost invariable twenty-nine lines to a page.

Z is the production of a large number of scribes. Up to f. 43, where a blank verso indicates that the model was broken up for simultaneous copying and that one scribe's portion ended before he could fill the last page, the situation is as follows. One scribe copied ff. 1–8v. His assignment seems to have contained more than the 464 lines that were ruled for his gathering, for beginning on f. 8r he wrote verses 408–468 as if in prose, continuing to the right-hand ruled margin, often ending the line in the middle of a word and occasionally even capitalizing the first letter of the next line when it was in the middle of a word. Folio 8v ends at 1.475, and a second scribe began the second gathering with 476 at f. 9r. He continued to f. 17r, line 3, where a third scribe took over at line

---

[1] I am extremely grateful to Professor Bischoff, who, in advance of his catalogue of ninth-century manuscripts, supplied me with his descriptions of the early manuscripts of Lucan. His kindness no less than his unsurpassed knowledge allowed me, amidst the intricacies of the textual tradition, this base of certainty.

The Text of Lucan in the Ninth Century

4 and went on to the end of f. 18r. There the second scribe returned and copied two leaves to the end of f. 19r, where the third scribe resumed copying to the end of f. 21v, the last leaf of the third gathering. At f. 22r a fourth scribe made his first appearance and became the copyist until on f. 30, line 20, a fifth scribe relieved him, but only until f. 31r, where the fourth scribe came back for another two leaves to f. 32v, line 14. The fifth scribe reentered at line 15 and remained on the job until the end of the sixth gathering, f. 43r, line 8, at 4.305. At f. 44r a sixth scribe appeared. No fewer than four more scribes seem to have shared the copying of the remainder of the manuscript.

The model was broken up at 8.742, for a scribe of Z, by skipping ruled lines on the recto and verso of f. 108, disposes forty-six verses over fifty-eight ruled lines to end at 8.742. A new scribe continued at f. 109r. Again on f. 130v, the last page of the seventeenth gathering, there are only twenty-two lines to 10.49, arguing for still another division of the exemplar, especially since there is a change of copyist at f. 131r. The several divisions of the model of Z seem to indicate that speed in copying was of the essence.

Z omits 10.287–317 from 135r and v, which begins with 10.282. In the margin, however, the note *quod hic deest inuenies in nouissimo loco et in fine decimi libri ubi est signum ueru* θ directs the reader to the missing lines, which follow the explicit to book 10 in the hand of the scribe who finished the text of the poem.

Marginalia and glosses stop abruptly after f. 6r, 1.329.

Z omits the following lines (I underline those omitted also by M, a closely related manuscript, and bracket those missing in at least one independent manuscript): 1.37, (436–440); 2.5, 31, 316, 446–448, 463–464, 727; 3.(146), 211, (167–168), 608; 4.(78), 171, (251), 677b–678a; 5.810; 6.22–24, (152), (188), (207), 296, 418, 562, 804, (816); 7.90, (103), (154), (200), (257–258), 607, 725, (747), (796), (820–822); 8.117, (124), 285, 306, 503; 9.35, (83), (87), (100), 201b–202a, (253–254), 256, 306–308, 362, 365–367, 375, 386, 477, (494), 579, 608, 612, (615), (664), 697, (924), 1014; 10.(8), 25, 296.

Z^2

Z is distinguished by extensive contemporary correction. From the general nature of the correction, especially the addition of many of the lines omitted in MZ, it is obvious that Z was compared with one or more other manuscripts. Like

The Manuscripts

the copying of the text, correction in Z was performed by a number of hands, some identical to those of the text. While diverse correcting hands might at first suggest diverse sources of correction, the number of scribes who took part in the copying of Z makes it less unlikely per se that Z^2 represents a single book. Further, in a negative way, the nature of the correction is uniform. That is to say, in no section more than in any other does Z^2 resemble any particular extant manuscript of Lucan. The siglum Z^2 may at least be limited in date to corrections made in the middle of the ninth century, for, as will be shown, we have another manuscript, A, that was copied from Z at about that time. On the basis of those corrections that are reflected in A, Z^2 can be recognized and limited to a terminus ante quem. The fact emerges from internal evidence that Z was corrected, in places at least, more than once before the manuscript was copied by A. At 2.31, Z omitted the line. Z^2 added it with *lumine* (RW), which is corrected by erasure to *limine*, found in ABrell. At 8.3, Z omitted the final word, which, in fact, he added to the next line in the form *(turbat) negandi*. Z^2 added in line 3 *negante*, perhaps shared by R, which may be a confusion of *negantem*, the reading of most of the manuscripts. But another corrector of Z, Z^{2b}, changed the word to *neganti*, which is also found in ABM. Similarly, at 7.739, where the final word of the line is clear in neither M nor Z, Z^2 had *uacabant*. This was corrected to *uacabo* by Z^{2b} and followed by AB. The reading is shared by QUVEW against *uocabo* YGPJ. This is the full extent of demonstrable corrections of Z^2 by a second hand prior to the copying of A. Since in neither case is Z^{2a}'s correction traditional, it is possible that Z^{2b} is the same scribe correcting himself, though I have noticed none of this elsewhere among scribes or correctors in the ninth century. By attributing the corrections of Z^2 to a single manuscript, I may be oversimplifying the situation. It is more convenient to think of the collation of Z^2 that is found in Appendix IV as the reconstruction of a single lost manuscript, though it may in fact be a collection of readings from several correcting manuscripts. The real benefit to be derived from employing the siglum Z^2 to represent a particular manuscript is that we may, as a result, consider those readings as deriving from a source that came into contact with Z at a particular time. It has already been conceded that the evidence for the text of Lucan is not usefully considered as the property of particular manuscripts. Z^2, as a single siglum, contributes to our understanding of the chronology of the development of the medieval transmission. The alternative seems to me to diffuse and de-emphasize an important source of evidence for the text of Lucan simply because it may not have been contained in a single manuscript. I use my own collation.

The Text of Lucan in the Ninth Century

M

Montepessulanus H 113 is described by Bischoff as follows: "saec. ix 2/4 z.t. deutlich in Schrifttyp von Orleans." M contains the complete text of Lucan on ff. 2r–108v, with one column to a page. There are thirty-seven or thirty-eight lines to a page. Book 6 ends on f. 63r with sixteen lines of text. The verso is blank, book 7 beginning on f. 64r.

M begins at f. 1r with the life of Lucan attributed to Suetonius, followed by the *argumentum* to book 1, which continues on to the verso. Then the epitaph *Corduba me genuit*... finishes the preliminary texts halfway down the verso page.

M contains the subscription of Paulus Constantinopolitanus after certain books. Housman (pp. xiii–xvi) has shown that the presence of this notice does not indicate a relationship between M and other manuscripts that contain it. Beyond that, in the absence of any information on what form Paulus' correction took, nothing relevant to the transmission of the text can be learned from the subscription.

Housman's account of the hybrid origins of M will be discussed later. In the following lists of lines omitted by M, I underline those also omitted by Z, and specify those also omitted by P after 9.84, when M and P show other close affinities. 1.(436–440); 2.(463–464), 571, 732–733; 3.(146), (167–168), 608; 4.(78), 171, (251), 667b–678a; 5.810; 6.(152), (188), (207), (816); 7.90, (103), (154), (200), 209, (257–258), 481, 607, 725, (747), (796), (820–822), 8.(124), 375, 9.(83), (87), 99MP, (100), (253–254), 353, 485–487MP, (494), 499MP, (615), (664), 805MP, (924); 10.(8), 312–313, 396b–398a. P breaks off after 10.107. In addition to these lines, 5.636–713 are not original: they were written by Bouhier and should not be designated as M. I use my own collation.

A

Ashburnhamensis, Parisinus bibl. publ. lat. "nouv. acq." 1626, is described by Bischoff as "saec. ix 2/4, aber die eingefügten Blätter 63 und 76–77, sowie die auf Rasur geschriebene Seite 64r sind jünger, ca. ix 3 oder 4/4; (West) französisch." The text is contained on ff. 2r–143v (f. 35 is numbered twice), at which point the text breaks off at 10.476 and is completed by a scribe of the twelfth century. The relationship of the added leaves to the model of A as well as to the manuscript copied from A will be discussed in Appendix I.

The Manuscripts
A² and Aᵛ

A received the attention of two correctors to whose dates a terminus ante quem can be assigned. One of them, A², alters the text and makes interlinear corrections; the second corrector, whom I shall refer to as Aᵛ, records variants at the appropriate places in the margin, correlating them to the particular word with the sign (./.) and introducing them with al(iter). These marginal additions represent a collation of a now lost manuscript against A, the inclusion of some 800 readings from a ninth-century book. Hosius had some notion of this and lists some of Aᵛ's readings.[2] No editor, however, has made sufficient use of this evidence, partly because it had not been noticed that the readings of Aᵛ can be dated to about the middle of the ninth century.[3]

The following lines are omitted in A: 1.436–440; 2.655, 675; 3.167–168, 211, 373–374, 619; 4.78, 251, 416, 638, 648; 5.420, 432, 546–547, 595, 795b–796a; 6.130, 152, 188, 450 (on an added leaf), 805; 7.90, 103, 200, 257–258, 356, 394 541, 841; 8.124; 9.83, 615, 979, 987; 10.296, 476–546.

I report A from my own collation.

B

Bernensis 45, written, according to Bischoff, "saec. ix Mitte oder 3/4, Fleury höchst wahrscheinlich," contains the text of Lucan on ff. 1v–52v in two columns of from thirty-seven to forty lines to a page. Unlike M, Z, A, which begin unceremoniously with an incipit of one line and proceed to the text of the poem, B has an elaborately produced, artistic title page. Folio 1r was originally left blank as a cover but now contains the Suetonian VITA LVCANI POETA (sic), the epitaph, and the *argumentum* to the first book, all written by a scribe dated by Homburger as of the tenth or eleventh century.[4] It is this same scribe, I believe, who added the scholia from the *Commenta Bernensia* as far as 3.286, some notes from the *Adnotationes super Lucanum*, and a number of scholia that are derived from neither corpus. Folio 1v begins with the title INCIPIT LIBER / PRIMVS MA/NNEI LVCANI / BELLI CIVILIS / FELICITER across both columns. The page is full of later, minutely written scholia.

---

[2] Hosius, pp. xxxii–xxxiv. C. M. Francken, *M. Annaei Lucani Pharsalia* (Leiden 1896–1897), 2 vols., p. xi, dates Aᵛ to the twelfth century. Hosius seems to have accepted this judgment.
[3] As proved in discussion of Aᵛ below.
[4] O. Homburger, *Die illustrierten Handschriften der Bürgerbibliothek Bern* (Berlin 1962) p. 99.

The Text of Lucan in the Ninth Century

B has suffered methodical correction, partly at least by a nearly contemporary hand. Since the same criteria that allow an identification for Z^2, A^2, and A^v cannot be applied to corrections in B, I shall use no siglum to characterize a ninth-century corrector.

B omits the following lines: 1.436–440; 2.655; 3.370; 4.78, 251; 6.96, 152, 188, 310, 450; 7.90, 103, 200, 257–258, 534; 8.124, 302–304; 9.83, 157, 422, 478–481, 488, 499; 10.296.

I report the readings of B from my own collation.

R

Montepessulanus H 362, in the judgment of Bischoff, was written "saec. ix 4/4; französisch." The text of Lucan is found on ff. 94r–267r with one column of twenty-three or twenty-four lines to the page.

R has nowhere been reported; I therefore describe it in some detail.

Folio 94r begins in the middle of the *argumentum* to book 1, *e]uocatos exercitumque* (sic). Following this, and covering four ruled lines, is the incipit: M ANNEI LVCANI / BELLO CIVILIS LIBER / PRIMVS INCIPIT. Then come the first twelve lines of book 1. The first part of the *argumentum* and perhaps the Suetonian life of Lucan had already been lost by the time the book reached the hands of P. Pithou, whose name appears at the top of the page. The entire piece of vellum was lost, for there is a lacuna at 1.264–309, which would have provided the eighth recto and verso of a quarternion beginning with the now missing first page. On f. 141v there are only three lines of text to 4.11, indicating that the model of R was at this point broken up for simultaneous copying. Up to that point there are a constant twenty-three lines to a page, except f. 116 with twenty-four. Beginning with f. 142 and extending to f. 204 (the equivalent of eight quaternions) there are twenty-four lines to a page, except for ff. 182–183, which have twenty-three. For f. 205r to 267r, where the poem ends, there are without exception twenty-three lines on a page. It should be noted that the third section contains the beginnings of books 8, 9, and 10, all without the *argumenta*, which are similarly absent from ZAB. Also for those three books the incipits are identical with those of ZAB:

M ANNEI LVCANI LIBER VII EXPLICIT INCIPIT
   LIBER VIII FELICITER   ZABR
M ANNEI LVCANI LIBER VIII EXPLICIT INCIPIT
   LIBER VIIII FELICITER   ZABR

The Manuscripts

M ANNEI LVCANI EXPLICIT LIBER VIIII INCIPIT LIBER X FELICITER	ZABR
M ANNEI LVCANI LIBER X EXPLICIT	ZBR (*deest A*)

Especially noteworthy is the reversal of word order in the explicit of book 9. After book 1, for which see above, the usual form of the title in R is:

M ANNEI LVCANI LIBER _____ FINIT INCIPIT _____.

Somewhere in the past a manuscript like Z was compared with one which had the *argumenta* for at least books 1, 2, 5, 6, and 7 and a different form of the title. Yet, the result of the formal imposition upon R of a manuscript representing a different tradition reflects the complexity of a contaminated transmission. For while the titles are altered and *argumenta* added, there is no correspondingly dramatic change in the character of R's text. We shall see some traces of the influence of a different tradition in readings throughout the ten books, but in peculiar readings and in other formal ways R remains closely allied to MZAB throughout. That the model of R or the exemplar of that model had interlinear notes becomes clear from the following additions found in the text of R, written by the first hand in spaces ruled for lines of the poem.

After 1.147 we find: *non contentus felicitate praesenti sed semper ad alia properans.* The note in the *Commenta* to 1.148 reads: *non contentus felicitate praesente ad alia properare (n. c. f. praesenti sed semper ad alia properans* scholion in B.) The note in B does appear between the lines but is preceded by *felicitates rebellos.* In any case, the scholia in B are more recent than the copying of R.

After 2.279: *accidente Catone partibus Pompei solus ubi Caesar uidebitur liber.* This is the note of the *Commenta* for 2.281, with *sibi* for *ubi*. B omits the note.

After 4.526: *tunc sol erat in geminis ad cancrum transiturus ergo Iuli mensis.* This is adapted from the scholion in the *Adn.* to 4.526: *tunc sol in geminis erat ad signum Cancri transiturus. significat autem Iulium mensem.*

After 4.645 we find: *dissimulat poeta Mineruam ho inuenit se consilium.* This is a corruption of *Adn.* to 4.646, which reads for *Mineruam ho, hoc Mineruam*; and *inuenias.*

After 4.656 R reads: *Hannibale deuastante Italiam hannibale.* The *Adn.* offer at 657 merely the gloss *Poenum hannibalem.* In the *Commenta*, however, after a lemma, POENVM-SCIPIO, we find *deuastante Italiam Annibale scipio in africa missus . . . (deblastante* C). This is further into the text than the scholiast of B carried the *Commenta*.

The Text of Lucan in the Ninth Century

After 5.132 R has: *deseruit Nero cum responsum nominis acceppisse (sic)*. This does not correspond to anything in *Adn.*; a lacuna in the *Commenta* prohibits comparison.

After 7.312 is found: *haec semper fuit clementia Caesaris ut uictis parcere (sic)*. No similar note appears in the *Commenta*; the *Adn.* offer at 313 *ille, inquit, unicat qui pius est animi, ut uictis debere credat ignosci. hanc clementiam Caesari in Caesarianis adsignat et Tullius.*

At f. 141v, where the scribe broke off at the third ruled line, a medieval *accessus*, probably of the twelfth century, has been added to fill out the page. R is heavily annotated. The comments are both interesting in themselves and may shed light on the state of the scholia in late antiquity. I include a short discussion of these notes in Appendix II.

Though mentioned by Beck, R has never been fully reported. I use my own collation.

F

Besides MZABR there exists a fragment of a ninth-century manuscript. Parisinus bibl. publ. lat. 10403, ff. 49–50, which I designate as F. It is Q in Hosius and Housman. Bischoff describes it as "saec. ix 2/4 ca., französisch." The leaves are bound into a composite manuscript containing varied texts of different dates. They contain the text of Lucan from 8.575 to 9.124. The two leaves are written in double columns and are bound so that f. 49v appears as the recto. On f. 49 there are a uniform fifty-six lines to a column:

	Col. 1	Col. 2
49v	8.689–745	746–802
49r	8.575–631	632–688

The four columns of f. 50 are of different lengths:

50r	8.803–855	856–9.25
50v	9.26–69	70–124

The Manuscripts

The leaves, now bound into a variorum book, were severely cut on the outside margins. As a result, the contents of about the first metrical foot and a half of 9.27–69, the last foot of 8.746–802, and up to the caesura of the third foot in 8.575–631 have been lost. Further, 8.623–631 are illegible because of the flaking of the ink. I have seen very clear photographs of these leaves, but I suspect that the script was more legible when Kalinka studied the text.[5]

Y

Leidensis Vossianus Q 16. For this manuscript I quote the description kindly provided by Mr. K. A. de Meyier of the library of the University of Leiden. "Parchment 10th century ... fo. 136. 25–26 lines of text; written by various scribes in Carolingian minuscules ... The MS. contains the ten books of Lucan, but as the beginning of book I has been lost, the text begins with I 248; between 80v and 81, VI 424–VII 299 are wanting, but not lost, for they have been written on f. 125 line 12 to f. 135v, line 4, after the end of Book X ..." This manuscript, known to editors from Oudendorp, has never been fully reported. From it we may see what happened in the tenth century to a book descended from a manuscript like MZABR. I use my own collation.

Q

Parisinus bibl. publ. lat. 7900 A is described by Bischoff as follows: "Dies sehr interessante Corpus scheint mir saec. ix–x und trotz seiner späteren Fugehörigkeit zur Bibliothek von Corbie in Mailand geschrieben." Q contains the text of Lucan on ff. 57r–94v of a manuscript that has works of Terence, Horace, Juvenal, and Martianus Capella. It is the earliest extant manuscript totally independent of Z. *De Bello Ciuili* is written in two columns of forty-eight to fifty-eight lines to a column except for book 9, which has thirty lines in each column. The absence of 8.267–313 might indicate the loss in the model of one leaf with twenty-three lines on each side, but there is no further evidence for any supposition about the model.

Q contains scholia throughout that cannot be identified with either established corpus. But, from what has been seen in the case of the scholia in R, this is not surprising (see Appendix II).

---

[5] E. Kalinka, "Analecta Latina," *Wiener Studien* 16 (1894) 85–93.

The Text of Lucan in the Ninth Century

The manuscript has long been known; and, though not used by Hosius, it is reported by Bourgery in the Budé edition. Bourgery's collation, however, is both inaccurate and incomplete. I cite Q from my own collation.

The following four manuscripts are known in detail by readers of Lucan using Hosius' third edition. I have relied upon the collations in that edition. Since they are neither new nor central to the subject of this paper, I describe them briefly.

G

Bruxellensis bibl. Burgundicae 5330–5332 (Gemblacensis), tenth century, contains the text of Lucan on ff. 1–131r in one column of thirty-two lines to the page. The text has suffered extensive correction and has been supplemented by a large number of variants in the margins introduced by *legitur et*. G contains many interesting readings both of the first hand and of correctors and might well repay closer inspection, especially in light of the four earlier manuscripts—ABRQ—whose evidence had never been accurately set out. There are extensive scholia throughout the text which, too, should receive more attention.

U

Leidensis Vossianus F 63, Oudendorp's "Vossianus Secundus," is of the tenth century and contains the text of Lucan on ff. 1–129r in single columns of thirty-two lines. It, like G, is heavily corrected and offers numerous variant readings by later hands; scholia appear in the margin throughout the text. The form and place of the Pauline subscription have been described by Housman. U has the *argumenta* to all the books except the first. It may be that the present f. 1 (formerly numbered 46) replaces an original page that had the *argumentum*, for it was attached to the manuscript at a later date. It contains the last two lines (5–6) of the epithet, a long scholion on *plus quam ciuilia* (verse 1) that is not found in either corpus of commentaries but may be an expansion of the note in the *Commenta*, and the *Vita codicis Vossiani II*. Mr. K. A. de Meyier, who admits that the various hands of U are difficult to distinguish, implies by his silence that there is no reason to suppose that this unique *uita* is not an integral part of the manuscript.

The Manuscripts

V

Leidensis Vossianus Q 51, the manuscript most highly regarded by Oudendorp, is also a tenth-century document. The text appears on ff. 1v–162v in single columns of twenty-five lines. There are corrections, variant readings, and scholia. The first page begins with the epitaph and contains an *accessus* essentially the same as that in R. Many of the rare and interesting readings in V can now be found in Q, an earlier manuscript. These two books share sixty-two erroneous readings absent in all other manuscripts before the eleventh century.

P

Parisinus bibl. publ. lat. 7502, tenth century, contains Lucan on ff. 155–206 with two columns of thirty-seven lines to the page. The text ends abruptly at 10.107, though damage has made portions of the last remaining leaves illegible. P begins with the title ARGVMENTVM LIBRI PRIMI, and goes on to give the Suetonian life, the *argumentum*, and the epitaph, before proceeding to the poem. It contains the Pauline subscription after all books except, of course, the tenth and has all the *argumenta*.

Though these four manuscripts—GUVP—were all written in the tenth century, it seems to me that P is the earliest. That it contains an extraordinary number of errors speaks for a careful scribe, since, when after 9.84 M is a copy of the model of P, M shares most of the errors. Further, a significant number of the errors can be attributed to a confusion of letters in capital script. For these reasons P is of especial importance. While it is not directly related to M for the greater part of the text, P shows closer affinities than QGUV to M and to Z.

For readings mentioned here, I shall report the following three manuscripts, which have been used intermittently or not at all by editors of Lucan. No claim of great value can be made for any of them, though all offer readings of interest to the student of Lucan whose knowledge of the textual tradition is limited to the editions of Hosius and Housman. Their evidence supports to some extent E. Fraenkel's view that manuscripts later than those of the ninth and tenth centuries can contribute to our understanding of the textual tradition of Lucan.[6] From them we can also get a better idea of the state of the text in the Middle Ages. I use my own collations, made from microfilms.

---

[6] E. Fraenkel, "Lucan, ed. Housman," *Gnomon* 2 (1926) 497–532.

The Text of Lucan in the Ninth Century

E

Parisinus bibl. publ. lat. 9346, saec. xi, contains the text of Lucan on ff. 3r–122v, with thirty-four lines to a page. E was used by both Lejay and Getty[7] for their editions of the first book. The first leaf of the present manuscript has been attached upside down and contains the first fifty-six lines of book 1 of Lucan in an earlier hand. This fragment has at 1.13 *potuit terrae* (*terrae potuit* rell.), 31 *descendere* rightly with ZP (*discendere* MR; *discedere* rell.), among other interesting readings. Folio 2r has the life of Lucan attributed to Vacca. This *uita* appears in C of early manuscripts and afterward in two books of the eleventh and twelfth centuries.[8] The *uita* seems to me to be in a later hand than that of the text of E, and I suspect that the original manuscript began with the poem itself on what is now f. 3r and was complete in fifteen quaternions to f. 122. The scribe, who added frequent scholia, also wrote in the margin the *argumenta*.

E shares fifty of those sixty-two special errors found in QV and no other manuscript of the ninth or tenth century (see on V above). This said, little more can be assumed about the relationship of these manuscripts, for in most important respects they have little in common.

W

Vaticanus Reginensis 1634, saec. xi–xii, contains the text of Lucan on ff. 1–126v. The first folio is a later addition (1.1–581). It contains thirty-seven lines to the page and ends in the middle of f. 8v. Folio 9r repeats 1.581, and the manuscript continues with thirty-two lines on each page. At f. 84v (beginning 7.719) after 7.742, there follow 8.479–9.207; f. 94r (beginning 9.181) goes to 9.207 after which follow 7.743–8.478 on f. 103v (beginning 8.452); 9.208 to the end of the poem follow 8.478. The chances are that the model had been bound with two quaternions in reverse order. From 84v to f. 94r there are six hundred lines including the *argumentum* to book 9; from ff. 94r–103r there are the same number of lines, though no *argumentum* exists for book 8. The number of lines cannot be divided by the sixteen sides of a quaternion and give a consistent number of lines to a page. Yet the 580 lines lost at the beginning suggest the missing gathering to have been one of about that number of lines, allowing perhaps for a *uita* or more ornate title page. W has the *argumenta* to the last two

---

[7] R. J. Getty, *M. Annaei Lucani De Bello Ciuili Liber I* (Cambridge 1940).

[8] Monacensis D 4d siue 4610 (saec. xi–xii) and Wallersteinensis I 2 (xi–xii) are mentioned by Hosius (p. 334) and Endt, *Adnotationes super Lucanum* (Leipzig 1909) pp. v sqq.

The Manuscripts

books only; this probably reflects the state of affairs in the model. Another curious feature of W is that at f. 61v, after 6.119, a line is left blank, and there follows the Suetonian life of Lucan. Its errors do not ally it with any of Hosius' manuscripts of the *uita*. It continues for eight lines on f. 62r; then come the six lines of the epitaph. Immediately following that, the poem continues at 6.118 (sic).[9] In the version of 6.118 on f. 61v, W has *castris* with MZABY; on f. 62r it reads *claustris* with the rest of the manuscripts. Scholia appear erratically throughout the manuscript.

J

Vaticanus Ottobonianus 1210 and Vaticanus Palatinus 869 together form one uniform text of Lucan of the twelfth century.[10] There are thirty lines per page. The Ottobonianus is numbered consecutively to the end of the poem at f. 124v but omits 1.483–2.274. These lines, comprising a complete quaternion, are found in the Palatine collection as a fragment under the number 869. Some palaeographical importance attaches to this manuscript; for at f. 41r, the beginning of the sixth quaternion, the text is written in the Visigothic script.[11] There are only two other manuscripts of classical authors copied in this hand.[12] A corrector, also identified by the unusual script, went over the first five gatherings as well as the rest of the book, though there are also corrections by a French hand.

There is ample room for scholia, though full advantage was not taken of the space. Occasionally the notes that do appear are written in geometric forms—triangles with the apex at the bottom, sometimes joined with another with the apex at the top.

Folio 73 is a smaller sheet in a later hand, obviously not a part of the original manuscript. It contains 7.144–203, omitting lines 174–175. Since the inserted

---

[9] One is tempted to assume a different exemplar from this point.

[10] This fact was noted by W. J. Anderson in *Revue Bénédictine* 43 (1931) 104–105. In their respective catalogues at the Vatican, the Ottonobianus is dated as twelfth century, the Palatinus as tenth. The later date has been confirmed for me by Dr. Claudio Leonardi of the Biblioteca Vaticana.

[11] Vat. Ottob. 1210 is described by P. B. Katterbach, "Ein westgotischer Kodex der Vatikanischen Bibliothek," *Vorreformationsgeschichtliche Forschungen Supplementband* (1925) 62–66. Dom De Bruyne had dated and identified the script of the manuscript in *Revue Bénédictine* 36 (1924) 7.

[12] They are Matritensis Hh 74 of Terence and Leidensis Voss. F 111 of Ausonius, a manuscript probably written at Lyons. There is no indication in J that it descends from a Visigothic class of manuscripts or that the unusual script has any implications for the tradition of the text.

sheet contains only fifty-eight lines instead of the sixty we would expect, we may be sure that there was no such omission in the original. Folio 78v ends with 7.505; in the left margin has been pasted a strip of parchment with lines 510–519 written as if prose by a later hand. An arrow directs the reader to insert these lines after 489. Lines 506–627, two leaves of J, are missing.

The following are fragments of ancient manuscripts. In reporting their readings, I use the apparatus criticus of Hosius and the articles of Detlefsen.[13]

N

Fragments of a single ancient manuscript, later erased and written over, exist today in two libraries. Vindobonensis 16 contains 5.31–91, 152–211, 272–301 and 6.215–274, 305–334; Neapolitanus iv A 8 has 5.332–390, 631–660 and 6.153–163, 168–178, 395–425, 545–576, 667–698. The original manuscript was written in rustic capitals in the fourth century.[14]

S

Vaticanus Palatinus 24, fourth or fifth century, is also in capital script and contains 6.21–61, 228–267, and 7.458–537.[15]

Brief as the ancient evidence is, we can learn from it something of the state of the text of Lucan toward the end of the Empire. Both books are idiosyncratic in that they offer readings that are neither correct nor, so far as the medieval manuscripts allow us to determine, traditional. Where the medieval manuscripts disagree, N and S sometimes support the less preferable readings.[16] So 5.155

---

[13] D. Detlefsen published "Der Wiener Lucanpalimpsest mit Berücksichtigung des Neapolitanischen und Römischen," *Philologus* 13 (1858) 312–357; "Der römische Lucanpalimpsest," *Philologus* 15 (1860) 527–538; "Der neapolitanische Lucanpalimpsest," *Philologus* 26 (1867) 173–194. I was able to check Detlefsen's work on the Naples fragment in Naples in 1963. The Vatican fragment I found impossible to read.

[14] E. A. Lowe, *Codices Latini Antiquiores*, vol. 3, p. 36.

[15] Ibid. vol 1, p. 22. Lowe also mentions Vaticanus 5755 (vol. 1, p. 12) as a seventh-century uncial palimpsest containing Lucan 8.60–524. He describes it as "very illegible." I was unable to read it at all. Of less import is the fragmentary survival of four lines of a fifth-century manuscript, Br. Mus. add. 34473, described by Lowe in *CLA*, vol. 2, p. 175.

[16] A glance at the readings of Vaticanus 5750, a sixth-century manuscript containing passages of Juvenal and Persius, reveal it to be similar in value to N and S. It is, like the ancient manuscripts of Lucan, as W. Clausen, *A. Persii Flacci Saturarum Liber* (Oxford 1956 p. x, describes it, "more notable for its antiquity than its usefulness." We should expect no more, for it was in antiquity that contamination brought about "normal" or vulgate texts.

The Manuscripts

limina MUVPW; *culmina* ZABRYQGEJN, or 7.487 *puras* Z²ABR cett.; *pura* MZPS. In one place where we have the evidence of both N and S, they are divided: 6.237 *tenentem* GJSE²; *trementem* MZABRN rell. (*prementem* U; *minacem* Y²). At 7.462, where other manuscripts are divided between *tempus quo noscere possent* ZRA^v cett. and *uultusque agnoscere quaerunt* Z²ABUW, we find in S VVLTVSQVONO. Housman adopts *uultus quo noscere possent* taking *quo* to mean *ut*; but this seems strained. It is more likely that S combines two already existing readings.[17]

C

Bernensis 370, now dated to the end of the ninth century,[18] contains a commentary without text on the *De Bello Ciuili* known as the *Commenta Bernensia*. For this commentary lemmata were supplied from another manuscript, and not infrequently the lemma will have a variant of the word explained in the commentary. C refers to the lemmata.

c

The *Commenta Bernensia* begin in f. 2r, following the *uita* attributed to Vacca of f. 1, with the Suetonian life of Lucan. For both the lemmata and the commentary I have used the edition of H. Usener, *Scholia in Lucani Bellum Ciuile, pars prior, Commenta Bernensia* (Leipzig 1869).[19]

adn.

Directly following the *Commenta* in C (ff. 125v–179v) is an abbreviated form of the so-called *Adnotationes super Lucanum*. The basic text of the work that goes under this title, published by J. Endt at Leipzig in 1909, is a twelfth-century

---

[17] This vexed passage has not, I think, been satisfactorily explained, in spite of the efforts of Housman and Fraenkel. The order of lines, the alternative half-line, and the lemma of the *Commenta*, TEMPUSQ.T.I.R.N.P., should all somehow be taken into account in elucidating the text here.

[18] See O. Homberger (above, n. 15) p. 16 n. 2.

[19] Homberger offers photographs of C and B. Chatelain, *Paléographie des classiques latins* (Paris 1894–1900), reproduces leaves of M (plate CLVIII), Z and A (CLIV), R (CLV), G (CLVII), U (CLX), V (CLVII), P (CLIX), N and S (CLIII). Reproductions of the two scripts of J are in Forster, *Mittelalterliche Buch- und Urkundschriften* (Bern 1946) XXII a–b.

The Text of Lucan in the Ninth Century

manuscript, Wallersteinensis I 2, which has continuous scholia with no text. A less than thorough investigation—for a proper edition of the scholia would be a long and exacting task—has led me to believe that, while there may well have existed in antiquity more than one set of scholia, they are not represented as such by the *Commenta* and the *Adnotationes* (see Appendix II). Nor is it certain that the scholia came down from antiquity in continuous form rather than in the margins of texts of the poem.

Chapter III
The Assessment of the Manuscripts by Modern Editors

With so great a variety of evidence—several kinds of scholia, ancient fragments, half a dozen ninth-century documents as well as many later manuscripts—the editor would naturally have to sift and reduce. That among the rejected manuscripts are found three of the five complete ninth-century manuscripts is itself remarkable. In this particular case, the state of affairs reflects a scholarly attitude that gained ascendancy in the second half of the nineteenth century. Housman avowedly reacted against that attitude; yet readers who are dependent for their knowledge of the manuscript tradition on the relevant sections of Housman's preface are bound to have a distorted notion of the work and aims of his predecessors.

The first critical edition, i.e., the first edition subsequent to the introduction of the so-called method of Lachmann, was that of Hosius, for Teubner, in 1892. In it he reported throughout the readings of five manuscripts, MBGUV, along with the ancient fragments and readings from the scholia, adding at random lections from six other manuscripts, among them Y and J in my *conspectus siglorum*. In the following two years he published articles supporting his belief in M as the *codex optimus*. Though, as I have suggested, his motive in adopting this procedure stemmed from a desire to bring to his text the order and simplicity he admired in Lachmann's *Lucretius*, there can be no doubt that Hosius realized the differences between the two traditions: he recognized (p. xiv) that the manuscripts of Lucan were contaminated. The temptation, however, to choose a "best manuscript" on whose readings he could depend in the absence of incontrovertible philological grounds when the tradition offered alternatives was, for Hosius, too great fully to resist. In this respect he shares his guilt with virtually all of his contemporary textual critics. Given his inapplicable method, however, his choice of M cannot be faulted. Following on Steinhart's work,[1] Hosius realized that M contained a more sincere, less interpolated text than that offered by the Leiden manuscripts (U and especially V) favored by Oudendorp.[2]

Yet, it should not be thought, as one naturally would from Housman's indignant account, that Hosius represented or informed the opinion of a large number of scholars. In 1894, Lejay produced an edition of the first book of *De Bello Ciuili*.[3] For it, he used ZAQP for the first time consistently as well as Hosius' MBGUV and five more Paris manuscripts of the eleventh century including 9346, E in this study. He also mentioned F, the Paris fragment, which, however, contains nothing from the first book. Lejay, too, tried to deal with the manuscripts in a way their character would not permit; but his standards were less restrictive, and he was able to criticize both the limitations of Hosius' method and his choice of M: "il a en tout cas négligé la seule source probable de cette recension [i.e. A] et a pris tout légèrement le parti trop simple de décider tous les cases douteux par autorité de M" (p. xcviii). Lejay, as we shall see, had a much better understanding of the nature of the problem. His edition was not used, however, by C. M. Francken, whose two-volume opus appeared in 1896–1897. For reasons as understandable as Hosius', though no more justifiable, Francken chose A as his authoritative manuscript. Beck, in his monograph of 1900,[4] though influenced by the Pauline subscription, was not partial to M, certainly not at the expense of, say, Z. Hosius, in his two subsequent Teubner editions (1905, 1913) continued to maintain that M could give succor to the undecided critic; but his view was far from being universally accepted, as we learn from Fraenkel (see note 17 above). Bourgery had prepared his edition before Housman's appeared, without relying on any single manuscript. Already in 1917 J. P. Postgate had understood the nature of the tradition: "The relations and consequently the genealogy of the different MSS are very difficult to determine. As to their authority it may be briefly said that none of them is entitled to a distinct preference over the rest, and that each reading that they offer is to be judged on its intrinsic merits."[5] It might, perhaps, be mentioned as a parallel

---

[1] G. Steinhart, "De Lucani Codice Montepessulano," *Symbola Philologorum Bonnensium in Honorem Frederici Ritschlii collecta*, fasc. prior (Leipzig 1864) 287–300.

[2] F. Oudendorp, *M. Annaei Lucani Cordubensis Pharsalia siue Belli Ciuilis Libri Decem*, vol. I (Leiden 1728), p. ***.

[3] P. Lejay, *M. Annaei Lucani de Bello Ciuili Liber Primus* (Paris 1894).

[4] F. Beck, *Untersuchungen zu den Handschriften Lucans* (Munich 1900).

[5] J. P. Postgate, *M. Annaei Lucani De Bello Ciuili Liber VII* (Cambridge 1917), p. c.

The Assessment of the Manuscripts by Modern Editors

that Housman's account of scholarly work on the manuscripts of Juvenal takes no account of the following accurate, if in some ways marvelously naive, judgment: "It, i.e. the Pithoeanus, is generally considered the most ancient and valuable extant (if it still be extant) MS. of Juvenal, but its readings are often hopelessly corrupt, and some editors seem to me not to have evinced sound judgment in relying, as they have done, almost exclusively upon it." Those words were written in 1873, more than a quarter of a century before Housman's *Juvenal*, by John Delaware Lewis, in a useful two-volume edition with commentary.[6]

It would seem that Housman took Hosius' conclusions about M to heart in opposition more than many other scholars in acceptance. And the result was not just a minor irony; it blinded Housman to some of the real merits of M and, consequently, to some extent, of Z. Hosius, himself, as well as W. B. Anderson, who could review the 1905 Teubner equipped with some of his own collations and in general approve, felt great dissatisfaction about the state of the manuscripts.[7] What caused the discomfort, though it was not so diagnosed, was the inappropriateness of feeling obligated to choose a *codex optimus* from among the highly contaminated manuscripts of Lucan. If Hosius had reported all the ninth-century manuscripts in full, Housman, who limited himself for knowledge of the variant readings almost completely to Hosius' apparatus criticus, might have more accurately seen the character of the tradition and reflected it in his own apparatus criticus, which is now but a neater, more sensible version of Hosius'. It could be argued that Hosius' main damage to Lucan studies was not having provided Housman with such comprehensive evidence as he did for the text of Juvenal.

By the time Hosius published the third edition of his Teubner *Lucan*, the process of *eliminatio codicum descriptorum* had brought about the dismissal of three ninth-century manuscripts, AB and the Montpellier manuscript cited by Beck as F (my R) but never fully reported. Since the true relationship among these manuscripts can now be shown with some precision, I shall trace in detail the steps by which it came about that the majority of the early manuscripts are not reported in modern editions.

[6] J. D. Lewis, *D. Iunii Iuuenalis Satirae* (London 1882), p. xii.

[7] W. B. Anderson in *CR* 20 (1906) 354–360. He maintained that M or Z or both might be at one remove from their common antecedent. He appealed to Hosius' hint of this possibility (Hosius, p. xxxv); but at that point Hosius was referring only to the divergences between Z and M which begin in book 9. His doubts about Hosius' simpler reconstruction are more than justified; see below, pp. 52ff.

The Text of Lucan in the Ninth Century

Of the ninth-century manuscripts Hosius knew accurately only M and B when he produced his first edition in 1892. So numerous and so striking were the similarities between the two that he had no hesitation about calling them *gemelli* (p. xiii). He did not account for those places where M and B are divided between traditional readings, a factor which alone would tend to vitiate the conclusion; but, compared with lack of discernible relationship of VUG with each other or with M or B, the more than eight hundred peculiar errors shared by MB provided strong temptation for Hosius' over-simplified assessment. With Lejay's edition two years later came information about Z and A, though already in 1891 Francken had published an article giving many of A's lections.[8] Lejay saw that all four ninth-century manuscripts were closely related. His reconstruction was as follows (pp. xci sqq.): Z is the model from which B was copied. In Z, 3.211 is omitted from the text but has been added in the upper margin before the first line of the page, which is 3.194. The added verse is prefixed with "h" to correspond with a "d" at the end of line 210. Of all the lines omitted in Z and added by Z^2, this alone bears a notation for suppletion after the previous line, rather than in the left-hand margin between the lines on either side of the omission. Though the notation is unique, it should be said that it is nevertheless without a doubt the work of Z^2. In B, line 211, absent from its proper place, is found between 193 and 194. The scribe of B, therefore, following the order of lines in Z, either did not notice that 211 was an addition or, finding no sign in the left-hand margin to guide him, left the corrector's verse where it appeared in the text he was copying, i.e., before 194.

This, it would seem, is an irrefutable proof of the dependence of B upon Z after correction. The only other explanation for the position of the misplaced line in B is the complete coincidence of lineation in an earlier manuscript, exactly the same omission (there is no obvious paleographic explanation for the omission of the line, which is, by the way, not omitted in M), and precisely the same means of correction. Barring these simultaneous coincidences, Z is a formal antecedent of B. Not that the latter must be a direct copy of Z, as Lejay asserted; indeed, it cannot be. Yet, removed by a certain number of transcriptions, B is descended from the extant manuscript Z itself. It is rare that such compelling proof is available for the necessary, formal relationship of one manuscript to another. Of all the arguments put forth by Lejay, and later by Hosius, to show

---

[8] C. M. Francken, "Selecta de Montepessulano et Ashburnhamensi Lucani," *Mnemosyne* 19 (1891) 16-40.

The Assessment of the Manuscripts by Modern Editors

connections between manuscripts, the misplacement of 3.211 is the one that is capable of no other reasonable explanation.

Lejay also noted that in B 3.244 appears both in its proper place, following 243, and again after 254. The first hand of Z wrote the line only in its proper place; but it is repeated by Z^2 in the margin at the top of the following leaf, f. 29v, which contains 253–282, with a sign designating that it belongs after line 254. The addition of Z^2 was later erased, but not, apparently, before the scribe of (an antecedent of) B, this time interpreting his directions correctly, wrote the line in both places. Lejay maintained that Z had been copied from a manuscript in which the line was to be found in its proper place but that Z^2 used for comparison a manuscript in which the line was omitted, but added in the lower margin of its page—a page ending with line 254. This line of argument carries less weight than the one above, for it is just as likely that Z was copied from a manuscript in which the line was already repeated, a manuscript in this respect like B. It is not possible to say in this case at what point in the transmission the error originated. From his annotation Z^2 makes it clear that he wants the line added where B in fact has it. If the scribe of B could countenance the repetition, so too might an earlier scribe. From this piece of evidence, then, Z^2 might as logically be following a manuscript with the format of B in these lines as creating one.

Lejay believed of A that it was the oldest extant medieval manuscript of Lucan; and the opinion was not a rash one, for a comparison of the scripts would indicate just that. Bischoff's descriptions of the manuscripts also suggest that A is older than Z or M. But the criterion of handwriting is not infallible: an older scribe might continue to the end of a long life writing in the script he had learned as a young man. In the present case, as we shall see, internal evidence proves the priority of Z. With A assumed to be the oldest manuscript, similarities between A and M would indicate that a source of M was compared against a manuscript like A; and such was Lejay's conclusion. On the basis of his study of MZAB he drew up the accompanying stemma (Lejay, p. xciv).

In this diagram Lejay hit upon a potentially more accurate and comprehensive design for the stemmatic representation of a contaminated tradition. MZAB are all felt to be the result of two antecedent manuscripts: a formal model and a manuscript used to correct that model. In this sense, it is far superior to the subsequent stemmata of Beck and Hosius, which picture only vertical descent without taking cognizance of the horizontal transmission, that is, of contamination. In detail, however, Lejay's stemma is far from satisfactory: it is confusing

The Text of Lucan in the Ninth Century

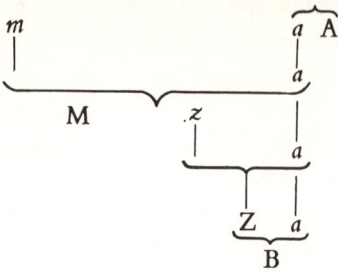

to find M, for example, placed without connection below the line; and too often a vertical and a horizontal line meet with no indication of what that union entails. If a stemma is worth making at all, it must be a good deal more specific and self-explanatory than Lejay's. He claimed that he uses lowercase letters to designate the antecedents of extant manuscripts, which he indicates by capital letters. But *a* is certainly not so represented in the stemma; it is not clear precisely how *a* is related to A and what the differences are, if any, among the various *a*'s. Yet in his verbal account of the transmission, too, Lejay seems to be somewhat confused about the process and results of contamination and, specifically, the state of B and its antecedents. On pp. xci–xcii he says, "C'est [Z] l'original direct de B," and goes on to make clear that by Z he here means the sum total of the readings offered by Z and Z^2 (p. xcv n. 1). If this is so, then according to the stemma the corrections in Z come from *a*; but, whatever *a* was like, the only characteristics B could derive from it would be the ones transferred into Z by Z^2, the corrector who used *a* and whose contribution we can see in the margins of Z. Thus, there should be no significant agreement in peculiar error between B and A or M or indeed any manuscript, unless that error is present in Z after correction. Yet, we find many errors shared by B with manuscripts that, according to Lejay, are antecedent to it but are not found in its direct antecedent, Z, before or after correction. In the following examples, the correct reading, found in ZZ^2, appears in parentheses.

2.468 arca *AB* (arce)   655 *om. AB*   3.167–168 *BRQYGV om. ZAMUPE*   417 fame *AB* (fama)   4.334 garamantas *MB* (garamantes)   613 libico *ABQYVEW* (libyco)   5.196 tenebris *MBPW* (tenebis)   355 dextris *AB* (dextras)   519 causantia *AB* (quassantia)   534 speriam *AB* (Hesperiam *Zmss.*; hisperiam *MZ*)   6.48 attollit *AB* (attollet)   302 Romana *MB* (Roma)   389 Oeta *AB* (Oetaeo)   393 silide *AB* (sidere)   413 locauerunt

The Assessment of the Manuscripts by Modern Editors

AB (locarunt)   450 *om. AB*   561 manus *MB* (manes)   7.670 ducti *AB* (duci)   8.475 Pelle *MBRP* (Pellaeae)   567 externis *ABJ* (externas)   10.356 foras *AB* (pharos)

None of these readings in B can be explained by Lejay's stemma; and the list is by no means exhaustive.

Perhaps Lejay meant to imply that only after correction was Z compared with *a*, so that *A* descends from $(ZZ^2)a$ rather than Za. Even so, unless *a* had undergone correction that altered its character, we should find nothing in B that was not among $(ZZ^2)A$. Thus, only if B was written by a scribe who had before him two manuscripts and chose word by word between them—and there is no evidence for this in the transmission of Latin texts—could (ZZ^2) be a direct antecedent. Yet, even then, B would be our source of evidence for the now-missing second manuscript. It is far more likely that B, or any other manuscript produced in a contaminated tradition, has a single formal model with marginal, interlinear, and textual corrections. This model cannot be Z as we have it with early ninth-century correction; therefore, we lack not only the formal model of B but also the manuscript used to correct that model. Yet B was affected by both Z and A and preserves characteristics derived from them.

The principle of *eliminatio codicum descriptorum* is that a manuscript may be ignored if it offers no traditional evidence independent of an extant antecedent manuscript. Neither the corrected Z nor the corrected Z with A allow the critic to dismiss B from consideration as Lejay's stemma suggests it may be.

A more serious defect in Lejay's argument, uncovered by Beck, will be discussed presently, Between the work of those two scholars chronologically comes C. M. Francken's edition, which received the memorable, if unflattering, attentions of Housman. Francken knew of MAB, realized that they were closely related to each other, and found that the connection between A and B was closer than the relationship between either of them and M. On the basis of the agreements of AB, he determined that B was copied from A. Here again, not only is the method inappropriate, it is misapplied. Francken allows for no special readings in B that are not found in A. All that is necessary to destroy Francken's reconstruction is a single example in B of a peculiar error or traditional variant shared by other manuscripts but not present in A. One need not search far; there are many such (see Appendix VIII).

In 1900 Friedrich Beck published the most extensive study to date of the many manuscripts of Lucan. Three major faults of technique and procedure mar his laborious reconstruction of the transmission: his collations were not sufficiently accurate; he derived his examples from too small and too restricted a part of the text, limiting himself for the most part to readings from the first book of the poem; and he forced himself, in the face of a great deal of evidence that he himself offered, to reconstruct for the textual tradition a single stemma of descent embracing all the extant manuscripts. He realized that M and Z, though they seemed to derive independently from the same manuscript, diverge over readings in which traditional variants are involved, and assumed properly that such variation must reflect a corrected exemplar.[9] The source of those corrections did not seem to interest him. He failed to understand that, once a corrected model is assumed, it is no longer useful to consider M and Z as deriving from a single source. Beck never took into account the corrector of that model—the scribe responsible for the variants and the manuscript he used for corrections. A similar procedural error detracts from his discussion of AB and the fifth manuscript of the ninth century, R, which Beck used for the first time.

His most important contribution to the understanding of the relationship of the earliest medieval manuscripts was his realization that A, in spite of the indications of its script, is not, as Lejay thought, the oldest of the manuscripts. His proof is as compelling as it is obvious (pp. 10–12), and it remains a little surprising that Lejay, who addressed himself forthrightly to the complex problems of the tradition, failed to notice it. The displacement of 3.211, by which Lejay realized that B is descended from Z, is also present in A. If A were indeed older than Z, then B might as easily have derived from A as from Z; but this would not explain how the state of affairs in Z came about. Z omitted 3.211 completely; either Z^2 saw in his correcting manuscript 211 following 210 and copied it in the margin at the top of the page with a notation that it belongs after 210, or he found it in a manuscript like A after 193 and put it in Z before 194. In the first instance, the coincidence that the logical place for Z^2 to copy in the omitted line is precisely the place where it appears mistakenly in another manuscript is hardly acceptable. The second possibility, no more palatable, disregards the notations of Z^2. Only one conclusion can be drawn logically from the facts: A, like B, derives from Z; and Z, therefore, is the oldest ninth-century manuscript. There need have been no great lapse of time between

[9] Beck, p. 27. This was accepted by Hosius, p. xxxv; but neither used this knowledge constructively to show the complexity of the tradition. Their concern was to present a simple stemma, eliminating from consideration as many manuscripts as possible.

The Assessment of the Manuscripts by Modern Editors

transcriptions. A scribe in the Renaissance at least could copy the complete text of *De Bello Civili* in fifteen days.[10] In the course of this discussion the existence of nearly a score of ninth-century manuscripts of Lucan will be adduced from the evidence of the five extant ones and the Paris fragment. The work was popular and frequently copied. As far as we know, wherever a copy was made, a second manuscript also existed, which a corrector could use for comparison. A is not appreciably more recent than Z, but Z is without a doubt the older of the two.

The conclusion offered by Beck on the basis of this chronological consideration was that Z is an ancestor not only of B, but of A as well. Bringing R into the discussion, he asserts that A and R must be copied from the same manuscript, a copy of Z which he calls α. This is a tacit correction of an earlier claim that A was copied from Z, but it is forced by certain agreements of AR against Z, ZA against R, and ZR against A. The logic of this, an attempt to show how upon occasion both A and R will agree with Z against the other, is faulty. Either the reading shared by Z and one of the others was in α, in which case the third should have it or a singular error, or it wasn't, in which case the agreement is not explained by α. The familiar problem has again arisen: the reconstruction fails to account for the facts. When faced with the difficulty of lines appearing in A or R that are absent ftom Z, Beck is forced to assume (p. 17): "Wie so oft früher die Kopisten von Hss. neben ihrer eigentlichen Vorlage eine oder schliesslich auch in den günstigsten Fällen mehrere Hss. zu Rate zogen und daraus andere Lesarten und in ihrer Vorlage nicht vorhandene Verse entnahmen, so benutzte auch hier der Schreiber von α einen anderen codex, in dem jene Verse standen." As with the second source of the model of ZM, Beck makes no effort further to understand the character of this independent witness and indeed in his stemma makes no attempt to characterize it. So far as the stemma is concerned, the reader must assume that AR and B, which Beck also derives from α, should be dismissed, by the principle of *eliminatio codicum descriptorum*, from consideration.

Like Hosius, and to a certain extent Lejay, Beck suffered from the malaise shared by so many nineteenth-century editors of Latin texts and was torn between the desire to be "scientific," to reduce the number of manuscripts necessary for the constitution of the text to a bare minimum, and the knowledge

---

[10] At the end of Vat. Lat. 1621 we find, "Explicit liber Lucani deo gratias. amen. quem scripsi in xv diebus ego P(etru?)s."

that there is evidence in the manuscripts he intends to discard not found in their extant antecedents. "Auch die Mss. Klasse α, scheint es, können wir fast aufgeben, da wir ja ihre Quelle Z kennen" (p. 58). Yet (p. 59), "Die beiden ältesten nämlich A und F [my R] sind wohl zu verwerten, um die Ueberlieferung vom α festzustellen, die ja . . . öfters von alters her beglaubigt ist." But the distinction between α and its antecedent Z is never investigated; it cannot be ignored, but finds no mention in the stemma. Thus Beck was unable to find a way effectively to deal with contamination in the Carolingian manuscripts of Lucan.

In his second edition of *De Bello Civili*, from which the third differs in minor details only, Hosius accepted in large part the results of Beck's investigation of the ninth-century manuscripts. He agrees with Beck's assertion that the model of MZ carried variants, but makes no greater effort than his predecessor to integrate that intelligence into his account of M and Z. To the arguments already adduced for the dependence of AB (he mentions R but does not deal with it) upon Z, he adds several others. I examine these in some detail, not in order to disprove the main point, that A is derived from Z after correction, but to show the inconclusiveness of the evidence that Hosius adduces. The following examples do not guarantee that Z is a formal antecedent of A, but they do offer some information about the second manuscript Z^2 had before him as he corrected Z.

4.171 is omitted in Z and added at the top of the next folio, which begins with 177, with signs indicating that the verse belongs before 178. In A and B 4.171 appears after 177. But 171 was also omitted by M, and it may therefore be assumed that the common source of MZ lacked it. Since it is certain on other grounds that A and B derive from Z, the position of 171 in those manuscripts is explained by the correction of Z^2. But why did Z^2 willfully insist that the verse should be inserted after 177 if that is not where he found it in his manuscript? A and B then show the order of lines in the second manuscript at Z^2's disposal.[11]

---

[11] The verse itself is probably an interpolation, as Oudendorp and later editors believed; it does not, however, as Duff claimed in his Loeb edition, rest on weak manuscript evidence. Only MZ (i.e. ζ) and Y omit the line. It was certainly meant by whoever composed it to stand after 171. Its place in Z suggests that it was omitted in the text of an antecedent manuscript and later added in the margin, but in such a way as to confuse a future copyist. It is not surprising that Z^2 should have suffered contamination; that seems to have been the fate of all early manuscripts of Lucan in the Middle Ages. That it, too, omitted 171 would indicate that Z^2 bore some special resemblance to ζ. This will be found to be not at variance with other evidence.

The Assessment of the Manuscripts by Modern Editors

At 8.570ff there is a displacement of lines in ZAB.

> 570 damnatum leto traherent ad litora Magnum
> non ulli comitum sceleris praesagia derant:
> quippe fides si pura foret, si regia Magno
> sceptrorum auctori uera pietate pateret,
> uenturum tota Pharium cum classe tyrranum.

570 Magnum Z^2*cett.*; magno *MZ*   573 *ante* 571 *habent ZAB*

The erroneous order of lines may be explained in two ways. In either instance, the scribe, after he had finished line 570 (*magno* in MZ only facilitates the confusion; it need not be solely responsible for it), looked down to the end of 572 (*Magno*); and he proceeded thence directly to 573. It is quite possible that he noticed his own mistake immediately and wrote the two omitted lines directly after 573 with or without directions for a future copyist (or indeed reader). It is also possible that he made no attempt to rectify his error but that a corrector discovered the omission in correcting the text and supplied the verses in the margin without designating sufficiently clearly between which two lines they should be inserted. The first explanation, that which involves only the scribe himself, is more likely to be correct in cases of inverted order of lines owing to homoeoteleuton.[12] From the frequency with which just this sort of displacement occurs, we would hardly be justified in using it to prove that AB descend from Z. Of itself the error at best indicates that the manuscripts are related.

Next, Hosius adduces 8.368f:

> illic et laxas uestes et fluxa uirorum
> uelamenta uides Parthus per medica rura

These lines appear in ZAB in the following form:

> 368   Illic et laxas uestes et fluxa uirorum
> 368a uelamenta uides et fluxa uirorum
> 369   uelamenta uides. Parthus per Medica rura

---

[12] See the many examples collected by W. Clausen in "Silua Coniecturarum," *AJP* 76 (1955) 48–49.

The Text of Lucan in the Ninth Century

The error is, of course, purely mechanical. The scribe, writing 369, confused the graphically similar *uestes* and *uides* and wrote out the rest of 368. Though such an error is unlikely to have occurred in three manuscripts independently, it argues only for common source and cannot be used to prove the priority of any particular book.

Hosius next cites 9.484ff:

>   sed nisu iacuit, uix sic inmobilis austro
> 485   qui super ingentes cumulos inuoluit harenae
>   atque operit tellure uiros. uix tollere miles
>   membra ualet multo congestu pulueris haerens.
>   alligat et stantis adfusae magnus harenae

487 haerens A^2cett.; harenis ZA   488 post 485 Z^2A; om. B   485-487 om. MP

The cause of difficulty at this passage is homoeoteleuton. MP completely omit the lines that the scribe overlooked when, completing 484, he cast his eye back not to the next line, which ends with *harenae*, but to 488, which ends with the same word. At this point M no longer provides a check upon Z or vice versa, so we may assume that Z correctly copied what was correctly written in his exemplar. But to the left of 485, Z^2 placed a sign (·/.), and another (· . ·) before 488. While, since A derives from Z, those signs dictate the order of lines in A, it must be that Z^2 found the lines in his manuscript as they now appear in A. That lineation, as has been shown above, is the common one after homoeoteleuton when one line intervenes; though the possibility that the exemplar, like M and P, omitted the lines altogether and that the corrector added the lines in such a way that they were next copied after 488 cannot be ruled out. In any case, Hosius' proof at best would indicate a common source; the chances are that the manuscript Z^2 used had the order 484, 488, 485-487. The error in B can have come about in a variety of ways. Homoeoteleuton with *haerens* and *harenae* could have brought him to grief at 488, or the correction of a model similar to Z may have induced him to omit 488 where it does not belong without persuading him to replace it where it does. Once again Hosius' evidence fails to prove his point, for the genesis of the error in A is older than, or at least independent of, Z.

The Assessment of the Manuscripts by Modern Editors

The same is true of the next example, 9.498ff:

> utque calor soluit, quem torserat aera uentus,
> incensusque dies, manant sudoribus artus,
> 500 arent ora siti: conspecta est parua maligna

499 *om.* MP

In A and B we find the following:

498 utque calor soluit, quem torserat aera uentus
498a exarsitque dies iam mundi spissior ignis
   iam plaga qua (quam *B*) nullam superi mortalibus ultra (ultat *B*)
   a medio fecere die calcatur et umor (humor *B*)
498d in noton omnis abit manant sudoribus artus
500 arent ora siti: conspecta est parua maligna

The intruded lines are adapted from verses 604ff of the same book:

> nunc olim factura deum es. iam spissior ignis
> 605 et plaga, qua nullam superi mortalibus ultra
> a medio fecere die, calcatur, et unda
> rarior

Both passages contain similarly affecting descriptions of the thirsty, hot trek of Cato and his troops suffering through the Libyan desert. At some point—we cannot say for certain if it was ancient or medieval—a reader, perhaps just because he noticed the similarity, perhaps for the sake of comparison, copied *iam spissios . . . rarior* in the margin of his book next to 499. Another reader later adapted these lines for insertion into the new context. *In noton umbra cadit* (9.539) or *in noton effugit umbra* (9.695) may have suggested the phrase of 498d. But the fact that the marginal addition was adapted both metrically and syntactically bespeaks a reader at home with classical Latin poetry. The problem of dating corrections does not allow of a simple solution. In general, the greater the knowledge of Latin needed to make the correction, the better the chances that it was made in late antiquity.[13] Though we occasionally find emendations

---

[13] Thus, Z^2's *uouere in* for *uouerunt* at 3.127 is likely to be ancient.

by ninth-century readers that indicate dexterity,[14] too much credit in general is given to scholars of this period for interpolations found in texts of popular authors. Even Lupus of Ferrières, best known and most highly regarded of the early Carolingian scholars, emended only occasionally—and then not well.[15] The chances are better that the lines were produced, suitable for a hexameter text, in an ancient edition.

In the upper margin of f. 119v, which begins with 9.497, Z^2 has written the verses as they appear in A, assigned them to follow 498, and deleted 499. To the left of the added verses, he wrote the following note: *isti uersus inuenti sunt in* ꝣ *uara pagina.* Either he read on and came across the lines in their proper place, which revelation he records as above, or else he is copying a note found in the margin of his exemplar. I have attempted to reproduce the figure before *uara*, as I cannot interpret it. In either case, A could as well be reflecting, through the correction of Z^2, an earlier manuscript. AB omit 499 because it is encompassed in 498d; it was for that reason Z^2 deleted it. MP, at this point probably copies of the same manuscript, both omit 499, *ob homoeoteleuton*, according to Housman; and it is possible that a scribe may have confused *uentus* and *artus*. It is, however, certain that, if an ancient manuscript offering 498a–d were then corrected by excision of the added verses, 499 could not be recovered.

Hosius' final piece of evidence for the dependence of A on the corrected Z concerns the transposition of verses after 7.488. Z exhibits the lines in the order found in most manuscripts, which dictates the numeration of modern editions. Folio 89r ends with 490; f. 89v contains 491–519, f. 90r begins with 520. Before 489 a "C" was placed by the corrector of Z, who wrote, in the right hand margin after the line: *dimissum ordinem require in sequenti pagina ad uersum incohantem Inde faces* (= 512) *Illic quoque suo miscet* (= 510). On the next page before 512 appears the letter "A," and after 520 the letter "B" with the note: *et hoc loco require superius in altero folio versus & quota pars et ceteri*, i.e. 489ff. If all these directions were written by the same corrector (it would be strange if he wrote both *Inde faces* and *Illic quoque suo miscet* without at least offering a preference unless he were faithfully copying a compound note), the letters still

[14] See K. Mueller, *Geschichte Alexanders des Grossen* (Munich 1954) 173f. But of correctors in the ninth-century manuscripts of Quintus Curtius, Mueller says that they generally limit themselves to marginal notes explaining or labeling contents: "seltener finden sich Worderklärungen oder Konjecturen." I should be confident in extending that observation to the ninth-century correctors of manuscripts of Lucan.

[15] See C. Beeson, *Lupus of Ferrières as Scribe and Text Critic* (Cambridge, Mass. 1930) 4.

The Assessment of the Manuscripts by Modern Editors

instruct the next copyist to transpose 512-520 and put them before 489. The copyist may have been clever enough to ignore both the letter and the first reference in the note and insert 510-520 between 488 and 489, as Hosius suggests was attempted; but it is hardly likely that, having puzzled out the obscure first note, he misunderstood the second so badly as to lift only 510-519 from their original place for insertion after 488. Yet the order found in AB is 488, 510-519, 489-509, 520. The note in Z is confusing; the order in AB is confused. But this is not enough to assure that the latter manuscripts derive from the former. Realizing the difficulties, Hosius acceded to Beck's qualification of an intermediary manuscript between Z after correction and A, an intermediary that was itself contaminated (Hosius, p. xl). In all of Hosius' examples, then, we find that similarities between Z after correction and A can be attributed at best only to a common source and that often A reflects the character of the manuscript Z^2 used in correcting Z.

In dealing with the interrelationship of ABR, Hosius takes issue in several details with Beck. Beck had rejected Francken's contention that B was copied from A by listing significant agreements between B and R against A. His assumption was that R is an older manuscript than B, contemporary with A (pp. 18-19). If so, all three manuscripts would have had to derive their readings from a common source: a source with interlinear variants accounting for agreements of AB against R and BR against A. The complexity of the interrelationship of the ninth-century manuscripts as revealed by the special readings they offer in conjunction with, or in opposition to, each other makes it desirable that the relative chronology of the manuscripts be established. Yet, especially when so short a period of time separated the production of each manuscript from that of its antecedent, even a competent palaeographer would be tentative in dating the manuscripts comparatively on the basis of script. Beck was neither so qualified nor tentative. Bischoff claims that R was copied about a quarter of a century after B, which means that the common readings of B and R might theoretically have been introduced into B as it descended from A and only subsequently, through B, found their way into the text of R. Only with significant agreements between B and M or Z or a totally unrelated manuscript against A could Beck convincingly have refuted Francken's contention that B is derived from A.

Hosius felt he had other grounds on which to criticize Beck's reconstruction. It is true that Beck did not make very clear whether, when he refers to Z as the ancestor of A, he meant Z, or Z after correction. Hosius assumed the former,

The Text of Lucan in the Ninth Century

perhaps not correctly. In any case, neither assumption accounts for the readings in ABR, and so Hosius, like Beck, had to assume an intermediary, which itself underwent correction, between Z and ABR. He went so far as to describe in general terms the character of the intermediary: "Accurata est effigies libri Z post correcturam ita tamen ut interdum etiam neglecto illius correctore priorem manum repraesentet"; and he further maintained that the corrections in some cases suffered correction. It will be shown by explaining the precise relationship of the extant manuscripts that Hosius' assumption is not necessary. The conclusion he drew from it, however, does neither justice to his understanding nor credit to his logic (p. xlii): " Quae cum ita sint, iam sequitur AB, ubi cum Z aut z [i.e. Z^2] concrepant, abiciendos esse; nam ubi ex fonte haurire possumus, non rivulis longe derivatis utemur; paucis locis ubi discrepant, si cum ceteris codicibus concinunt, sua auctoritate carentes nihil proficiunt, si singularia praebent, suspicionem aut corruptelae aut interpolationis plerumque movent." At the very least, Hosius should have seen that A helps in determining the age of corrections in Z; further, if he credits A with readings divergent from Z that appear independently in other manuscripts, there is no reason why singular readings that do not appear in unrelated manuscripts should be automatically dismissed. The lack of corroboration for a reading may speak more for an accident of the transmission than the uniqueness of the lection. If A partially reflects a source other than Z, it is unwise to limit the extent of that reflection theoretically. Realizing as he did that the manuscripts with which he was dealing were closely, but not directly, connected and that the evidence points to intermediaries that were themselves corrected against other, now lost, manuscripts, Hosius should have abandoned entirely and confidently strict adherence to the "method of Lachmann" rather than attempt to explain away particular difficulties. Instead, he forced himself to make assumptions about the ninth-century manuscripts that ran contrary to his initial and finally unqualified view.

Any hope of a successful resolution to the problem was swept aside when, in 1926, A. E. Housman applied his exceptional talent to the text of Lucan and his distinctive scorn to the most recent editor and his highly regarded manuscript, M. It was once said of Richard Bentley that he treated manuscripts as if they were Fellows of Trinity College: the remark refers to his professional dealings with both. Housman treated the excellent Montpellier manuscript as if it were a contemporary German scholar, and his attitude borders on the hysterical. Absent is any attempt to amass and judge the evidence; absent, too, is any mention of three of the five ninth-century manuscripts. What he offers instead

The Assessment of the Manuscripts by Modern Editors

is diatribe disproportionately severe and a dismissal, rather than an appraisal, of the manuscript evidence.

It seems then to have been a feature of critics working on the text of Lucan that they had fixed general impressions of the tradition—whether the scientific order of Beck and Hosius or the chaos welcomed by Housman—but only the most indistinct understanding of the relationships among the existing manuscripts. Needless to say, it is precisely the details, the welter of variant readings, that must be explained coherently and in orderly fashion to give credence to the general theory.

Chapter IV
Re-examination of M and Z

I propose now to return to the ninth-century manuscripts, examine them afresh, and present a conclusion more in keeping with the evidence.

Lejay realized that M and Z are closely related to each other. Hosius noticed and maintained in his second edition that the similarities between them ceased early in book nine though his claim that Z, not M, deviated from the common model is at best fanciful. Housman was first to point to the lack of close allegiance in the first 481 lines of book 1. Like Hosius, Housman believed that M and Z are, from 1.482 to 9.85, independent copies of a single exemplar, and, on a first examination of M and Z, one is likely to accept this evaluation of the relationship between them. For the first 481 lines they show no close affinity; they agree against GUVP in the following places, where in some instances, the reporting of other unrelated manuscripts robs them of their privacy:

246	deriguere *MZAQ*	diriguere A^2BR*rell.*		d. *Y.*
253	latii *Rcett.*	latia *MZAB*		
277	at Z^2AB*cett.* et ad *MZ*	sed *QGA*^{v}		l.o. *R*
317	dimittet *Rcett.*	dimittit *MZABE*		
349	derunt *MZABE et* deerunt *RQGUVW*	desunt *YPJ*		
350	neque *MZABRQYEJ*	nec *GUVPW*		
414	aestuet Z^2AB*Rcett.*	aestuat *MZEW*		
427	latio *MZABRE*	latios *QVPJ*	latiis *YGUW*	
435	cana *QGUVPEWJ*	canas *MZABRY*		

Re-examination of M and Z

In the same portion of the text, besides a number of individual errors on the part of M or Z alone of the kind that continues throughout the text, the following readings show M and Z divided, each supported by unrelated manuscripts:

64	accipio *MVP*	accipiam *ZABRGUEWJ*		d. QY
103	frangat *ZABRVPE*	franget *MGUJ*		l.o.W, d. QY
138	haerens *MGUVPWJ*	haeret *ZABRE*		d. QY
140	umbram *MGUVPWJ*	umbras *ZABRE*		d. QY
141	et *MVP*	sed *ZABRGU(?)EWJ*		d. QY
181	tempora *ZABRUVPE*	tempore *MQGWJ*		d. Y
209	iubam et usato graue *ZA²BRQGJ* iubas et uasto graue *PE*	iubas et uasto *M(?)Z²UVW* iubam et uasto *A*		d. Y
320	micantes *ZABRP*	minantes *MYGUVEWJ*	mincantes *Q*[1]	
349	nec *ZABRGJ*	neque *MQYUVPEW*		
356	munera *ZABRQYUVEWJ*	munere *MGP*		
359	si licet *ZABQGVP*	scilicet *MRYUEWJ*		
416	ducat *MCYVP*	tollat *ZABRGUEWJ* et tollit *Q*		
429	foedere *MG(?)UEJ(?)*	sanguine *ZABRQYVPW*		
453	datum *GPE*	datum est *ZABRQYVWJ*	datur *MU*	
481	hunc *GU*	tunc *ZABRCQVEW*	nunc *MYPJ*	

This list is more extensive than that of Housman and is, so far as I know, complete.

After 9.85 the close resemblance between M and Z, which begins at 1.483 and is characterized by more than twelve hundred agreements in peculiar errors and variants, suddenly ceases and M bears a resemblance to Parisinus 7502 (P), a tenth-century manuscript, only slightly less striking than its similarity to Z over the previous six thousand lines. There can be no doubt that it is M, the later manuscript, that changes its affiliation; that what was until this point an exemplar closely related to Z is no longer available to M. This does not prevent some fortuitous agreements between the two, sometimes even to the exclusion of P, but they are in readings which could easily have been arrived at by independent, coincidental errors on the part of any two scribes.

Between 1.482 and 9.85 the similarities between M and Z are strikingly

[1] This reading speaks for a model of Q with interlinear corrections.

numerous; in approximately six thousand lines there are more than twelve hundred agreements against the other manuscripts used by Hosius and Housman, including omitted words and lines and nonsense readings which can only be explained by the presence of the same nonsense in a common source. It would seem that, as Housman claimed, M was copied from the model of Z after that model had been truncated at the beginning and the end, the latter loss being made up by a manuscript antecedent to P. His explanation of how this came about is not the only possible one. "It may be asked why the two losses, I 1–482 and IX 86–X 546, were not made good from one and the same manuscript. Because Books I–VI and VII–X were copied by different scribes, and the copying was probably simultaneous" (Housman, p. xii note). It is perfectly possible that a scriptorium with two complete manuscripts of Lucan would set two scribes to work creating a third copy based on the truncated model of Z. The quest for new manuscripts was an earnest one. In the first portion of the text 477 lines are involved—436–440 being a twelfth-century addition—and the loss of a quaternion with thirty lines to a page would account for those lines and a title. On the other hand, the model of Z, after Z was copied, may have undergone partial correction. It is not infrequently noticed that the initial interest of correctors and annotators flags. Thus, Z is heavily annotated over the first six leaves, but very irregularly thereafter. In two manuscripts as alike as M and Z any tampering with either one over a short span of the text will result in glaring discrepancies.

Granting Housman's premise, however, he was still delinquent in not pointing out that in about 175 places in the central portion of the text M and Z disagree in readings where each has the support of unrelated manuscripts. He does, in forgiving M its popularity with Hosius—for that is his tone—offer a small number of individual readings in which each excels the other; but he gives no account of how it came about that these divergences occur in that portion of the text for which he claims that M and Z have a single source. He must have been aware of the difficulty, for he had read discussions of it in Beck and Hosius; and his apparatus criticus acknowledges the disagreements between the two manuscripts in traditional variants. Beck, followed by Hosius, offered the explanation that the model of MZ had undergone correction and therefore carried variants interlinearly. Since their interest was to simplify the tradition, they made little of this fact; but Housman was not wedded to the notion of a single stemma. The conclusion should have been inescapable to him: if M and Z have a single source, that source represents more than a single manuscript.

When M and Z disagree in a traditional variant, it is impossible to say which

Re-examination of M and Z

preserves the reading of the first hand of the exemplar, and which the interlinear correction. Even if it could be ascertained that in every case Z gave the reading of the exemplar, the corrections must nevertheless represent lections found in another manuscript of approximately the same age as the exemplar which it had been used to correct. Housman especially, who realized that the tradition of the text of Lucan was one of readings, not manuscripts, should have welcomed an additional independent source; and this should have been true of the first 482 lines and 9.86 onward as well. But Housman was unwilling to abandon the rhetoric that could characterize M as "a king of shreds and patches," or the polemic that underlies the smug and disingenuous conclusion (p. xiii) "Of all our six manuscripts (MZGUVP) it is the one we could dispense with." Housman had no intention of dispensing with M; not just because it offers independent evidence for 1–482; not just because it records the antecedent of P for four hundred more lines after P breaks off in book 10; but because the evidence of M is of interest and importance throughout. He concludes this unsatisfactory section of his preference on a conciliatory note, "I am saying nothing against it..." and goes on to say something in its favor. "In I 483–IX 85 it is quite equal to Z, excelling it and all in the lections II 245 *derige* (*di-*Z), 707 *classi*, III 410 *ulli*, V 43 *uobis*, VII 93 *potui*, while Z in its turn excels in II 51 *Suebos* (*uos* M), III 510 *maris*, IV 186 *det*, V 680 *gemitu*, VI 274 *cumulo*" (p. xiii). One is tempted to attribute to a certain uneasiness with the forthrightness of his exposition the sloppiness of this compilation. It is trivial (2.51, 2.245, 3.410—where *nuli* in Z is a slight error in copying after *non*: a common source would have read *ulli... aurae* against *ullis... auris* in the rest of the manuscripts, and Z has *aurae*), inaccurate (5.680 is on a page lost in M and copied from another manuscript by Bouhier in the eighteenth century), and arbitrary (3.510 and 6.274 are more likely errors by the scribe of Z than correct readings). Further, at 7.93 *potui* is the reading not of M, but of M², although M had *potuis sine* against *potuit sine* in all other manuscripts including Z. With a larger selection of manuscripts, Z's *det* at 4.186 would be shared by WJ as well as ABR against *dent* QGE, *dat* MYUP, *dant* V. At 5.43 *uobis* is also read by W. Of Housman's list, only M's *classi* at 2.707 remains unique and right. The attraction of M is this: throughout the text M offers readings found in other, later and unrelated manuscripts but absent from Z; and M is at least half a century earlier than those other manuscripts. Z may well be a more complete copy of a common source, but it is through M that we learn of traditional variants available to readers of that source at the time Z was copied from it.

The Text of Lucan in the Ninth Century

To acknowledge that a manuscript was copied from an exemplar that bore the marks of a corrector is to be committed to a kind of investigation not covered by handbooks on textual criticism like that of Paul Maas. In the first place, the family as a metaphor for the relationship between manuscripts, at best inelegant and inaccurate, is especially misleading when applied to a textual transmission like that of Lucan. When a scholar claims that one manuscript is the father of a second, he implies that the second manuscript has acquired all the characteristics of the first, or all that the accuracy of the scribe permits. This would depend on a single set of characteristics and imply, for a closed tradition, a kind of transmission by parthenogenesis. In a contaminated tradition there is no such pure set of inherited characteristics. A new manuscript would have two direct antecedents: the exemplar, which it will follow in format and a majority of its readings, and the manuscript with which that exemplar was compared and from which readings were transferred into the text and between the lines of that exemplar. The new manuscript would thus also have two sets of characteristics, by which it can in some respects resemble its formal model and in other respects the correcting manuscript. It has not been sufficiently well realized that except for inadvertence, when a scribe becomes confused and incorporates a gloss or interlinear variant into the text, no newly copied manuscript has more than one of the possible alternatives at any given place in the text. This means that the copyist of a corrected manuscript must, in places where the original and correcting hands are both legible, choose between the two readings; and no inviolable pattern of preference can be demonstrated. Thus, in the case of M and Z, if they descend from a single corrected source, the variety of readings may include the following: both copy the reading of the text, both copy the reading of the corrector; one copies the text, and the other the corrector; one copies the text, and the other offers his individual aberration; one copies the corrector, and the other offers an individual aberration; both offer aberrations. And it must be added that the aberrations may be completely independent or may be based on either of the two possible readings in the text. Such diversity of variation may well warm the heart of a geneticist; it brings no comfort to the critic concerned with tracing the transmission of a text back to what must ultimately have been a single autograph manuscript.

What, then, can be established about the common source of M and Z? That there was such a source can be demonstrated by the common omission in the two manuscripts of the following verses, lacking in no other manuscripts: 3.608; 5.810; 7.607, 725. To these should be added 2.463-464; for it is unlikely

Re-examination of M and Z

that the only possible mechanical cause for omission, namely, homoeoteleuton (462 *Libonis*, 464 *paternis*) would have influenced two scribes independently. Of all the manuscripts I have examined only MZ omit these verses. In addition to a number of other words, MZ leave out the following: 2.47 *superi*; 3.303 *fata*; 6.801 *uinclis*, 806 *uitae*. It has already been mentioned that about twelve hundred times between 1.483 and 9.85 MZ agree in error against the other manuscripts. A number of their common errors derive from the confusion of similar letters in capital script; I enclose the correct reading in parentheses. 1.600 TOTAM (LOTAM), 628 LEGIENS (TEGENS); 3.325 MITTES (MILES); 4.612—a textbook example with four mistaken transliterations—CEFONAEI PROLEGIT (CLEONAEI PROIECIT), 688 CONCILIVS (CONCITVS); 5.413 PORTIVS (FORTIVS), 737 CENAS (GENAS); 6.480 DEPENSO (DEFENSO); 7.317 SELLAVIT (SATIAVIT),[2] 707 PLEREVITA (FLERE VETA), 730 VILES (VITES). But errors such as 4.59 *uices redies* (*uicere dies*), 5.88 *caelique atitur* (*caeli petitur*), 5.739 *in dulcior* (*mihi dulcior*) indicate that there were minuscule errors in the model and, thus, that the model was itself copied from a minuscule manuscript.

Besides the places where M and Z disagree in offering traditional variant readings, certain errors show traces of the corrected state of the source when both of its copies were written. I refer to such examples as the following: 5.322 *dete legit* MZ, where the correct reading, *detegit*, was mistakenly transliterated from a capital manuscript as *delegit* and corrected by *te* written above and to the left of *le*. 3.718 *superest* cett.; *superes est* ZM. The source had *superes*, the corrector writing *est* over *es*. It is, of course, impossible to know whether the correction was made in the source or whether the source read exactly what is found in ZM after mistaking a correction in its own corrected model. The examples just offered might suggest the latter possibility, since they exhibit Z and M copying exactly the same letters. So, too, at 8.673 *rotareuolui* for *rotare*. It cannot be said whether the gloss *uolui* appeared in a second hand in the source or whether the source copied the gloss in its exemplar.[3] 10.122 *toris* MZ[2]ABYGUWJ; *toros* QVE; *torios* Z.[4] At 8.9 Hosius' critical note reads *sui precium* VGU; *sui facinus*

---

[2] This example is perhaps doubtful. I assume an original error of TI to LL.

[3] Hosius, who distinguishes between consonantal and vocalic *u*, should in his critical note to this word have written *volvi*, not *volui*.

[4] Since M is at this point no longer a descendant of the same manuscript, we cannot tell whether the model had *toris* (*o* over *i*) or *toros* (*i* over *o*) or *torios*. Hosius cites *torios* and *rotareuolui* in his second note on p. xxxv. He also cites 3.58 *caelum lucemque*; *caelumque lucemque* Z; *caelumque* M. Perhaps he envisaged *caelumque* in the source, with *lucemque*

The Text of Lucan in the Ninth Century

PU; *facinusui* (sic M; *sui facinus* Z) *pretium* MZ. In both manuscripts *facinus* has been erased by a corrector. The source must have contained *sui pretium*; its corrector added *facinus* in such a way that M thought it should precede *sui*, Z that it should follow. Had the corrector been more thorough, MZ would both have adopted *sui facinus*; we would then have had no reason to doubt that the source itself read *sui facinus*. This kind of example makes one aware of the dangers of attempting to reconstruct a manuscript, for often there is no way, as there is here, of checking the truth.

I now turn to places where Z and M offer different readings, but where each is supported by at least one unrelated manuscript or where one offers a unique and right reading.

Book 2

213	aquae *MYPE* et aques *W* et aqua *ZC*		aquis *Z²ABRQGJ* et aqui *U*
245	derige *MQE*		dirige *Zrell.*
257	corrupti *MVP*		corruptis *Zrell.*
707	classi *M*	classis *ZGP*	classes *Z²rell.*

Book 3

36	annona *ZABRQGUVEJ*	annonae *MYPCW*
427	priori *ZABRQ*	priore *Mrell.*
459	inanis *MG*	inanes *Zrell. C*
539	posset *MYGPEJ*	possit *ZABRQUVW*
575	conserta *MZ²ABRQYUWJ*	conferta *ZGVPE*
663	illis *MP*	illi *Zrell.*

---

written above the word and the original *-que* marked for excision; i.e., a correction of the source's mistake in going from *-(u)mque* to *-(e)mque*. But this is more circumstantial. At 9.531 *locum* MZ²ABRGUPW; *polum* QYVEJ; *pocum* Z, the state of the source is obscure. though Z's reading makes it likely that both variants appeared in the model. Again at 9.576 we cannot confirm the reading of Z's model by comparison with M. 5.386 *ceperit* M(?)Z for *repperit* may be a variant rather than a gloss.

Re-examination of M and Z

Book 4

45	praeducere *MUV*		producere *Zrell.*	
46	ex *ZQUVPEJ*		et *MABRYGW*	
158	cauae *MGUP*		caua *ZABRrell.*	
177	propinquum *MGEJ*		propinqui *Zrell.*	
186	det *ZABRWJ et* dent *QGE*		dat *MYUP et* dant *V*	
201	steterint *ZABRcett.*		steterant *MUVP*	
274	constet *MQGUVP*		constat *ZABRYEWJ*	
314	distentas *MQUVPEWJ*		distensas *ZABRYG*	
451	laxas *MGJ et* laxa *PW*		laxe *ZABRQYUV*	
671	regna *MQGVEWJ*		regni *ZABRYUP*	
762	ille *MUP*	illi *ZABRYGJ*		illis *QVEW*

Book 5

155	limina *MUVPW*		culmina *Zrell. N*	
421	remis *ZABRYVEWJ*	remi *MQP et* remo *V*		mali *G*
725	remotam *MYUP*		remota *Zrell.*	

Book 6

212	facta *Zcett. et* fracta *C*	fixa *MUVP*	
466	praeducunt *MQYGVEW*	producunt *ZABRUPJC*	
492	labor *Zcett.*	pauor *MUVP*	
505	cantu *Zcett.*	caelo *MUVP*	
601	mihi *MUVP*	tibi *Zrell.*	
604	uulgato *MQGUPW*	uulgatae *ZABRYVEJ*	
686	confudit *MGJ*	confundit *Zrell.*	
687	multum *Zcett.*	primum *MVP*	
752	percussae *Mcett.*	percusso *ZQP*	
781	infernam *Zcett.*	aeternam *UVP* (externam *M*)	

Book 7

93	potui sine M^2 *et* potuissine *M*	potuit sine *Zrell.*
145	gigantas *MZ²ABRQEJ*	gigantes *ZYUVPW*

The Text of Lucan in the Ninth Century

351	uolunt *MYU*	volent *Zrell.*
563	contenta *Zcett.*	contempta *MZ²ABR*
622	ictus *MUW* (istus *P*)	ictu *Zrell.*

Book 8

39	uector *MZ²ABRYGEW* et rector *QVJ*	uictor *ZUP*
133	litora *ZYGUVPEJ*	litore *MZ²ABRQW*
293	nostro *MWC*	est nostro *Zrell.*

Of the 173 places between 1.483 and 9.85 where M and Z disagree and each is supported by manuscripts not otherwise closely related, the foregoing are the most important.[5] In the remainder of the readings P is the manuscript that more than any other supports an otherwise unique reading, agreeing nineteen times with M and twenty-two times with Z.

Up to this point I have worked on the assumption, accepted by editors to date, that there was a single source for the two manuscripts in the central part of the text and argued that this manuscript remained internally unchanged from the time the scribe of Z used it as his model to the time when the scribe of M did. In its trip from somewhere in Luxemburg to Orléans, it lost several gatherings from the end and perhaps one at the beginning. This assumption is tenable if the source manuscript had been corrected and contained interlinear variants. The double readings in Z alone and in M and Z point, independently, to this likelihood. It is also possible that a manuscript bearing corrections, from which Z was copied, was further corrected, as well as truncated, before it reached Orléans, or indeed that Z's model was copied and that copy, itself corrected, went to the scriptorium where it was copied by the scribe of M. There is some formal evidence that M is not an independent copy of the model of Z.

It has already been pointed out that the scribe of the first gathering of Z, in order to get to 1.475 by the end of the eighth verso, wrote lines 408-468 with no regard for the ends of verses. Since lines 436-440 did not exist in the ninth century, it must be assumed that the scribe had a section of the text, most likely a gathering, containing 470 lines of text plus the title. Thus, if the independence

---

[5] At 5.44 all manuscripts have *exhausto* against *exacto* in N. Z's *exhaucto* may be no more than a peculiar error. Possibly, however, it reveals a trace of the ancient variant in the common ancestor of MZ.

Re-examination of M and Z

of M for the first 482 lines indicates the loss of a gathering, it would be a gathering with different lineation from that of the model of Z. 483 *agitantibus* MZ (for *a gentibus*) heralds for Housman the beginning of the use of a single source, 481 *nunc* MYPJ, *tunc* ZABRCQVEW; *hunc* GU the last diversity caused by independent sources. It might be argued that though *nunc* vs. *tunc* appears to be a true variant, initial letters in lines of verse are potentially less stable, especially if entered by a rubricator. Before 481 the last disagreement between M and Z is at 453. This instance loses weight as an argument against a single source for M and Z, because the variation in M may be owing to partial contamination of its model. It is, however, a place where evidence of a formal nature for a single antecedent might be forthcoming and is not.

It was assumed earlier that a scribe of Z broke off in the recto of f. 43 and left the verso blank because the section of text he was given to copy ended with 4.305, while another scribe began copying another section with 4.306 at f. 44r. Although this is mere assumption, it is hard to suppose that a supervisor would tear a bifolium rather than divide the model at a gathering. Between 1.475 and 4.305 there are 2,023 lines of text; within these limits nine lines are omitted by MZ and may thus be considered to have been lacking in a common source. The titles are identical in the two manuscripts, but take up nine lines in M and seven in Z. We may posit something like 2,022 ruled lines in a common exemplar. Just as the abrupt stop in f. 43r of Z indicated that the model was broken up at a gathering at that point, so the partially filled recto and the blank verso of f. 63 in M should mean that the model could be conveniently divided at the end of book six so that a different scribe, working at the same time as the first, could begin book seven at the beginning of a gathering on f. 64r. On the same assumptions used to arrive at the 2,022 lines between 1.475 and 4.305, there are 2,158 ruled lines to be filled between 4.305 and the end of book 6. If there were consistency in a common model in the size of gatherings and the number of lines to a page, the discrepancy between 2,022 and 2,158 ruled lines would preclude immediately the possibility of a common source. Even assuming three quaternions and a ternion of a manuscript with thirty-four lines to a page (i.e. 2,040) followed by four quaternions (2,176), we cannot resolve the discrepancies. And thirty-four lines to a page cannot be made into a gathering that would account for 1.1–475. The reconstruction of a manuscript's format is uncertain at best, depending on a consistency that is all too often lacking in extant manuscripts. Yet the evidence of format provided by M and Z as described above hardly encourages the assumption of a common exemplar.

The Text of Lucan in the Ninth Century

A displacement of lines at 8.570ff in Z has already been mentioned. Z has 571–572 after 573, and it was suggested that the erroneous lineation is a common sort when alternate lines end in the same or a similar word. However, Z also has lines 571–572 in the ruled lines following 536, where they are crossed out. With this, the probability arises that the two lines were omitted in Z's model because of homoeoteleuton and added by a corrector at the top of a page beginning with line 537. This would assume a model with a folio beginning at 537 and continuing to at least 573, thirty-seven lines omitting 571–572. M, itself, has 37. It might seem illogical that a corrector, noting an omission at the bottom of a page would add the verses in the upper margin. Yet Z omits 3.608 on f. 35v, which contains 607–637; Z^2 supplied the missing verse at the bottom of the page. That the scribe of Z first treated the corrector's addition as part of the text and later as a correction albeit not quite in the right place is not inconsistent with his disciplined lack of concern throughout with the content of what he was copying: copying was a mechanical art. A manuscript beginning a leaf with 8.537, however, does not account for a peculiarity in M, namely that 549–552 are absent from their proper place but stand after 525. The cause of this displacement must be mechanical; the lines make no sense in their new context. The only explanation for their location is, as above, that omitted lines in the model were added by a corrector here in an upper margin of a page beginning with line 526. It should be stressed that the explanation covering the two relocations is hypothetical; the behavior of scribes need not be logical. What seems impossible is to provide an explanation that would account for both displacements stemming from the format of a single exemplar.

Finally, it was observed that at f. 108 a scribe of Z spread forty-six verses over fifty-eight ruled lines at the end of a gathering (marked XIIII). The last line, 8.742, presumably was the end of a gathering of the model he was given to copy. Yet the most satisfactory way to account for the divergence of M from Z after 9.85 is to assume that the model of M was there truncated and that the scribe of M had to seek another manuscript to complete his text. But, again, it is most likely that a manuscript becomes truncated at the end of a gathering. Only 215 lines and one title separate the place at which it is logical to posit the end of a gathering in the model of Z and in the model of M.

The problem posed by our inability to reconcile the indications of format in M and Z is no small one. While any one of the difficulties described above could be passed over for lack of positive evidence, the cumulative effect offers one no confidence in predicating the existence of a common model for M and Z. That

Re-examination of M and Z

they have a common ancestor is attested by double readings and twelve hundred common errors. The divergences in places where traditional variants occur can be explained by assuming a single corrected model. But if such a directly antecedent model did not exist, corrections may have appeared in any number of transcriptions between Z and M. The twelve hundred common errors need not argue for a single source. An independent and contemporary copy of the model of Z may have contained many more. In the section between 1.483 and 9.85, M omits only six lines not also omitted by Z; in the same interval Z lacks nineteen lines that are present in M. Previously the assumption would have been that M was more careful; it is also possible that a number of those lines, absent in Z's model, were added by correctors in subsequent transcriptions.

The complexity of the problem should affect only editors insisting on the reconstruction of a stemma; it does not disturb Housman's basic assumptions on the manuscript tradition, except for the rash generalizations that served as ammunition in his war on Hosius. Had he been in possession of the facts, he would have realized that the sources of ninth-century evidence are more numerous than Hosius' apparatus criticus suggests. Presented schematically, the relationship between M and Z, assuming a common model, appears in the accompanying diagram. Lowercase Greek letters indicate lost manuscripts.

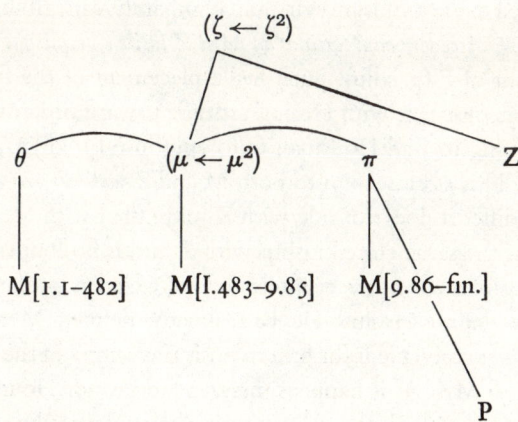

Lines descend from the formal model to its copy. Horizontal lines show the direction of contamination, readings from one manuscript introduced into another. Sigla followed by a superscript 2 should be thought of not as correctors, but as contemporary manuscripts. Parentheses indicate that readings from the correcting manuscript were already in the formal model when it was copied.

Even when M and Z agree in a reading, we cannot be certain whether they are following ζ or both accepting a correction by ζ^2. When they do not agree, it is impossible to say at any point whether M or Z has the reading of the first or second hand in ζ, which we know to have been corrected, or whether ζ offered only the reading we find in Z, while M shows the influence of μ^2. In such cases, each reading must be accompanied by its siglum, and the reader should be aware that both readings were available in the same place and at the same time in the ninth century. The source of readings in M to 1.483 is probably not μ^2, but another manuscript older than M. The source of the last section in M may still be identified with an antecedent of P; but, since ζ probably ended a gathering at 8.742, it is more likely that the loss and suppletion took place in a copy of ζ than in that manuscript itself. But, whatever manuscripts are reflected in the hybrid production M, they lack only formal integrity. With this account of M and Z, the shreds of which M is, according to Housman, king are seen not to be despicable for their mixed origins and the trinity (at least) which M represents must be respected in all its beings.

Similarly oversimplified is the treatment of the Paris fragment F both in Housman (both assign to it the siglum Q). The value of this fragment may be thought restricted in view of its brevity and comparative illegibility. Historically this is not the case. *Accedere eum tertium ad M et Z facile sibi quisque persuadebit* was Hosius' judgment of F (p. xliii). Such facile placement of the fragment in the tradition is not inconsistent with Hosius' attitude toward ordering manuscripts; it is more surprising to find Housman following him (p. xii): "From VIII 575 to IX 85 Q [my F] is as close akin to both M and Z as they are to one another, and when they differ it does not side with Z more than with M. From IX 86 to 124 Q maintains the same close kinship with Z and is no longer akin to M." I suspect that Housman was not very interested in Q, except insofar as it aided him in his polemics against Hosius. He had already defined M and Z as twin brothers, and it was convenient for him to posit F as a copy of the same exemplar that was model to MZ. As it happens, neither Hosius nor Housman is correct. As must be the case with all the manuscripts, the evidence should be presented in sufficient detail either to affirm suppositions of relationship or to make clear the contrary.

There are over thirty places where F agrees with MZ against all, or almost all, the other extant manuscripts. A complete list will be found in Appendix III,

The Assent of the Modern Editors

but mention of 8.787 *inusta* MZF against *inustis plena* rell., 818 *non* MZF against *super* rell., the omission of *illud* by MZF in 871, and 9.36 *Maleon* MZF against *Malean* rell. make it clear that MZF have in their past a common source. So far the claim of Hosius and Housman seems valid; but there are also about forty places where MZ agree in error between 8.575 and 9.85, where they lack the support of F. Since a reading common to MZ must be thought of as having occurred in their common ancestor, that manuscript cannot be the one from which F derives. Again I relegate to an appendix the complete list of errors in MZ not found in F, mentioning only a few in the narrative. Theoretically, of course, one such would cast doubt on the validity of Hosius' reconstruction. Yet, we find F agreeing with manuscripts independent of MZ at 8.653 *digna fui*, at 833 *plangens*, and at 9.59 *fletum* as opposed to *fui digna* MZABR, *plangis* MZABR, and *fluctum* MZ.

F, then, is not a third copy of a single manuscript from which also M and Z were copied. It is, however, closely related to them. It shares readings with MZ and even MZABR; but, when those manuscripts disagree, F shows no special allegiance:

Book 8

660	accersere *GUVJ*	arcersere *MZAB*	arcessere *RFQYPEW*
704	die *MZ²ARUVWJ*	dies *ZBFQYGPE*	
761	nullo *MZABRQVEW*	nudo *FYGJ et* mundo *P*	n.l. *U*

As to its allegiance when M and Z disagree before 9.86, Housman is not quite correct, for F shares eight readings with M and six with Z. From 9.86 onward, F agrees with Z four more times in error. Yet, it must also be mentioned that at 9.122, where ZABRW read *et medias* for *medias*, F sides with M.

When Z², a near contemporary of Z, corrects Z, F agrees more frequently with the corrector than with the first hand. Yet, at one place (8.786), it may reveal the original reading of M and Z: *semusta* (*m* in ras. M²) MYGUVPWJ; *semiusta* (*mius* in ras. Z²) ZABRQE; *sed iusta* FC.

F also has readings independent of the other ninth-century manuscripts. Some of the examples in the appendix will show F disagreeing with not only MZ but also ABR. So, too, 8.724 *tunc* MZABRUVW; *nunc* FQYGPEJ.

Though F underwent correction, a number of its unique readings stand unchanged. At 8.703 for *cladesque omnes*, it reads *clades omnesque*; it transposes word order at 713 from *raptim tumulum* to *tumulum raptim* and at 719 from *quaesitum corpus* to *corpus quaesitum*. A full report of the readings of F may be found in Klein;[6] the foregoing suffice to show that no extant manuscript is derived from it.

No single manuscript can be reconstructed to cover all the readings of the ninth-century manuscripts, though they share characteristics that distinguish them, even after extensive correction, from QGUV or P, which are themselves diverse from each other. F, as we have seen, is related to MZ, but no more closely than those two are related to each other. All were written in the first half of the ninth century. Their evidence is often redundant; but, where the three do not agree in a reading, their value is independent and equal. Their relationship may be shown by the accompanying scheme.

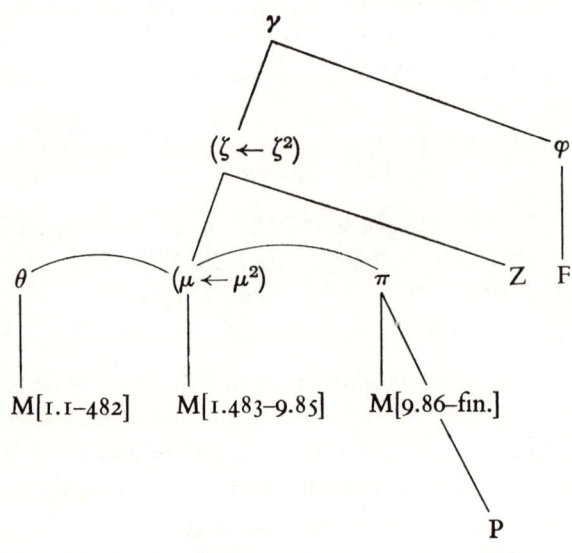

[6] J. Klein, "Zu Lucanus," *RhM* N.F. 24 (1869) 121–126.

Chapter V
Re-examination of ABR

The three remaining manuscripts of the ninth century, ABR, all have Z as a formal antecedent. Were the transmission of the text of Lucan purely vertical—had there been no comparison, no correction of manuscripts—these three books would be mere replicas of Z, distinguished only by the vagaries of their individual scribes and the scribal errors they perpetrated in copying. They would, then, indeed be *codices descripti* and fully worthy of the silence with which they now are treated. This is not the case; for different reasons, all these manuscripts are of interest and contribute independently to the constitution of the text of Lucan in the Carolingian period.

Their dependence on Z and, therefore, their interdependence is assured by the displacement of 3.211 to follow 193. The order of verses can be explained only by a manuscript that lacks 211 in its proper place and supplies it in the hand of a corrector at the top of a page beginning with verse 194. Only Z fulfills these conditions. It was on this basis that Beck, followed by Hosius, dismissed A and B from serious consideration. Yet, even in his final edition, Hosius records several readings of A and B in his apparatus criticus. Similarly, Beck in his study would not commit himself to the utter dependence of these manuscripts on Z and, thus, their utter worthlessness as witnesses. A clear conflict existed between the desire for an ordered, streamlined tradition and the nature of the evidence. The difficulty arose from the failure precisely to define the relationship of ABR, not only to Z, but also to each other. Beck properly despaired of a single direct source for ABR; but in his attempt to sort out the problem he allowed himself several confusions and misrepresentations. Most damaging of the former was that he did not take the corrections of Z^2 into account in deriving A from Z. He thus precluded the possibility that he would so much have liked to be able to

The Text of Lucan in the Ninth Century

accept, namely, that A is a direct copy of Z. Then, by his judgment that R is a contemporary of A, older than B, he had to conclude from divisions of allegiance like ZA vs. R, ZR vs. A, AB vs. R, and BR vs. A, that none is copied directly from Z or from each other. He ended up with the accompanying

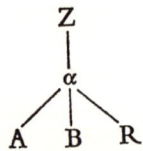

stemma, admitting that α had undergone contamination, i.e., had been compared with another manuscript and contained interlinear corrections that might explain divergences in the allegiance of ABR. His stemma—of the design conventional for direct, uncontaminated descent—does not reflect the complexity of the transmission it attempts to describe. As it stands, it cannot account for the variety of evidence engendered by comparison of a manuscript with an independent source. Nor in his discussion did Beck acknowledge the conclusion of the assumption the evidence forced him to accept. If α was corrected against another manuscript, the descendants of α would reflect a tradition independent of α's formal antecedent, Z. Yet as a mere copy of Z after correction by Z^2, α could offer no evidence independent of Z and the readings added and altered by Z^2. Those characteristics in A, B, or R, which are independent of Z and Z^2 and individual scribal error, must in Beck's reconstruction be attributed to a correcting manuscript which introduced readings into α. No such manuscript is represented in the stemma or acknowledged in Beck's final notion of how the tradition should be presented. In other words, with a diagram such as the one which follows, which follows the conventions described on p. 55, Beck would better have represented the tradition as he reconstructed it. This account of the relationship of A to Z claims nothing not acknowledged by both Beck and Hosius; it does, however, insist on the importance of two manuscripts now lost, Z^2 and $α^2$. Hosius conscientiously reports corrections of Z and, by citing A (as opposed to Z or Z^2), acknowledges $α^2$. But he made no attempt systematically to distinguish the hands or ages of correctors in Z, nor did he ever examine A to see precisely what it contained other than what it inherited from Z after correction. Z^2 in Hosius' apparatus criticus—and therefore in Housman's—simply refers to readings not by the first hand. For example, 7.257–258 and

Re-examination of ABR

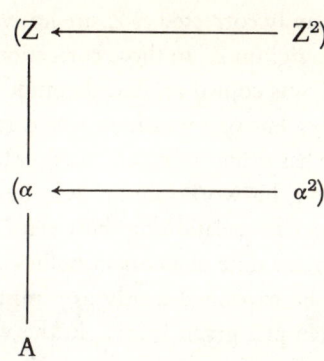

10.122a are attributed to Hosius to Z^2, though they were introduced into Z in the twelfth century. That Housman does not attribute them to Z^2 is not a mark of discrimination, for neither does he credit Z^2 with 6.207, an addition anterior to the copying of A.

In our attempts to recover, isolate, and present ninth-century evidence for the text of Lucan, the readings that can be subsumed under the siglum Z^2 and limited to the first half of the ninth century have a particular importance. Attention to the evidence of correcting hands for the currency of traditional readings throughout the Middle Ages is in itself, as Fraenkel maintained, mandatory for an editor. Yet, when such corrections are not limited in age or distinguished one from another, neither is the source; there is always the possibility that agreements between an early manuscript and correcting hands in later manuscripts may not be independent. The evidence of Z^2, on the other hand, is ipso facto independent of Z and virtually coeval with it.

Our sure knowledge of Z^2, the manuscript(s) used to correct Z, is limited to the readings that have been introduced into Z. It may sometimes be tempting to argue from the silence of Z^2 where a traditional variant in Z is not corrected or an omitted line not added; and, doubtless, the absence of correction will at times be owing to the fact that the manuscript(s) represented by Z^2 shared Z's reading or omission. In book 7 lines 90, 103, and 200 are all omitted by Z and not added until after A was copied. Since Z^2 did not transmit these lines, we are in no position to say whether they were in his correcting manuscript. Line 90 is omitted by ZM, 103 by ZMUP, 200 by ZMP. If we could presume that Z^2 lacked these lines, it would not be the only indication that Z^2 was more in character with ZM than the majority of the tenth-century manuscripts; but the inference here is far from compelling. Arguments based on what is not found, even in a manuscript so heavily corrected as Z, are not valid. What can be done in most cases is to limit the siglum Z^2 to those corrections definitely—or almost certainly—made before A was copied around the middle of the ninth century.

When a later scribe adds a line or a word, or even certain letters, he can often be identified in time; if he has made an erasure, set dots under letters, or written, for example, an *i* above an *e*, his work cannot easily be distinguished from that of an earlier corrector. Once the relationship between Z and A is established, it can be used as evidence for the time of a correction in Z. Often A will contain a corrupt reading that can be explained neatly as a misinterpretation of a correction in Z, as in the examples given below. In the vast majority of cases A agrees with a correction in Z against the first hand. Yet it cannot be argued that a copyist will consistently prefer corrections at the expense of still legible readings of the first hand. A's failure to reflect a reading of the corrector of Z cannot in and of itself be used as a criterion for dating the correction. The behavior of copyists in choosing readings is somewhat idiosyncratic, though they lean heavily toward corrections. The fact does emerge that they make clear choices. Their concern is to transmit a single reading, rather than to record the possibilities.

When attempting to assess a corrector and the material at his disposal, one is gratified to find nonsense-readings imported into the text. Any copyist can produce nonsense through inadvertence or the inability to read accurately the text before him. When a corrector creates order out of chaos, it might be assumed that, endowed with a certain talent, he was using his own ingenuity to correct the text. When a corrector introduces nonsense into the text, there can be only one explanation: he is transmitting faithfully into one manuscript what he has seen in another. When Z^2 wrote over *mittendis* at 3.317 *miciendis*, he indicated that he was collating unquestioningly from another manuscript. Similarly at 2.567 the corrector's own Latinity did not persuade him to write *omina* for *omnia*; he misread a manuscript or transmitted its error. So, too, *inplere* for *implete* at 4.144. No number of such readings, nor the addition of lines omitted in Z or MZ, can preclude the possibility that at times Z^2 did stop collating and instead turn to conjectural criticism. Within the space of thirty-five lines in book 6, there are four distinctive readings, found only in Z^2 and its dependents among the manuscripts I report:

81	pabula Z^2AB	gramina *rell.*	
100	perempta Z^2ABR	cadentum *rell.*	

Re-examination of ABR

101	manent Z^2ABR	iacent *rell.*
114	rumpere rictu Z^2ABR	frangere morsu *rell.*

pabula looks like an ancient gloss and is found in the correcting hands of two manuscripts (M^2G^v). *perempta*, too, is found elsewhere, as a variant in M. *rumpere rictu* is unlikely in the extreme to have flowed off the inspired pen of the same scribe who wrote *streni* over *sternit* (ZM) at 7.100, where the other manuscripts read correctly *sterni*. In the latter case, he was not thinking about a word; he copied letters. He wrote *streni* and *rumpere rictu* for the same reasons: he saw, or thought he saw, them in another manuscript. The presumption is, then, that he wrote *manent* above *iacent* for the same reason.

It seemed unwise to encumber an already dry narrative with long lists of variant readings and the manuscripts in which they are contained. On the other hand, for an accurate assessment, the evidence must be presented in its entirety. I have therefore relegated to appendices the full lists of readings which make up as complete a collation as is possible of now lost manuscripts. For Z^2 I have given by line number the places where a casual error in Z was corrected before A was copied. If another manuscript shares this untraditional error, it is given in addition. Casual errors not reported by Hosius in his third edition are given special mention. The longer lists give the places where Z^2 introduces into the ninth-century tradition readings that must have existed in late antiquity or where Z^2 imports its own nonsense, or the nonsense of another manuscript, into Z. The Z^2 reading is given first. The collation of Z^2 is found in Appendix IV.

Some attention, perhaps, should be given to readings which look to me as if they might be by a Z^2 hand, but which are not reflected in A. There is no assurance that a scribe will always accept the correction in his exemplar, but far less confidence can be given to such readings than to those whose dating can be guaranteed by their presence in A. I mention a few:

7.510 illic quaeque suo miscet gens proelia telo.

quaeque A^2BR *cett.*; quoque ZA; quippe Z^2?

The correct reading is that given by the majority of the manuscripts, *quoque* is Z's aberration dutifully passed on to A. *quippe* in Z^2 may have begun as part of an explanatory note. The question is whether the corrector Z^2 found *quippe* in his text or whether he mistook a suprascript note for a correction. In other words, Z^2 was probably, like every other ninth-century manuscript of Lucan we know of, corrected. This fact should neither surprise nor disturb. On the other hand, 8.717 seems to indicate that the manuscript used to correct Z itself derived from a corrected manuscript. The reading of the majority of manuscripts:

> 8.716f quaestor ab Idalio Cinyraeae litore Cypri
> infaustus Magni fuerat comes.

717 infaustus Magni *MZ cett.*; infaustusque fugae $Z^{2?}G^2$

seems to be guaranteed, as has been noticed, by *Aen.* 6.166 *Hectoris hic magni fuerat comes*. *fugae* at some point was written above the line in a text as an explanation; the next stage was a metrical emendation to allow *fugae* into the text. This development is more likely to have occurred in antiquity and to have appeared as a part of the text in Z^2.

> equitum proparate cateruae,
> 2.498–499 ite simul pedites, ruiturum ascendite pontem.

499 ascendite *MZ cett.*; escendite $Z^{2?}CP$

By the tenets of textual criticism, the rare and more exquisite word should be preferred. Housman, acknowledging this, accepts *ascendite* as better suited with *pontem*, though it can be argued that how the reader visualizes the actions, depends on the verb he accepts, and *escendite* might heighten the contrast with the adjective *ruiturum*.

> 2.653ff sufficerent aliis primo tot moenia cursu
> rapta, tot oppressae depulsis hostibus arces,
> ipsa, caput mundi, bellorum maxima merces,
> Roma capi facilis.

654 oppressae *MZABRQYGWJ*; infestae *UVP*; obsessae $Z^{2?}adn.^v$

Here we have the explicit statement of an ancient scholar that *obsessae* as well as *oppressae* was found in manuscripts of the late Empire. *oppressae*, however, is to be preferred; whenever Lucan uses the verb *obsideo*, its object is a person, and, where he uses the participle, the noun it agrees with is a person. 3.349–350:

> nec pauet hic populus pro libertate subire
> obsessum Poeno gessit quae Marte Saguntum

Re-examination of ABR

is not an exception. *Saguntum* stands specifically for the inhabitants of that town.

> 1.228ff sic fatus noctis tenebris rapit agmina ductor
> impiger, it torto Balearis uerbere fundae
> ocior et missa Parthi post terga sagitta
> Vicinumque minax inuadit Ariminum ...

229 it $Z^{2?}VPEM^2$ et; *rell*.

Housman, acknowledging that *it* was more likely to be corrupted to *et*, still accepts the majority reading as being better suited. The rhetorical balance achieved by *et ... et* in the same place in their lines introducing parallel ablatives of comparison is certainly attractive. On the other hand, it is not easy to imagine the difficulty of interpretation that would induce a reader intentionally to break the balance by substituting *it*. Housman may be using a casual error to improve the author.

Besides corrections of Z^2 that inform the text of A and a few probably early corrections, such as those just mentioned, not reflected in the copy of Z, there are other correctors of Z who worked in the ninth century. They, however, in altering readings, so changed the text as to obliterate the original reading. In these cases, if A does not agree with the correction in Z, that correction must postdate the copying of A. In an apparatus criticus, then, they would be designated, if at all, by Z^3. One example of this kind of correction is found in 3.382:

> aggere diuersos uasto committere colles

diuersos uasto *MZG*; diuerso uastos $Z^3CRQYUVPEWJ$; diuersos uastos Z^2AB

The eventual correction of Z was to *diuerso uastos*, but once the *-s* of *diuersos* was erased, it could not have found its way into A. Probably Z^2's manuscript did have *diuerso uastos*, but his correction, changing *uasto* to the accusative plural, was incomplete. Similarly the additions of complete lines at 7.90, 103, 200. These are added interlinearly and could not be avoided by a copyist. Yet, they do not appear in A, and so, though early, they cannot appear as Z^2.

Of the lines omitted by Z, Z^2 supplies all but 1.436–440, 3.167–168, 4.68, 151, 6.152, 188, 7.90, 103, 154, 257–258, 8.124, 9.83, 615, 10.296. A true evaluation of its contributions can be gained only by studying the readings that it possesses earliest of our ninth-century manuscripts. I do not intend to examine them here, for this is not a critical study of the text. It will be seen, however, that while Z^2 records some rare and interesting readings, very often it exhibits, in contrast to Z or MZ, a less exquisite reading.

Of considerable interest here, on the other hand, are a number of readings in A that result from a confusion as to the intention of the correction in Z. Such examples provide added proof of the formal relationship of A to Z. They also show how readings that may on the surface look like valid alternatives to the text can develop from technical misunderstanding. The following examples are by no means exhaustive; others will be apparent in the collation of A.[1]

1.642 *nulla cum* MZVA^v; *nulla sine* Z^2A^2R rell. C. Z^2 wrote *sine* between the two words and placed dots under *cum*. A, not noticing that *cum* should be omitted, wrote *nulla sine cum*.

2.27 *sed iam* Z^2A^2 cett.; *nec tam* MZ. Z^2 wrote *sed iam* directly over *nec tam*. In A we find *sed*; *iam* is written in an erasure, the first letter of which was *n*. We may assume that A originally had *sed nec tam* (or perhaps *iam*).

2.269 *fulminibus* Z^2A^2 cett.; *fluminibus* MZ; *ful-* between the initial and the first minuscule letter Z; *fulluminibus* A.

2.554 *hostis* Z^2A^2 cett. A^v; *hosti* MZ. Z^2's upright *s* over the *i* with the hastas of the two letters joining caused A to write *hosts*.

2.620 *compositum* Z; *oppositum* Z^2A^2 rell. Z^2 put *op* between *c-* and *-om*. A saw and wrote *copompositum*.

3.127 *uouerunt* A^{2}cett.; *-re* over *-runt* and *in* added Z^2; *uouererunt in* A. The variant in Z^2 *uouere in*, entailing an *-ere* perfect, probably goes back to antiquity; it appears nowhere else in the manuscripts of Lucan.

3.359 *ad axen* MZ cett.; *in axen* Z^2A^2BRYEW. Between *a* and *d* Z^2 wrote *in* above the line. A has *ad indaxen*. The first *d* is not explained, Since A^2 corrected to *in axen*, this is the reading, possessed by BR, of a manuscript independent of Z^2. It is now found in the later manuscripts YEW.

3.414 *Ipse* Z^2A^2 cett.; *Pere* Z. Z^2 inserted *ipse* between the initial letter and *-ere*. *Ipsere* A.

4.499 *transibit* Z^2A^2BRYGUPEJ; *transisset* MZQVW; *transisibitset* A. Z^2 had written *ibit* above *-sset*. We note here as in other cases that the agreement of B and Z^2 is owing to nothing of internal transmission, but to the accident that A^2

---

[1] See Appendix V. Where A^2 corrects A to Z^2's reading, A has confused Z^2's correction of Z.

Re-examination of ABR

read what Z^2 did. If A^2 had seen *transisset* in his correcting manuscript, he would have erased *ibit* in A's conflation and the manuscripts would have divided *transisset* MZA²BRQVW; *transibit* Z²YGUPEJ. And, of course, if A were lost or not considered, the reading would, as it now stands, be used to show B's affiliation to MZ.

4.677 *autololes* Z²G; *autolopes* ZA²BR rell.; *autdolopes* P; *audolopes* Y. Z^2, knowing the correct reading, put an *l* above the *p*, but the hastas joined, and the scribe of A saw *b*. His *autolobes* was corrected by A^2 to the conventional *autolopes*. If we could not see the exact state of Z, we might logically conjecture a confusion of B and P in capital script.

5.769 *non* Z²A² cett.; *nos* MYW. Z appears to have written *n s(olim)*, a tiny *o* having been added between *n* and *s*. Z^2 also put a dot under the *n* and wrote *non* above the line. Before correction, A had *non nos*.

6.94 *pati* Z²RQGUVPEJA^v; *patens* MZA²BYW; *patiens* A. Z^2 wrote *ti* above *tens*; A simply replaced the *t* of *patens* with *ti*.

6.281 *ut* ZRCVWA^v; *et* Z²A²BMQYGUPEJ and *&* over *ut* Z^2: *ut et* A.

6.375 *undae* Z²A² cett.; *undas* MZ. Z^2 put an *e* over the *a* without, as it appears, deleting the *s*: *undes* A.

7.101 *meis* Z²A²BR cett.; *malis* MZ. The correction of Z^2 is written above and to the left of *malis* in Z. A has *meis malis*.

7.130 *mortis uenturae* Z²A²BRYUW; *et mors uentura est* MZQGVPEJA^v. Z^2 wrote *mortis uenturae* over *mors uentura est*, leaving the ampersand in Z undeleted: *& mortis uenturae* A.

8.155 *iam* MZUP; *non* Z²A²BRQYGVEWJ. Z^2 wrote *non* over the *-am* of *iam*. A had *ianōm*.

8.240 *famuli* Z²QYGVEJ; *famulo* UPA^v; *famulos* MZ; *famulus* W. Z^2 read *famuli* in his manuscript; he therefore marked *-os* for excision with dots, merely changing *o* to *i*. The result is *famulis* ABR.

8.268 *ut nequeam* Rcett.; *ut nequem* M; *unequem* Z. Z^2 added a *t* between *u* and *n* and an *a* over the *e*. A wrote *ut nequam*. B, as will be seen, is formally descended from A. In A, an *e* has been written over the *a*. B has *nequem*. One may wonder whether A^2, like MZ, had in his manuscript *nequem*, in which case B read as directed, or whether A^2 meant to restore *nequeam* by the same method of correction that Z^2 used, in which case the error has gone full circle via two misinterpreted corrections.

8.318 *Maeotida* Z²A² cett.; *Maeotides* MZ. Z set dots under *-es* and wrote an *a* directly above the *e*. A ignored the dots and copied *Maeotidas*.

The Text of Lucan in the Ninth Century

8.392 *moriare* Z²A² cett.; *moria* MZ. The loss of final *-re* is not infrequent in early manuscripts of Lucan. Z² knew the correct reading, for he added *-re* over the *a*. The scribes of A, misunderstanding the correction, replaced *a* with *-re*, to read *morire*. So at 9.471, where Z reads *qua* for *quia* and Z² adds the *i* over *a*, the copyist created *qui*.

9.79 *terens* MZQGUVPEA^v, *tenens* Z²A²BRYWJ. Z² wrote *n* above *r*; A copied *ternens*. A² erased the *r*.

9.430 *petimus ab* ZQWC (*petemus ab* MUP); *petiuimus* YGVEJ. It would seem that Z² had something like the latter in mind when he set dots under the *ab*. But that is the full extent of his correction. A copied *petimus*, omitting *ab*. Were this an isolated case, it would indicate only common source. I suspect that the error began with a haplography of *ab* before *orbe* with an *or* ligature. Some scholar emended to *petiuimus* to make meter. It may be that the model of Z² was not thus corrected.

In all the above examples, and there are others fully as obvious, we can see what the scribe of A did when confronted with a corrected reading in Z. In some cases, like 8.392 *morire* and 6.94 *patiens*, we are entitled, on the basis of this knowledge, to leave the unique reading of A(B) out of an apparatus criticus. What is of tremendous interest is the faithfulness with which the scribe of A tried to preserve what he saw in his exemplar. It may be said that his faith was greater than his care and that both impress us more than his attention to Latinity. But the ignorant scribe is more likely to report accurately the evidence of his predecessor than an educated copyist or scholar. It is important to try to assess the character of a particular scribe before crediting him with emendation.

One more bit of evidence that both shows the relationship and comparative chronology of Z and A and supports the contention that for A copying was primarily an occupation of the hand, not the mind, is found at 4.636, where A offers *telluris uiribus egne ille*, with *egne* erased by A². There is no traditional variant, possible gloss, or contextual reason to account for *egne*. In Z, however, on f. 49, on the verso of which this line appears, an oblong hole in the parchment has affected 2.636–639. In 636 *uiribus* is written to the left of the hole, *ille* to the right. I suspect that the scribe of A saw a part of the word *regna* (4.577) visible through the defective leaf from f. 48v and copied what he saw, namely, *egne*. Folio 48v begins with 567, f. 49v at 625; the lines in question, then, 577 and 636, would be ten and eleven lines respectively from the top of the area of their folios ruled for text. Since each leaf was ruled separately, and not uniformly,

Re-examination of ABR

there is no intrinsic difficulty in the discrepancy of one line. *Segnior* in 580, on the other hand, does seem as if it would be too low. Though as presently bound the manuscript does not line up with (*r*)*egna* directly under the hole, this does not seriously invalidate the argument. The book has been re-sewn and re-bound since 850.

In examining readings in A that resulted from a scribe's mistaken notion of a correction by Z^2, I have assumed no intermediary between Z and A. Beck, followed by Hosius, was forced to posit α because he did not understand the relationship between Z and ABR. He did not realize that R, as will be shown, is dependent on A and that readings held in common by those two manuscripts speak for that dependence rather than a common source. When ABR, AB, or AR share a reading, we can attribute that reading to A. We must then address ourselves to the question of the source of readings originating in A, a copy of Z after correction. Again I relegate a full listing to an appendix (see Appendix V). All but the following will immediately suggest a casual error in copying by the scribe of A.

Book 2

426 culta *ABREWJM²U²*   tecta *rell.*   dexta *P*

Book 5

379 dalmatico *ABGVEJ*   delmatico *MZRQYUPW*
625 astra *Acett.*   anstre *M(?)Z*   anstra *Z²*

Book 6

451 obducit *(A)B*   abducit *MZRQYEWJ*   abducet *GUVP*
474 non expulit *(A)BREWG^v*   non extulit *Z²QYGUVPJ*
     non explit (non ex *in ras. Z²*)*Z*   non extulit (tulit *in ras. M²*)*M*

Book 8

852 imbriferas *ARMCA^v*   imbrifera *Z²A²BQYGUVEWJ et*
                                    umbrifera *ZP*

The Text of Lucan in the Ninth Century
Book 10

245 fluctus *ABRMUVW*   fluctu *ZCYGEJ* et flatu *Qc*   d. *P*

This is a full list of readings that could be attributed to a corrector of a lost intermediary between Z and A. For 6.451 and 474 see Appendix I. *Dalmatico* (5.379) and *astra* (5.625), as well as *imbriferas* (8.852) where the following word begins with *s-*, cannot be given much weight. This leaves 2.426 and 10.245 that might tempt an editor to report them in an apparatus criticus (see Appendix I). It is, however, inconceivable that a corrector, no matter how perfunctory, would apply himself to the text of Lucan and add only two readings with any claim to traditional value. These few possible readings are much better attributed to random cases of probability in a welter of impossibilities. Except for them, there is no reason to assume an intermediary between Z and A. A, then, is a *codex descriptus*. Yet, it has already been of importance in allowing us to date many of the corrections in Z to the first half of the ninth century. But even when Z^2 has been established, when it is acknowledged that Z^2A give no more information than Z^2, A should not be discarded, for it contains evidence of two independent manuscripts not appreciably more recent than itself.[2]

That there are corrections in the text of A is not surprising: all the ninth-century manuscripts of Lucan are heavily corrected. However, the dating of corrections is so difficult on the basis of script alone that a siglum A^2 would have little value as a representation of early evidence. Once again, however, internal evidence allows us to limit A^2 to a terminus ante quem, for it can be shown that B, a manuscript written in the third quarter of the ninth century, is a descendant of A. This time it is not A^2's entry that demonstrates the relationship, but the correction of another man, whom I refer to as A^v. A^v was no ordinary corrector, but a collator who introduced into the margins of A some eight hundred readings demonstrably taken from another manuscript. It was his practice never to change the text or insert variants interlinearly. Rather, he marked the word in question in the text and after a similar marking in the margin wrote *al(iter)* and the variant he found in his second manuscript. Thus, when at 9.944 he found in the text of A:

    iamque procul nemorum rara est attollere frondes

[2] 2.126 *uestae* A^2BRM(?); *dextrae* CQYGUVPEWJA^v should be mentioned. A is illegible. Z omits the word, Z^2 is silent. The normal assumption, that A read what A^2 does not, i.e. *dextrae*, must be here suspended.

Re-examination of ABR

rather than make two changes in a single line, he wrote in the upper margin the line as his manuscript had it:

iamque procul nemorum rarae se tollere frondes

with his mark (/.) before the line and to the left and just above the first word of line 944. In A f. 132v begins with line 939. B has, after line 938:

iamque procul nemorum rarae se tollere frondes

later crossed out, and after 943:

iamque procul nemorum rara c̄ adtollere frondes.

Thus we have evidence of a sort as compelling as that which determined the relationship between Z and A to show that B is a formal descendant of A. Consequently, when we find a reading shared by A^2B, we may assume that A^2 represents a corrector working before B was copied and thus using a manuscript of approximately the same age as A.

The same A^v is responsible for the erroneous order of lines in B at 3.165ff. Lines 167–168 are omitted in MZAUPE. In A they are added in one continuous line by A^v at the bottom of f. 30r, below 169. But A^v's clear marking indicates that the added lines should be inserted between 165 and 166. Lines 167–168 appear in B in the following order: 165, 167, 168, 166. Whether A^v here reflects the state of his manuscript or has placed the mark of insertion incorrectly is impossible to determine. The order he imposed follows that of lines omitted by homoeoteleuton; but, though the lines are left out by unrelated manuscripts, no mechanical reason for the omission suggests itself, and only B and the closely related R exhibit this order.

Once the relationship between A and B has been determined, we can see again how corrections in the earlier manuscript cause confusion for the scribe of the later. I refer to such peculiarities as: 4.119 *paludes* mss.; *pludes*(*a* over *p* A^2)A: *apludes* B. 6.7 *alea* mss.; *alia* MZP; A^2 extended three horizontal lines from the vertical hasta of the *i* into the following *a*; B read this as *ali*. 4.276 *aperit* mss.; *aperi* (*t* over *i* A^2)A; *aperti* B. 9.92 *ferre* mss.; *terre* Z(*t* erased A^2)A; *erre* B. 10.97 *inire peto* mss.; *intrepto* Z (*i* erased, *t* corr. to *i* A^2)A; *ni repeto* B.

The Text of Lucan in the Ninth Century

At 5.276 B has *uit**e*, where all other manuscripts agree on *uitae*. The two erased letters are illegible and no alternative reading suggests itself. With the fact established that B is a formal descendant of A, we may look to the latter manuscript for assistance. Indeed, it provides the solution to the problem of B's reading. With the other manuscripts A has *uitae*, but the *a* is of the open variety commonly, though by no means exclusively, written by the scribe of A. B, then, doubtless saw and originally wrote *uitice*. In the case of B's descendance from A an intermediary will be assumed; the origins of mechanical errors of this sort need not be found in A itself. I refer to readings resulting from mistaken letter forms such as the following. At 8.238 the manuscripts read: *uolet* YQGUVEWJ; *uolit* MZ; *ualet* Z^2ARP; *uidet* B. The intermediary scribe must have copied *ualet* as *uiclet*, the *cl* being read as *d* either by a corrector, who closed the gaps between the letters, or by B himself. B seems to have had trouble with open *a*, *ic*, and *u*, which also resembles the open *a*, since at 6.41, where Z^2 and A read *tescua* for *tesqua*, B had, before correction, *tescica*. This same confusion is in part responsible for the readings of B at 6.563; for *laeua morienti*, A has *leua *orienti* (*m* in ras.); in B is found *letimorientem* with an *a* written above the line between *i* and *m* by B^2. The whole difficulty is not explained, but it seems likely that *leu-* was read as *leti*. Since we find the closed *a* here in A, we must assume that the intermediary copied it using an open *a*.

Another place where B preserved what A read before correction is at 9.175, where B's *bucerta* was copied from A which now reads *buceta* (*ta* in an erasure of three letters). Similarly, 9.219 *Tarcon**motus* after an erasure; *Tarconthmotus* B.

Once more, it cannot be decided with certainty whether A^2 was a single corrector or a number of hands. It may be assumed that the sigla A^2B represent a reading earlier than B. Neither siglum is recorded in the most recent editions of Lucan. There are about 275 such entries, recorded in Appendix VI. While in many cases A^2 merely corrects casual errors in A, often those inherited from Z, it also provides evidence of sincere, if mindless, concern to correct A when A differs from the correcting manuscript; and it introduces, chronologically for the first time, a number of variants which by their presence in unrelated manuscripts are proclaimed as traditional. The number of nonsense-readings, as was the case with Z^2, cannot guarantee against freehand correction, but the extent to which A is marred by petty error, even after A^2's work, argues against A^2's having applied his own critical faculties to the text to any extent. A glance at Appendices VII and IX on A^v and R will give some indication of the number of mistakes that remained in the transmission from Z through Z^2, A, and A^2.

Re-examination of ABR

As examples of unreflective copying by A^2, the following may be cited:

Book 2

345 mutarin A^2R et mutari et B et   mutarim rell.
     mutari ZAA^v

Book 3

645 tibi A^2BRM ibi rell.

Book 4

612 proieiecit A^2B et proleiecit A proiecit Z^2Rrell. et prolegit MZ
672 athlans A^2BR et atlans Z^2ACP atlas rell.

Book 5

708 consortis A^2Z et consorti A et   consertis rell.
     consortes B

Book 6

6   ali A^2B et alia $MZAP$ alea rell.   n.l. R

Book 7

28   somnos A^2BR somnus rell.
732 reuocet A^2B reuocent rell.

Book 8

327 crassu A^2B crassos Z^2Arell. et grassos MZ

When to such entries as the above are added those where A^2 corrects nonsense resulting from A's misunderstanding a correction of Z^2, as for example at

The Text of Lucan in the Ninth Century

2.27, 3.359, 4.242, 677, 6.147, and 7.101, there remain a comparatively small number of instances in which A^2 provides the earliest evidence of ancient variants in the ninth-century tradition. That is to say, even after the labors of A^2, a copy of A, specifically B, looks much more like Z or M than like the tenth-century manuscripts, GUVP or Q. Nor, in view of the number of corrections of peculiar errors of Z, ZA, Z^2A, and A, is this fact likely to be owing to chance. The manuscript used by A^2, if we possessed it, would be remarkably similar to Z and M and the fragmentary F.

The same could not be said of A^v, the manuscript used by the corrector who limited himself to the margins of A. All decipherable entries of A^v are collected in Appendix VII. Since they are antecedent to the production of B, these readings can be limited in time to between about 850 and 875. It is easy to establish that A^v was not, as he would not be expected to be, a conjectural emendator. In several places he introduces nonsense into the margins of A, nonsense he saw, or thought he saw, in his manuscript:

Book 1

214	pumceus A^v	pumceus *rell.*

Book 3

57	signe A^v	segne *rell.*
272	lagsus A^v	lapsus *rell.*

Book 6

291	superi A^v	super *rell.*
757	rectu A^v	rictu *rell.*

Book 7

84	si(natus) A^v	senatus *rell.*
698	gessisse A^v	cessisse *rell.*

Book 9

213	iuiram A^v	iubam *rell.*

Re-examination of ABR

Assuming, then, the sincerity of A^v's collation, we would attribute the following glosses to the text or margins of A^v's correcting manuscript, rather than to A^v's own attempt to explain the text:

1.397	fluminis A^v	uosegi $G^2U(?)$	uogesi *rell.*
3.154	apertas A^v		reclusas *rell.*
4.424	ratibus A^v		trabibus *rell.*
6.262	tyrannum A^v		dominum *rell.*
8.170	syriam A^v		libyam *rell.*

The origins of none of these can be determined; their presence, however, gives some indication of the nature of A^v's correcting manuscript. Also of particular interest in A^v are the rare readings shared with scholia or the fragments remaining from ancient manuscripts. Among these may be cited:

Book 4

595	python $A^vVadn.$	typhon *rell.*

Book 5

157	prodiderat A^vQGEN	prodiderant *rell.*

Book 6

24	scopulisque uomentibus A^vGJSM^2	scopulisque mouentibus Z^2ABRY	
	scopulis remouentibus $QUVPEW$	scopulis reuomentibus M	*l.o.* Z
221	admentauit A^vPN	amentauit *rell.*	
552	ferarum A^vN	luporum *rell.*	

The manuscript from which the readings of A^v derive would have been of some value to the editor of Lucan. The point has already been made that the corrections introduced into A by A^2 do not, in a later transmission, significantly disguise the character of A. The same could be said of the far more extensive efforts of the correctors designated by Z^2. A, the copy of Z after correction, maintains its striking affinity to Z and M. In both cases we must draw the conclusion that the correcting manuscript(s) had much in common with the manuscripts with which they were compared. Had A^v been a corrector rather than a collator, the next copy of A would not nearly so closely resemble Z, M, or even A. Of the tenth-century manuscripts, G would supply the most suggestive resemblances, though A^v and G cannot be thought of as closely related. At the monastery in which A^v worked, there resided a manuscript unlike in character all the ninth-century manuscripts we have examined or reconstructed so far.

From the disagreements between A^v and A^2 like (book 6):

798	constrictae A^vcett.A	constrictas A^2BRW
811	ducimus A^vMZA	ducibus A^2BRrell.

it may be assumed that corrections made in the text of A by A^2 preceded the collation by A^v. This fact completes the information we have on the ninth-century history of the text to this point. Z was transported from its more northerly home to a monastery in western France, where it was copied by the scribe of A. From the similarity of the correctors of Z to the text hands, we may be sure that Z arrived at A's monastery already heavily corrected. Soon after A was produced, it was corrected at the same or a nearby monastery. Next, A^v compared it with his correcting manuscript, though, again we cannot say whether that manuscript and A^2's were both in the same library. The next fact we have about A is that it lost several leaves that were recopied either from the original pages or a very similar manuscript. Then A was copied, and from that copy B was produced at Fleury. Whether A itself ever got to Fleury is impossible to determine.

We have already seen the value of B as evidence for the age of two correctors in A. The question now is of the precise relationship between B and A. Once more, a collation of B is given in an appendix so that all the evidence will be at hand (see Appendix VIII). While the list includes casual errors, a strikingly large number of which are shared by R, there are a number of corrections of A and readings found independently in unrelated manuscripts:

Re-examination of ABR

Book 1

154	perstringens *BRGPWJ*	praestringens *MZAUVE*	d. *QY*
359	scilicet *BRMYUEWJ*	si licet *ZAQGVP*	
600	cybelen *BRcett.*	cybeben *MZAP*	
608	admonet *BRPW*	admouet *rell.*	

Book 2

185	effundit *BRQE*	effudit *rell.*
517	quantum *BRUPWJ*	quanto *MZAQYGVE*
567	omnia *BRcett.*	omina Z^2A

Book 3

101	omnia *BRYWJ*	omina *rell.*	
160	regni *B(?)MP*	regi *rell.*	
199	bellum *BU*	nilum *rell.*	l.o. *R*
658	eiectat *BQYGUVEWJ*	electat *MZARP*	

Book 4

182	quod *BUP*	quid *rell.*
335	sicorum *BRMZP*	sicorim Z^2*rell.*
452	illam *BRMZ*	illa Z^2*rell.*
568	dispectant *BRYU*	despectam *rell.*
625	urguere *BRMZ*	urgueri Z^2*rell.*

Book 5

59	ptolomee *BRcett.*		ptolemee *MZAP*	
72	parnasus *BRQYUVEWJ*		parnasos *MZAGP*	
74	fatidici *B et* fatidicae *A*ᵛ		thebanae *rell. et* thebani *C*	
159	fingit *BP*	fingis Z^2AR *rell.*	finges *MZ* (fugis *U*)	
196	tenebris *BMPW*		tenebis *rell.*	
210	locuta est *BYUVE*	locutae *MZAGPW*	cuncta est *J*	n.l. *RQ*
233	annis *BQY et* rannis A^2R	rhamnus Z^2AGVEJ	ramnos *UP* (ramnum *M(?)Z*)	

The Text of Lucan in the Ninth Century

333	senes *BR*cett.	senex *MZAC*	
399	fastos fastis *GJ* *BMYUVPEW*	fastus *ZQA*ᵛ *et* faustus *Z²AR*	
588	nec *BVPEJ*	ne *rell.*	
588	manus *BYW*	manum *rell.*	
765	dimissa *BRGUVPJ*	demissa *MZAQYEW*	

Book 6

35	domus *MBUVPE*	domos *ZAQYGWJ*	l.o. *R*
41	tescita *B et* tescua testa *MZ* *Z²AR*rell.	pascua *S*	
126	quam *BQUPEJ*	qua *MZARYGVW*	
244	putatis *BR*cett.	putastis *Z²AE*	
286	tremente *BRQVJ et* premente *MZE*	trementi *Z²AGUPW*	
506	proprior *BRMZPW*	propior *Z²AQYGUVEJ*	
746	nox *BMZ*	non *Z²AR*rell.	
785	patrumque *BYU(?)P*	patremque *rell.*	

Book 7

3	cursumque *BMZQUVPW*	currumque *Z²ARYGEJ*	
183	tumultu *BCUA*ᵛ *et* tumultum *QYGVPE*	tumultus *Z²ARWM² et* tumultis *Z*	n.l. *MJ*
225	habenis *BRWJA*ᵛ	habenae *rell. et* habena *QE*	
395	quod *BRQYUVPE*	quo *MZAGWJ*	
548	regnum *BMZY*	regum *rell.*	l.o. *R*
555	ac *BVW et* hac *G et* ae *P*	a *MZARQYEJ et* ā *U*	
857	effudere *BRZ²*cett. *et* effundere *A*	effure *MZ*	

Book 8

59	dolor *om. BMZ*	habent *rell.*
61	depressa *B*Bern. 601	decepta *rell.*
118	quidquid *BRQGEW*	quid quod *MZAYUVPJ*

Re-examination of ABR

133	puppim *BYGUJ et* puppi *P*	puppem *rell.*	
224	decurre *BZUJ et* decurrere *rell.*	discurrere *PRW*	
240	ruptis *B et* ruptos *Z²ARW*	raptos *ZYUVEJM² et* raptus *GPA*ᵛ	
		et rapto *Q*	n.l. *M*
254	rursus *BRcett.*	rusus *MZA*	
260	recipitque *Bcett.*	receptique *MZARP*	
275	qua *BMZ*	quas *rell.*	l.o. *Q*
499	nilonque *BYGPJ*	nilumque *rell.*	
597	septimus *BRQYUPEJ*	septimius *MZAGVW*	
609	septimum *BMQYPJ*	septimium *ZARGUVEW*	
704	dies *BFQYGPE*	die *MZARUVWJ*	
844	reuulsus *BQG*	reuulsos *rell.*	

Book 9

175	magna *BMZQ*	magni *rell.*
317	superni *BMPE*	superne *rell.*
583	cauendum *BRMPW*	cadendum *rell.*

Book 10

84	quam *BRcett.*	qua *MZAP*
181	patronem *BQYEWJ*	platonem *ZARGV et* platona *MU d. P*

The extent of the foregoing list makes it likely that B is not a direct copy of A, but that a manuscript intervened and underwent correction from an independent, though similar, source. Since we shall see that R descends not from B but from A, there is a further reason—the many agreements of BR—to suppose that B had a direct antecedent other than A. The relationship then may be shown in the diagram on the next page.

Such readings as appear for the first time in B and corrections of errors in A left unchanged by A² should be given the siglum β^2, for, aside from scribal error, nothing would appear in β that is not in A(A²). There are some places where B agrees with Aᵛ, yet in the great majority of cases B ignores the marginal variants; it might be best to suppose that B never was influenced by Aᵛ's marginal corrections, but that β^2 had the same reading. It is also noteworthy that B occasionally returns to a reading found in MZ, M, or Z. This hardly suggests a close relationship. Especially in a tradition as contaminated as that of

The Text of Lucan in the Ninth Century

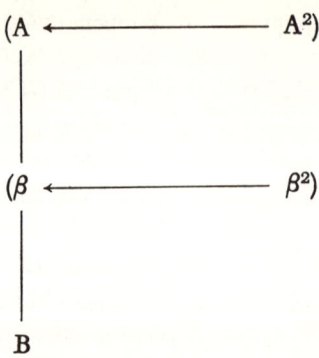

Lucan, readings are not the personal property of manuscripts. If B shares a reading with M at one place, it may agree with U in another. All that can be said is that the manuscript used to correct B must have had many of the characteristics that distinguish MZ and Z^2 and A^2 from the tenth-century manuscripts QGUVP.

It may seem odd that in his first edition Hosius could maintain that M and B were *gemelli* in view of the fact that B is at the remove of two scribes ($A\beta$) and three correctors ($Z^2A^2\beta^2$) from a manuscript (Z) not at all identical to M. We have already seen how Z^2 and A^2 bring about divergences between Z and B; and, generally speaking, as B loses the character of Z, so it has less in common with M. It remains true, however, that compared with GUVP—the tenth-century manuscripts employed by Hosius and Housman—and Q, a manuscript perhaps slightly earlier than any of the other four, Z^2A^2 and β^2 must have been rather closely related.

With knowledge of Z and A, Hosius altered his reconstruction, under the influence of Beck. But he also tried to show that AB cannot derive from the same manuscript. Besides the agreements listed by Beck of BR against A— from which develops an argument vitiated by the dating of R as later than B— Hosius pointed to 8.59, where *dolor* Z^2cett. is omitted by MZB. The scribe of A must have found *dolor* in his model; but, if B was copied from the same model, the absence of *dolor* in B cannot be explained. Therefore, determined Hosius, A and B could not derive from the same manuscript independently: *accepit ergo B suum contextum ex Z per alienum internuntium* (p. xl). The affinities between Z and B are indeed remarkable; but B also shares readings with M and other manuscripts other than A. The assumption that a reading found in Z and B must have

Re-examination of ABR

derived from Z itself was, in the light of what Hosius knew about the contaminated transmission of these manuscripts, imprudent.

In this case, the difficulty is of Hosius' own making. The manuscript assumed by Beck as the source of AB would have had itself to contain variant readings in order to fulfill the conditions both of having been copied from Z after correction and of containing the readings found in AB but not in ZZ^2. Theoretically—and Beck's entire reconstruction is theoretical—the intermediary manuscript could cover all the conditions found in AB. Even the omission of *dolor* could thus be explained hypothetically. Assume that the intermediary manuscript reflected Z^2 at this point with *dolor*; the corrector, using for comparison a manuscript that omitted the word—a manuscript like M in this respect—marks the word for excision by placing dots under it. A then ignored the notation, while B followed directions. Conversely, if the scribe of the intermediary followed the first hand in Z and did not incorporate *dolor* from above the line, but the corrector of the intermediary added the word from another manuscript then A was alert enough to copy the interlinear word into his text, while B ignored it. We have seen that B is a copy of a manuscript copied from A after some correction. The word *dolor* is not questioned in A, and, therefore, presumably, would have appeared in the next transmission. But that copy was compared with a manuscript that omitted the word, the corrector noted the absence either by erasing *dolor* or placing dots under it, and the scribe of B, whether by choice or necessity, left it out. To see just how inconclusive individual readings are, consider 8.268 *nequeam* Z^2A^2 *cett.*; *nequem* MZB; *nequam* A. We can see the form of Z^2's correction: the *a* that he wrote over the *e* to be added instead replaced it, which explains A's error. A similar misunderstanding of the correction in A gave rise to B's reading, which is only accidentally identical with that of MZ.

Again, description of the method used by a textual critic to establish the relationship between manuscripts may serve as a caveat. When the tradition of an author comes to the Middle Ages in a state of contamination, readings cannot be thought of as belonging to a particular manuscript. When a Carolingian manuscript is known to be the copy of a corrected minuscule manuscript, there is far more opportunity for suggestive agreements and divergences between it and another manuscript of the same age. What has been possible to determine is formal relationship, based on the evidence not of readings which, whether right, wrong, or impossible, were introduced and removed haphazardly in successive transcriptions, but of mistakes in placement of lines which can only be attributed to the physical state of a particular manuscript and a particular form of correction. This is how we know that B is a formal descendant of A; only then can an examination of the readings in B serve to determine more specifically that relationship.

The existence of β would be helpful only insofar as it would show whether scribal error in B arose from B or β copying. β^2 is the manuscript we should like to have, though, unless the corrector who inserted its readings into β, whence we have them in B, was quite remiss, we should find it very similar to the other ninth-century manuscripts. It is also possible that β^2, like Z^2, represents more than one corrector; in the case of A^2 and β^2 the sparseness of correction argues against this, but all we can be sure of is a terminus ante quem for those corrections known and accepted at a datable stage of the transmission. Since we have no dependent of B, it would be dangerous for any but the most expert palaeographer to date corrections in B; and even then erasures and changes made with a few strokes of the pen would be elusive.

We have, so far, seen that there existed a number of manuscripts of Lucan which were with varying assiduousness compared one with another so that special readings, whether true of false, sensible or impossible, were transferred, but not systematically, from manuscript to manuscript. Each had something to add to the others. The sum total of lections from these manuscripts, however, would lack a large number both of correct readings and of variants which almost certainly go back to antiquity. The agreements between β^2 and any other manuscript are fleeting. In the next transmission the work of a corrector would rearrange the correspondences.

β^2 was not just a conglomeration of readings found in other manuscripts. Certain corruptions were imported into the text by β^2. It is, in fact, usually impossible to know, when B in error diverges from A, whether the fault is one of mechanical error in the scribe of β or B, or whether such readings were deliberately imported into the text of β by β^2. A^v shows how faithful a corrector can be in introducing the errors, even sheer nonsense, of one manuscript into another. It is significant that virtually no true readings or traditional variants are found in the text of B for the first time, except:

2.517	quantum *BRUPWJ*		quanto *MZAQYGVE*		
7.395	quod *BRQYUVPE*		quo *MZAGWJ*		
10.181	patronem *BQYEWJ*	platonem *ZARGV*		platona *MU*	d. *P*

Re-examination of ABR

This, of course, is not to say that there is nothing more in β^2 that is of interest, for β^2 led B back to some good readings lost in Z^2, A, or A^2, but already known from Z. It must be remembered that, wherever B and Z agree in a reading not in A, B owes the reading not to Z but to β^2. The evidence does not permit the possibility that Z and β^2 were one and the same manuscript. B shares a number of readings with Z, but so does it with M and P.

It may be said that β^2 resembled B more closely than A^2 did A. Yet, it is hard to believe that the carelessness of the copyist of A and the scribe of B was responsible for all the corruptions in B. The scribes of the ninth-century manuscripts may have been indifferent to the coherence of the Latin they wrote, but they cannot be accused of undue sloppiness. Most of the variants that B shares with manuscripts other than A, even in error, should be attributed to β^2. Besides agreements of BR, which will be discussed presently, I refer to such readings as:

Book 1

324 lapsum *BErl. 304 et Bern. 601 (saec. xii)*   lassum *rell.*

Book 4

182 quod *BUP*   quid *rell.*

Book 7

555 ac *BVW et* hac *G et* ae *P*   a *MZARQYEJ et* ā *U*

Book 8

61	depressa *BBern. 601*	decepta *rell.*
260	recipitque *Bcett.*	recepitque *MZARP*
499	nilonque *BYGPJ*	nilumque *MZARQUVEW*
670	semianimis *Bcett.*	semianimus *MZAR*
704	dies *BFQYGPE*	die *MZARUVWJ*
779	aurora *BV*	aurorae *rell.*

The Text of Lucan in the Ninth Century
Book 9

741	uirtus *BG*	uirus *rell.*	
761	discernere *BQE*	discere *rell.*	

Doubtless, the source of error in each of the foregoing is different for B and the manuscript(s) with which it shares its reading. In some cases the scribe of B may well himself be responsible, though that is hardly likely in, e.g., 8.499 or 704.

Something more can be told about the model of B from a small number of readings that show corrections in the exemplar imperfectly incorporated into the text. Some may well have derived from A after correction. At 2.715 A's *Phasidis* is corrected to *Phasidos* by an *o* written over the *i*; B has *Pasidios*. At 2.417 the manuscripts read *Libycas...harenas* RYQGWJC; *Libycis...harenis* MZAUVPE. A² wrote *i* over the last vowel in each word; B's text is graced with *Libycias...harenias*. Other such readings cannot have developed directly from A. At 2.712 where the phrase *tracto in litora bello* occurs, for *in*, *ad* is found in Z²ARWJ. But MZ also made the error, common when dactylic words of the third declension comprise the fifth foot of a hexameter, of changing to the ablative singular from the accusative plural. A reads *ad litora* from Z², but B has *in litore ad littora*. At 6.425 *Pythia* QGVJ; *Cynthia* Z²(A)RUPE is probably an ancient variant. Z has *Cythia*. A² deleted the *n* with a dot and for some reason wrote an *h* over the *C*; this in itself would not be the genesis of *Pinthia* in B, which seems rather to be an amalgamation of the two standard variants. Finally, at 7.482 all the manuscripts read *agit* except ZP, which have *ait*. It is likely that β²'s exemplar also read *ait* and that he therefore set an *i* over *agit* in β², for B and in turn R read *aigit*.

Though Montepessulanus 362 (R) is demonstrably related to MZAB, of all the five manuscripts it shows most independence. That it descended formally from Z is indicated by the displacement of 3.211 to follow 193. It also shares many special readings with B. On these grounds, Beck, who cited R in 1900,[3] attached little value to it; Hosius just mentions it. Thus, a ninth-century manuscript of Lucan, known for over half a century, has never been reported. For that reason, I shall present its readings more extensively than I have in the

---

[3] Beck, p. 6. He offers readings of R (his F) almost exclusively from book 1.

Re-examination of ABR

case of the manuscripts already discussed. Most striking are the agreements in error of BR against A:

Book 1

99	ducum non sponte *BR*	non sponte ducum *rell.*	d. QY
103	sic ubi mare *BR*	mare sic ubi *rell.*	d. QY
217	undis *BR*	undas *rell.*	
374	dextris *BR*	castris *rell.*	
472	uires *BR*	linguas *rell.*	
474	uires *BR*	turmas *rell.*	

Book 2

202	immensa *BR*	immissa *rell.*
434	palmas *BR*	rupes *rell.*
517	quantum *BRUPWJ*	quanto *MZAYQGVE*
529	morituri *BRY*	moturi *rell.*
560	docet *B et* ducet *R*	uocet *rell.*

Book 3

131	populumque *BR*	populi *rell.*
203	tellus gelido *BR*	gelido tellus *rell.*
242	repletis *BR*	repletos *rell.*
510	temptari *BRP*	temptare *rell.*

Book 4

114	habent *BR*	habeant *rell.*
299	sonauerunt *BR*	sonuerunt *rell.*
426	feret *BR*	ferat *rell.*
470	capta *BR*	captae *rell.*
481	uita *BRQ*	uitae *rell.*
492	socii *BR*	sociis *rell.*
763	aures *BR*	hostes (-is) *uel* hostem *rell.*

Book 5

223	redigere *BR*		rediere *rell.*
430	crimen *BR*		primum *rell.*
453	excutiet *BR*		excutiat *rell.*
736	peti *BR*		petit *rell.*

Book 6

46	reuiset *BR*	recusant *P*	reuisat *rell.*
87	*u.o. BR*	medias *MZA*	medios *rell.*
111	cedisse *BR*		cecidisse *rell.*
159	fortunae *BRP*		fortuna *rell.*
301	tendit *BR*		tenuit *rell.*
563	morientem *BR*		morienti *rell.*
673	medulla *BRW*		medullae *rell.*
725	mori non posse *BR*		non posse mori *rell.*
727	immoto uiuo serpenti *BR*		immotum uiuo serpente *rell.*
783	diuersa *BR*		diversi *rell.*
786	belli *BR*		bellis *rell.*

Book 7

16	fuga ex *BR et* fugax A^2UJ	fuga $Z^2AQYGVPEW$	fugas *MZ*
96	genturi *BR*		gesturi *rell.*
136	solo *BR*		sole *rell.*
178	noctes *BR*		noctem *rell.*
262	*u. o. BR* (gladiosque *MZAQPEW*	gladiisque *UV*	gladioque *YGJC*)
749	caecos *BR*		caesos *rell.*

Book 8

184	aequora *BR*	aequore *rell.*
197	secantem *BRA*^{v}	secante *rell.*
645	prosperas *BR*	properas *rell.*

Re-examination of ABR
Book 9

383	frontibus *BRY*	fontibus *rell*.
1013	crimine *BR*	crimina *rell*.

Book 10

282	nilo *BR*	nile *rell*.
491	tantas *BR*	tinctas *rell*.

This collection of shared readings, so often in disagreement with all other manuscripts, and particularly the four examples of altered order of words and two of omitted words, seems to show without a doubt a close connection between the two books.[4] The possibility suggests itself that R descends from B and that the readings they share originated with the sloppiness of B or β or with corrections by β^2.

The similarity between B and R is so great that it is natural to expect at 9.938ff, a displacement similar to the one encountered in B. At 938, after and above the *H* of *Hoc*, a dot was placed, similarly after the *A* of *Auxilio* in 939. Otherwise nothing seems unusual. Line 944 appears in the form suggested by A^v and followed by B at 938a:

Iamque procul nemorum rarae se tollere frondes.

The following line in R is erased, but some of its words or letters can be recovered.

Iam. p(ro) ..l..........s..d..ll... frondes

That is:

iamque procul(? nemorum rarae?) se adtollere frondes

If a scribe were copying A and read the sign of A^v correctly, he might well have added the verse from the upper margin after 943 and before the version of 944

---

[4] The reduced number of agreements in the last three books should perhaps be attributed to the flagging interest of a corrector. However, it might also be related to the change of *titulus* in R after book 7 (see p. 16). However, if this is so, it is only in respect of special readings shared with B that R changes character between books 7 and 8.

found in the text. It is unfortunate that the words *nemorum rarae* cannot be made out; for, except for ZAB, all the manuscripts have the order *rarae nemorum*.[5] The correction in the model of R, in the form of a whole line now erased, may possibly have been made to cover that variant. However, the version of 944 that remains in R is found in its proper place in no other manuscript, and *se adtollere* appears only in A^2B and the later G. R, then, seems to descend not from B but from A.

The problem is a serious one; for, if R descends from another copy of A, the many agreements in peculiar error between B and R offer no obvious explanation. If R derives from B, the absence of 938a can be explained, as it is crossed out in B; but the second version of 944—that of A after correction—had no reason for being in its present position. The only solution that presents itself is that all the readings shared by BR stem from β^2 and that another manuscript copied from A was, like B, compared with β^2. It is inconceivable that two correctors would independently cull the identical readings from a single manuscript, but no such explanation is necessary. We have no way of knowing how many other readings in B, not found in R, or in R, but not in B, also derive from β^2. The hypothesis that B and R have a common source in β^2 would also explain why R so often agrees with B before contemporary correction when the nature of the correction is such as to force a copyist to write the corrected reading. It is not a wholly happy solution, depending as it does on a transmission that must be diagrammed in the following manner. Yet this is

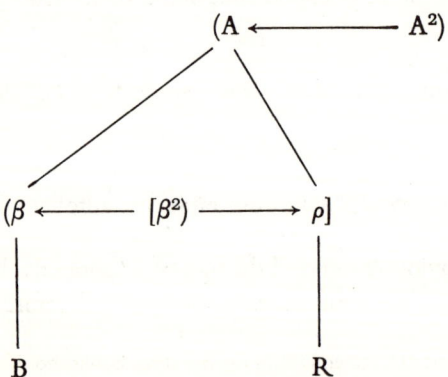

[5] *nemorum uisae* appears in Q and as a variant in G.

Re-examination of ABR

far from impossible. A was copied twice, at least, after A^v corrected the text, for R descends from A but not through B. The presence of another manuscript, β^2, used to correct one copy of A has already been established. If ρ was copied from A at the same scriptorium at which β was, β^2 would be available to a corrector of ρ.

This would at once satisfy the two basic points, namely, that B and R are intimately related and that R does not derive from B. That R has the same order as B at 3.165ff (i.e., 165, 167, 168, 166) offers no difficulties, for that would be the expected order in any copy of A after corrections. Agreements of AR or A^2R need not be mentioned, since they are expected. In such cases, the absence of B may be owing to an individual aberration in B or the acceptance by the scribe of B of an interlinear correction from β^2 that either did not get into the text of ρ or was rejected by the scribe of R, who used ρ as his model.

Even with the acceptance of the above stemma, one type of interrelationship of manuscripts is left ambiguous. When R agrees with a reading in, say, MZ, there is no way of telling whether that reading was present in β^2 or whether another corrector of ρ should be posited, one having available a manuscript like M or Z. I have shown earlier (above, p. 17) that R is copied from a manuscript which had interlinear glosses and scholia. The similarity of some of the scholia with B is not relevant, for the notes in B have been dated by Homburger as a much later addition. This being the surest base of knowledge, we must reconstruct backward. R derives its scholia from a manuscript which I shall call σ. But R is also formally a descendant of a manuscript like A which I have designated as ρ. Thus, the simplest reconstruction will impose the scholia and some lections of σ on ρ:

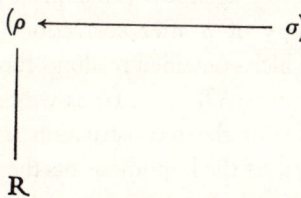

It may be that a manuscript already once corrected might also receive readings, glosses, and scholia from another source; but, for the sake of order in the stemma if nothing else, I shall assume that the manuscript into which the scholia were written was a copy of ρ:

The Text of Lucan in the Ninth Century

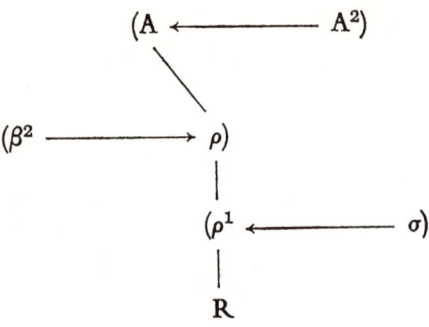

But this does not explain the special agreements of R with Z, M, and ZM together. In Appendix IX, which shows the readings in R not dependent on A or A^2, there are a small number of agreements with Z.[6] Similarly, but more frequently, R holds a reading in common with M.[7] Finally, there is an even larger number of places where A and B agree against MZ and R sides with MZ.[8]

It is conceivable that all the differences between R and A, A^2, B, derive from the manuscript β^2 except for a certain number of scribal errors which accidentally bring R into accord with M or Z or both. These would be lections transferred into ρ but ignored by the corrector of β. More likely, however, ρ (or a descendant of ρ as corrected by β^2) was compared with another manuscript similar to all the ninth-century manuscripts discussed thus far except σ, and contamination at that level is responsible for most of the readings shared by R and M or Z or both. Thus we would emend the previously suggested stemma as shown on the next page.

To sum up thus far: ρ descends from corrected A, to account for the repetition of 9.944 in R. ρ was corrected against β^2, to explain the agreement in peculiar error between BR. A copy of ρ after correction (ρ^1) was compared with another manuscript (ρ^2) which contained readings found in M and Z individually or in concert, but not in $A(A^2)$ or, so far as we can tell from what we find in B, in β^2. This last part of the reconstruction is least demonstrable and, therefore, least satisfactory; yet the hypothesis fits the facts and accounts for the

---

[6] E.g., 2.253; 6.68; 7.421, 615, 812; 8.744; 9.29, 406, 575; 10.426.

[7] E.g., 1.359, 490, 670; 2.637; 3.286, 320; 4.178, 520, 579; 6.329, 776; 7.579, 732; 8.142 424; 9.269, 456; 10.455, 459, 469.

[8] E.g., 2.431; 3.135, 263, 308, 328; 4.172, 486, 610, 634, 636, 672, 745; 5.350, 379; 6.62, 450, 451, 481, 683; 7.100, 120, 240, 272, 286, 462, 623, 690, 847, 861; 8.108, 141, 192, 360, 629, 788; 9.3, 104, 271, 440.

Re-examination of ABR

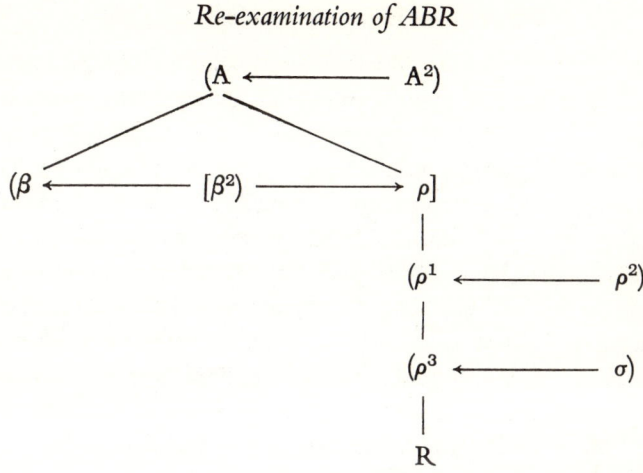

evidence suggestive of various relationships. With what we know of the earlier manuscripts, we may imagine that ρ^2 was a manuscript much like the ones discussed previously, exhibiting readings within the range we have come to expect from the ninth-century books.

The first major deviation in the remarkably restricted transmission of the ninth-century manuscripts came with σ toward the end of the century. All the manuscripts designated by ρ with suprascripts would have closely resembled A and, therefore, B or M or Z. σ, with which ρ^3 was compared, was a manuscript of a very different character. It contained scholia, which MZAB do not: the *argumenta*, also not associated with the ninth-century manuscripts; and a number of readings—by no means always preferable—that are not attested in MZZ²A²β² or, where available, in F. There had been external influences on this cluster of manuscripts earlier, and it is a matter of chance, for example, that the manuscript from which M derives for the last two books and the ones that provided the *vita* and the *argumentum* at the beginning of book 1 in M had no greater influence on the body of the text. Again, had a ninth-century copyist of A incorporated the variants of A^v from the margins, a manuscript of quite different character would have resulted. My stemma, which has the minimum number of hypothetical manuscripts to account for the evidence, includes about twenty codices prior to R and has no place for A^v. Of these only π, the common antecedent of P and M from 9.85 onward, is demonstrably independent of the others. And P is closer than QGUV to ζ and Z^2. It is a matter of chance, and perhaps geography, that the ninth-century manuscripts we know were corrected

The Text of Lucan in the Ninth Century

against manuscripts so similar. Much of what makes MZAB distinctive would have been lost had any of them been extensively corrected against σ. Until a manuscript of that cluster, ρ^3, was compared with σ, the group displayed a noticeable uniformity, suggesting isolation or a "closed tradition," though it is difficult to believe that the variants they exhibit can be derived from a single manuscript, however fully corrected that source may have been. It is not even wise to consider the identifiable character of MZAB as consistently and faithfully ancient; at the first stage, $\zeta \leftarrow \zeta^2$, choices were made—some evidence was added, but some was lost. Our earliest tangible evidence for a different sort of evidence is R, through σ. In more than one hundred cases where MZAB agree in error, R is the first manuscript to attest the correct reading. In some cases the reading of MZAB results from error, but ancient variants are also involved.

In about seventy places, R offers a reading that it shares with other manuscripts against the lection of MZAB also supported by unrelated books. These would come under the heading of traditional variants, though some involve no more than a change in spelling. I refer to such readings as the following:

Book 1

| 50 | iuuet *MZABGUJ* | iuuat *RVPEWM²* | d. *QY* |
| 424 | remusque *MZABYU* et romusque *P* | remisque *RQGVEWJ* | |

Book 3

23	innupsit *MZABYUPEW*	ennupsit *RQGVJ*	
113	possint *Z²ABQGVE* (possit *MZY*)	possent *RUPJ*	n.l. *W*
609	pectine *MZABGUPEJ*	pectore *RQYVWA*ᵛ	
629	et *MZABE* (at *QW*)	sed *RYGUVPJ*	

Book 5

89	mundoque *MZABGE*	mundique *RQYUVWJ*		n.l. *P*
112	maiore *RQGUVEWJ*	maiora *MZABP*		
383	summo...honori *MZP*	summo...honore *Z²ABQGVE*	summum...honorem *RYUWJN*	

Re-examination of ABR

549	notam *MZAB*	nota *RCcett.*	
617	illo *MZACPJ* (illa *B*)	ullo *RQYGUVEW*	
782	belli *RPWErl.* 304*A*ᵛ	bella *cett.*	*n.l. Q*
801	carinae est *RQYGVEWJ*	carina est *MZABUP*	

Book 6

109	turgentibus *MZABGUPWJ*	surgentibus *RQYVE*
321	dimisso *RQGUVPJ*	demisso *MZABYEW*
508	Erictho *RYGUVWJ*	erecto *MZABCQPE*
565	figens *MZABQYVP*	fingens *RGUEWJ*

Book 7

199	numen *MZABQYGEWJ*	lumen *RUVP*	
280	triumphi *MZABUVPJ*	triumphum *RQYGEWA*²	
310	hoste *RYGPEJ*	hostem *MZABQUVW*	
471	crastine *RYUVPJ*	crastina *MZABQGEWS*	
536	fundunt *RQGVEWSM*²	fundent *Z*²*ABYUP et* fundet *Z*	
			n.l.M, d.J
575	confundere *RQVEA*ᵛ	contundere *MZABYGUPW*	*d.J*
623	qui *RMZ cett.*	quis *Z*²*ABQE*	

Book 8

177	surget *MZABUVW*	surgit *RQYGPEJ*
179	descendet *MZABEW*	descendit *RQYGUVPJ*
385	uirorum est *RQGUVPEW*	uirorum *MZABYJ*
779	praemissa *RQYGUJ*	promissa *MZABFVPEW*

Book 9

605	quam *RYGVWJ*	qua *MZABQUPE*
982	ne *MZABYUVEW* (nec *P*)	non *RQGJ*

In the type of division of which the foregoing gives a sample, when a variant not a correction is at issue, R more often than not offers a less good reading. And

The Text of Lucan in the Ninth Century

here we are on more familiar grounds with respect to contaminated manuscripts. For the contrast, which would become more pronounced as copies of R got further removed from manuscripts like MZAB, is between honest errors in transmission (which have often been corrected in R) and deliberate variations in the text producing less exquisite, more easily comprehended contexts (of which R is frequently guilty).

Chapter VI
Conclusion

Our more detailed examination of the ninth-century manuscripts of Lucan has shown that only one of them may accurately be judged a *codex descriptus*, and that none may be dispensed with. On the contrary, each offers at least some evidence independent of the others for the presence and frequency of particular readings in the ninth century. This information, not available in Hosius, will help the reader to understand the nature of the textual tradition of Lucan. MZABR, with the related lost manuscripts adduced in this study, can be regarded as a group, united by some six hundred uncorrected errors and the lack of a certain number of correct readings and ancient variants. The contrast between the manuscripts of the ninth century and those of the tenth century, QGUVP, is still remarkable, but not nearly so great as when the earlier manuscripts were represented only by MZ. Often a reading known to readers of Hosius from one or two tenth-century manuscripts will be found to appear in earlier books. There are editors who feel that, faced with a contaminated text, they need be less restricted by manuscript evidence in the application of their judgment and taste in selecting and conjecturing readings. It seems to me more logical, since the editor's judgment should, in part, be informed by the nature of the tradition with which he is working, to assume that a highly contaminated tradition, represented by a large variety of readings in a great many manuscripts, argues rather against the complete loss or suppression of a true reading until the eleventh or twelfth century. This is not to say that there is no place for emendation in Lucan; but that, in view of what we know about the tradition, the absence of the correct reading is more difficult to explain. Thus, at 2.387, *Venerisque hic maximus usus,* / *Progenies* where Bentley conjectured *unicus*, we should hesitate before rejecting the evidence of all the manuscripts. Bearing in mind that Lucan is not the most careful of authors in his choice of words, we may suspect that Bentley is improving on the poet rather than the manuscripts. If the textual tradition were like that of Catullus, where all the evidence —all the truth transmitted—reposes in a single manuscript, there would be greater justification for accepting the emendation. Hosius' apparatus criticus, emphasizing as it does rare readings by the suppression of early and independent corroboratory evidence, suggests that the tradition is less stable than in fact it is.

Similarly, we should remark the almost complete absence of early medieval emendation in the text of Lucan. Again, this is not to deny the possibility of sufficiently competent Latinists in the ninth century; we know there were some. But the fact remains that there is no trace of one in MZABR, and the editor must keep that fact in mind. So, too, the clear proof in conflated readings (like 4.499, *transisibitset*) that scribes took the greatest care faithfully to reproduce their models is important for the editor to remember when evaluating his evidence.

In general, the relationship of the ninth-century manuscripts to each other as described above tells a great deal about the behavior of copyists in the early Carolingian period. Manuscripts were copied, corrected against other manuscripts, and used as models for fresh copies. And the process seems endless. On the basis of five extant books, MZABR, some sixteen other manuscripts of the ninth century have been reconstructed in the stemma, and at least three more can be adduced (A^v, F, and the model of F). The large number of manuscripts implied by this reconstruction is reflected in extant catalogues of the early Middle Ages (e.g., those published by G. Becker, *Catalogi Bibliothecarum Antiqui*, Bonn 1885). It has been shown that one book, A, was copied twice and that a single manuscript, presumably from the same scriptorium, was used to correct both copies.

The textual tradition of Lucan seems to be unique among those which are known to have suffered contamination in antiquity. We should expect to find a number of early manuscripts that could not be classified together, each offering a few unique, correct readings. This is the case with Persius and Juvenal, except, of course, for the Pithoeanus; from the apparatus criticus of Hosius it would seem, too, to be the case with Lucan. But MZABRF can be classified as a group, though the variety of readings they offer is too great, it would seem, to derive from any single ancient manuscript, even allowing for interlinear

Conclusion

variants. Their sources were closely related, and further contact with manuscripts of a different sort, like QGUV, were minimal, so that a remarkable degree of homogeneity was maintained over five or six stages of copying and correction. Errors remained, but inferior variant readings were not introduced until the last recoverable stage of copying. Only then are corruptions corrected but at the same time easier readings begin to replace more exquisite ones. R looks more like the kind of manuscript we would expect to find; by the middle

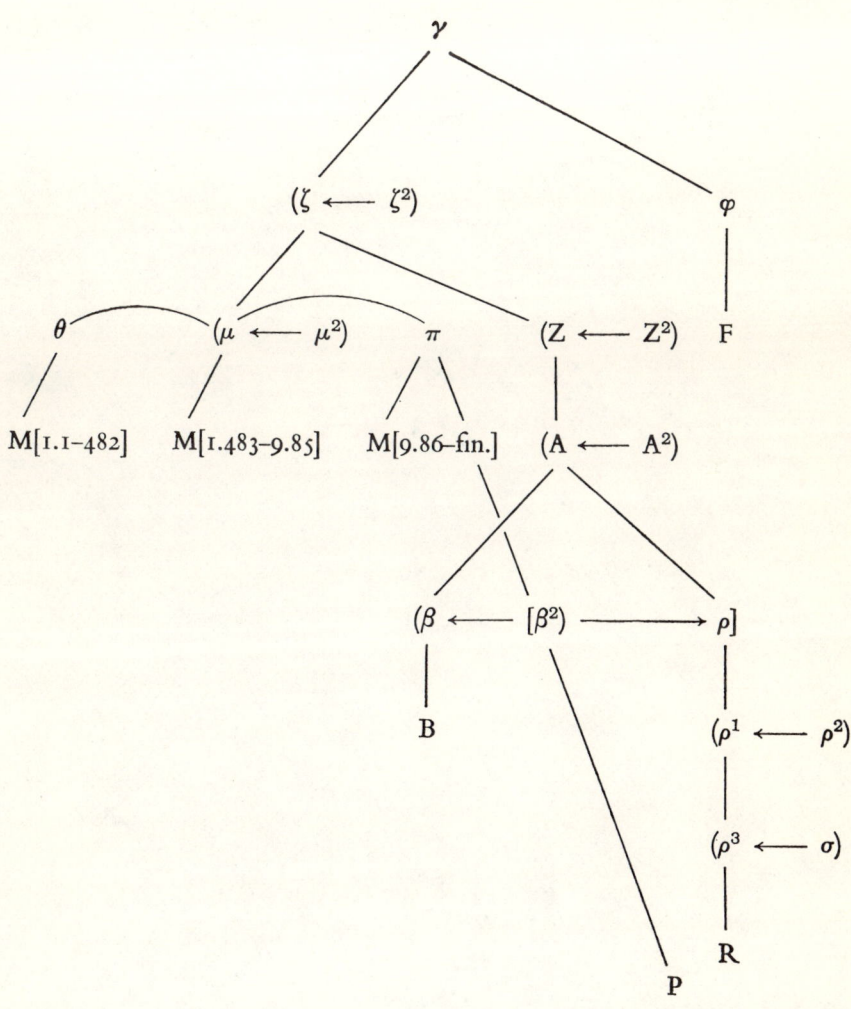

The Text of Lucan in the Ninth Century

of the tenth century its descendants would resemble QGUVP—showing fleeting allegiances with one manuscript or another, but incapable of being classified with any. The accidental isolation of MZAB and the model of R delayed this progression toward vulgarization. Had a manuscript of a different nature been available for purposes of comparison earlier, it would doubtless have been used. As it is, the ninth-century manuscripts of Lucan give a unique insight into the transmission of texts in the early Carolingian period.

Appendix I
The Added Leaves in A

Folios 63, 76, 77 are all leaves added to A by a scribe, according to Bischoff, in the third quarter of the ninth century. Further, f. 64r is written by the same hand on a leaf that had been entirely erased; f. 64v is in the hand of the original scribe of A. In this appendix I shall refer to the later scribe as A^s. We are concerned here with the relation of A^s both to the exemplar from which A was copied, i.e., Z, and to the copy of A that was the formal antecedent of B.

First, the make-up of the manuscript and the position of the added leaves should be described. The gatherings in A are as follows: 2–9, 10–17, 18–25, 26–33, 34–40 (consistent, for two leaves are numbered 34), 41–48, 49–56, 57–64, 65–72, 73–79, 80–87, 88–95, 96–103, 104–111, 112–119, 120–127, 128–135, 136–143. The last part of the text, written in the twelfth century, is on two leaves.

The gathering containing f. 63 is made up as follows:

```
60_____ / _____61
59_____ / _____62
58_____ / _____63
57_____ / _____64
```

Folio 58 is part of the original manuscript. Either it was part of a bifolium of which f. 63 was lost and replaced, or the two leaves were separate from the beginning, a condition better explaining the loss of f. 63. The state of f. 64r—"auf Rasur geschriebene"—may result somehow from the loss and replacement of the previous leaf, but f. 64r has a peculiarity of its own. All the leaves of the gathering to this point, including f. 63, have twenty-eight lines to the page. So, too, f. 64r, 5.518–545. Yet the verso, written by A himself, begins with 543.

Appendix I

The irregularity in lineation is in the original manuscript. Maintaining twenty eight lines to the page, it should have begun f. 64v with 546. The scribe of A omitted three lines, lines that were available to A^s. This single error is unlikely to account both for the insertion of f. 63 and the rewriting of f. 64.

The loss of 76–77 is easier to explain. They represent the inner bifolium of the tenth gathering:

```
76_____ / _____77
75_____ / _____78
74_____ /
73_____ / _____79
```

The absence of the two correctors, A^2 and A^v, from the added and palimpsest leaves offers a terminus post quem for A^s. Yet, the resemblance between A^s and B is as great as that between A and B, and the divergences are no more frequent or major. Thus, the loss and suppletion occurred after A was corrected twice, but before it served as the model for a manuscript antecedent to B. The designation A^{s}B after a reading would, in this respect, describe precisely the same evidence as AB elsewhere in the text.

The next question is where A^s got his text for the inserted leaves. It may be said at the outset that A^s resembles no manuscript of Lucan unrelated to A. In fact, on all of f. 63, 5.462–517, there is no reading in A^s which is not also in Z after correction by Z^2. On the palimpsest leaf there are six places where A^s offers a reading not found in Z, but these are all slight errors found in no unrelated manuscripts.[1] All may be attributed to A^s. To this point nothing forbids A^s from having as his model either Z, from which the rest of A was copied, or the original leaf of A, which may have become detached and stained and thus needed recopying.

The evidence of ff. 76–77 is similar. In this portion of the text there are fourteen readings at variance with Z after correction of which none appears in an independent manuscript.[2] Again, we may assume that A^s, not his exemplar,

---

[1] 5.519 *causantia* (*quassantia* mss.), 522 *haud* (*aut* mss.), 528 *pauperies* (*pauperis* mss.), 531 *caesaream* (*caesarea* mss.), 534 *speriam* (*hesperiam* mss.; *hisperiam* MZ), 541 *duxit* (*deduxit* mss.).

[2] 6.393 *tuque* (*teque* mss.) *silide* (*sidere* mss.), 396 *aequore* (*aequorea* mss.; *aequoreo* GP), 397 *omnem* (*omen* mss.), 408 *cirrhaea* (*cirrhaeaque* mss.), 413 *locauerunt* (*locarunt* mss.), 416 *moueri** (*moueri* mss.), 427 *aera* (*aere* mss.; *aethere* MZ), 431 *magnorum* (*magorum* mss.; *maiorum* MZ), 433 *u.o.* ABR (*fidem* mss.), 450 *l.o.* AB (*habent* mss.), 451 *obducit* (*abducet* GUVP; *abducit* MZRQYEWJ), *alienus* (*alienis* mss.), 474 *non expulit* ABREWG^v (*non extulit* mss. M^2; *non explit* [-*n ex-* in ras., *tu* super *p* Z^2]Z).

The Added Leaves in A

is responsible. Three of these readings are perhaps worthy of notice:

> 6.451   Abducet superos alienis Thessalis aris

Abducet *GUVP*; Abducit *MZRQYEWJ*; Obducit *A^{s}B*

The future is preferable, the prefix *ab-* necessary. *Odbucit* cannot be correct: the question remains of whether it is likely to be traditional. Initial letters, whether rubricated or more heavily printed, are more vulnerable to distortion and open to a different kind of visual error. No independent source records *obducit*. While the present ending does not necessarily ally A^s's reading to that of Z, it does not stretch probability to assume that a transmitted *abducit* was corrupted to *obducit* by A^s.

> 6.474   nilum non extulit aestas

non extulit *mss.*; non expulit *ABREWG^v*; non extulit (non ex- *in ras.* M^2)*M*; non explit (-n ex- *in ras.*; tu *super* p *Z^2*)*Z*

expulit would seem, if less from Z^2's reading than from G^v, to be traditional. The decision here to be made is whether for A^s's reading a source independent of Z must be adduced or whether it may be assumed that A^s unconsciously re-created *expulit* from Z's correction. The only other place where such an independent source need be assumed is at 6.476, where *ara* MZ, for *arar* in other manuscripts, is corrected by Z^2 to *arax*. Here, there is some difficulty in assuming that Z or A itself was A^s's model. Yet, to posit an independent source for seven pages of text merely for the benefit of a single reading seems extravagant.

Appendix II
The Scholia in R

The manuscripts from which M and Z descend seem not to have contained scholia. Bernensis 370, a late ninth-century manuscript, offers both the *Commenta Bernensia* and another set of notes, the *Adnotationes super Lucanum*. R is the earliest manuscript to have in margins and between lines scholia in a contemporary hand. Further, it is evident that an antecedent to R contained notes (see the discussion of R above).

The tendency of scholars is to accept the *Commenta* and the *Adnotationes* as two separate bodies of scholia stemming from antiquity. Yet, it is not clear that either originated as a self-contained corpus or, indeed, that the contents of either should be considered disparate or entirely ancient. Discrepancies between the notes and the lemmata in the *Commenta* may indicate that at one time a set of scholia existed independently of a text. But it may be equally well argued that notes, no less than readings, were transferred from manuscript to manuscript and that the *Commenta* represents a collection of such notes taken from a particular manuscript at a point in time when there was not complete agreement between the notes and the lines to which they were assigned. That is to say, if a reading were corrected in a text, the note might well be left unaltered.

I am led to scepticism about the integrity of the two bodies of scholia by what, on the basis of the alleged integrity, would have to be called the catholicity of R. Of the scholia I have transcribed from that manuscript, several seem to stem from the same source as corresponding notes in the *Commenta* but also display some independence. For further comparison I add some of the notes in B, similar in nature, though at least a century later.

The Scholia in R

R	Comm. Bern.
1.59 ut non uideas Romam idem ut placidus sit. occulte autem dicit numquam placabilem eum ibi fuisse.	ut placidus sis. sed adlusit ad caluitiem. an occulte dicit: numquam pluet si tu ibi sis (quin placidus sis id est caluus *B*)
1.642 secundum Epicureos dicitur qui dicunt mundum constare de atomis et nulla ratione regi.	secundum Epicureos qui constare mundum atomis non aliqua ratione praedicant ... *et* [non aliqua; et nulla] *B*
2.364 et haec suppara [ ]estis socerdotalis angu[ ]ab humeris usque ad[ ]induebantur nupturae[ ]s qua etiam uiri plerumque[ ]ur.	... alii "uestes angustae sine manicis pube tenus qui(bus) uirgines nupturae induuntur ... (facit autem hoc supparum et haec suppara. est autem uestis angusta sine manicis. pertingens ab humeris usque ad renes. qua inducebantur nupturae uirgines. qua etiam plerumque induuntur uiri ... *B*)
3.202 Quia Hister fluuius in multa capita diuiditur qu[ ]unum capud abluit Peucen insulam et ciuitatem ei[	ubi sparsam mari Peucan regionem multifidi Histri unum caput alluit. (in multis capitibus diuiditur Hister fluuius. unde unum caput per ipsam Peucen insulam currit. *B*)

So too, the slightly corrupt 1.58:

unde proximo feras auxilium ciuibus et allusit eum de hernia	ut de proximo urbi et ciuibus auxilium feras. adlusit ad herniam eius. (de proximo ciuibus et urbi feras a(u)xilium. simulque allusit ad ernian eius. *B*)

In some places R and B substantially share a note related to the *Commenta*, but not directly.

Appendix II

R	Commenta
1.636 Tages iste dicitur cum terra araretur subito nat[ ]libros[ ]aruspicinae.	... hic Tages dicitur cum terra araretur subito natus. hic auguriorum libros scripsit. TAGES aruspicinae disciplinam ... ferunt ... (hic Tages dicitur, cum terra araretur, subito natus et scripsit libros artis aruspicinae. B)
1.639 Nigridus (sic) mathematicus Figulus dicitur eo[ ]a Grecia dixit se didicisse se orbem ad celeritat[	Nigidius Figulus ideo hoc nomen accepit, quod reuersus a Graecia dixit se didicisse orbem ad celeritatem rotae figuli torqueri ... (idem Adnotationes cum qui ideo et regressus) (Nigridius mathematicus Figulus dictus quod ... B)

Adnotationes

2.368 Fescinnini primum in populo Sabinorum inuenti sunt.	solitos sales dixit de nuptiis iocos, qui Fescennini dicuntur, inuenti primo ex oppido Sabinorum Fescennino ... (Fescinnini ioci inuenti primum in oppido Sabinorum Fescennino B)

Occasionally, when B diverges from the *Commenta*, R will offer a reduced version of B's note.

R	Commenta
3.206 Cum Apollo et Minerua contenderent de [ ]ciuitate iudexque fuisset adhibitur. et[ ]Apollinem iudicareret ciuitas priuata o[	Apollo et Minerua cum de ipsa ciuitate contenderent deis caelestibus praesentibus eandem arbitrum acceperunt. quae cum secundum Apollinem iudicasset, oliua priuata est a Minerua.

The Scholia in R

> (iudex qui secundum Apollinem cum iudicasset ipsa ciuitas oliua est priuata a Minerua. Cum Apollo et Minerua contenderent de eadem ciuitate. iudexque fuisset adhibitus. et secundum Apollinem iudicaret. ciuitas oliua priuata est a Minerua. B)

In the following places R displays a scholion elsewhere found only in B.

	R	Commenta
1.52	adulatur Neroni Lucanus sicut Virgilius Augusto diuinos ei promittens honores.	An deus immensi uenias maris; Virgilius. (adulatur Lucanus diuinos ei promittens honores sicut et Virgilius Augusto: an deus immensi uenias maris. B)
2.369	]tiale solebant scurre[ ]ocose honesta iocular[ ]ridere.	(die enim nuptiale solebant scurre sponsos iocose honesta iocularitate deridere B)
3.210	et ipse est aurifer fluuius qui miscetur Mea[ ]unde Virgilius: atque auro turbidus Herm[	flumina quae arenas aureas trahunt. (Ipse aurifer fluuius miscetur Meandro de quo Virgilius: atque auro turbidus Hermus. B)

I omit the many places where R offers notes from the *Adnotationes* and B is silent, for B's scholia are mainly derived from the *Commenta*. Yet B offers some notes that are not found in the latter body of scholia; and again we may wonder how separate in origin these two sets of notes were. I give one example, partly to show that R did not get its text from the source of B.

	R	B
3.285	consuetudinem dicunt Persarum hanc fuisse ut procedentes	consuetudinem dicit hanc fuisse regibus Persarum ut procedentes ad bellum

Appendix II

ad bellum singulas sagittas extra urbem certo loco dirigerent, omnes post finitum bellum redivent et singuli singulas tollerent ut ex his quae remansissent occisorum numerus inueniretur. (*sicut Adnot. quae* loco certo *et* finitum proelium *habent*)	singuli singulas sagittas extra urbem loco certo dirigerent finito bello redeuntes singuli singulas tollerent ut ex his que remansissent occisorum numerus inueniretur

Finally, here is one of the notes in R which seem independent of B, the *Commenta*, and the *Adnotationes*: 1.43, *Seruilia bella dicitur quia serui insurrexerunt contra dominos suos, quos ultus est Pompeius.*

I conclude this discussion of the scholia with the full evidence of the four sources in question on 3.257 to show in what a confused state the tradition of the scholia really is.

R	*Commenta*
3.257 Duo flumina apud persidos (*sic*) oriuntur Tigris et Euphrates. quos nisi in[ ]mesopotamia separaret, esset in[ ]utrum Eufrates dicerentur an Tigris *Adnotationes* EUFRATES duo Persidos flumina, Eufrates et Tigris, inter quos posita Mesopotamia terra nominatur. DIVERSIS FONTIBVS EDIT ambo flumina unum habent ortum, quae diuidit terra et nomina dat duobus. Quod si non Mesopotamia separaret, esset incertum, utrum Eufrates diceretur an Tigris.	Tigris et Euphrates oriuntur in Persida. ... PERSIS fluuius de quo oriuntur Tigris et Eufrates, inter quos sedet Mesopotamia. qui de uno exeunt set in diuersum currunt (*et* Hinc Mesopotamia dicitur, quod media sit inter duo flumina ... meson medium. Potamus fluuius. *B*)

The Scholia in R

It may well be that, with the diverse nature of the wording of the notes and the overlapping of the two sets of scholia, we do ourselves a disservice by assuming that either the *Commenta* or the *Adnotationes* is a formal, coherent commentary handed down as such from antiquity. The *Adnotationes* do not after Bernensis 370 appear as a group without text until the twelfth century in Wallersteinensis I 2, which J. Endt (*Adnotationes super Lucanum*) held to be the best representative of the independent tradition. Meanwhile, notes of the sort found in manuscripts like R, B, and other early and useful manuscripts, but which are not in continuous form, are largely ignored. Less reliance should be put on the concept of continuous notes, and more interest taken in the notes themselves. Many will, no doubt, be proved late or derivative, but they ought to be known. Many of the notes in R may be ninth-century, e.g., at 8.92 *illos casus qui acciderunt Crasso in Assyriam ego tuli in castra*. Only when all the notes in the early manuscripts are collected will it be possible to judge them accurately.

Appendix III
On the Relationship of F to M and Z

F often does agree with MZ in error. Thus:

Book 8

607	recidit Z^2cett.	recedit MZF
617	fletu Z^2cett.	fletum MZF
662	trepida QYcett.	trepide MZABRF
763	auerte Z^2cett.	aduerte MZF
779	praemissa RQYGUJ	promissa MZABFVPFW
787	inustis plena Z^2cett.	inusta MZF
794	condi Z^2cett.	condita MZF
812	barbariem YGVJ	barbariam MZABRFQUPW
815	contentum Z^2cett.	contentus MZF
818	super Z^2cett.	non MZF
824	immerito Z^2ACYUVPEJA^v	merito MZA^{2}BRFQGW
	carmine QYcett.	carmina MZABRFC
826	aestate Z^2cett.	aetate MZFY
830	Aethiopum Z^2cett.	Aethipum MZF
841	dignam Z^2cett.	dignum MZF
	uerebitur Z^2cett.	uidebitur MZF
843	beatus Z^2cett.	beate MZF
847	feralibus Z^2cett.	ferialibus MZF
848	nimiis Z^2cett.	nimis MZF
	mouenti Rcett.	mouente MZABF
862	uictoris Z^2cett.	uictori MZF

The Relationship of F to M and Z

864 fulmen *QYcett*.   flumen *MZABRF*
870 illud *Z²cett*.   om. *MZF*

Book 9

3   semustaque *Z²cett*.   semiustaque *MZFR*
4   degeneremque *Z²cett*.   degenerumque *MZF*
36   Malean *Z²cett*.   Maleon *MZFU*
77   tendunt *QYcett*.   tendent *MZABRF*
100 habent *Z²cett*.   om. *MZFQPE*

Such, besides a few where the error is negligible and common to many scribes, are the agreements in error of MZF. Hosius gives 8.870 *qua sit* mss.; *quas et* MZF; but Klein reports F as offering *quasq*. At 7.611 *alium* in F derives from the same source as *altum* (MZP) against *alnum*. At 8.848, where ZF have *terra* for *terrae* mss., M omits the word. In addition to these common errors, there are a few correct readings shared by these three manuscripts against most of the others. I refer to:

Book 8

693 sorori *MZA²BRFUW*   sororis *Z²AQYGVEJ* (soleri *P*)

Book 9

67   iusta *MZAFGUP*   busta *A²BRQYVEWJ*
73   hinc *MA²BRFUEW et* hin *Z*   hic *Z²AQYGVPJ*

So far the claim of Hosius seems valid; but there are also about forty places where MZ agree in error between 8.575 and 9.85 where they lack the company of F. Since MZ for that section derive from a single manuscript, which I call ζ, their common errors may be supposed to have stood in ζ. If as Hosius and Housman asserted, F is another copy of ζ, it should share these errors with MZ. I offer a small selection of the readings in which the error of MZ, i.e., of ζ, is not shared by F. Theoretically, of course, one such instance would be enough to proclaim the independence of F.

Appendix III

Book 8

633	meus *Fcett.*	metus *MZU*	
647	culpa *Fcett.*	culta *MZABR*	
653	digna fui *Fcett.*	fui digna *MZABR*	
833	planges *FPE*	plangens *QYGUVWJ*	plangis *MZABR*

Book 9

6	lunaeque *Fcett.*	lunaque *MZU*(?)
39	classi *Fcett. et* classis *MZ*	clausis Z^2ABR
59	fletum *Fcett.*	fluctum *MZ*
74	litore *Fcett.*	limite *MZABR*
84	Hunc *Fcett.*	Nunc *MZABRE*

As to its allegiance when M and Z disagree before 9.86, Housman is not quite correct, for F shares eight readings with M (8.576, 595, 631, 690, 754; 9.44, 67, 71) and six with Z (8.751, 794, 848, 860, 868; 9.45). From 9.86 onward, F agrees with Z at 86 *nobis* ZF (*uobis*), 89 *aliquid* ZF (*aliquis*), 92 *reliquit* ZF (*relinquo*), 104 *uulnera* ZABRFYQGEWJ (*funera* MUVP). But it should be mentioned that at 9.122, where ZABR W read *et medias* for *medias*, F sides with M. Not that one doubts Housman's claim that M represents a different exemplar after 9.85, but the evidence of F is not so clear-cut as it might appear. Where Z^2, a contemporary manuscript, corrects Z, F agrees more frequently with the corrector than with the first hand. Yet, at one place it may reveal the original reading of MZ: 8.786 *semusta* (*m* in ras. M^2) MYGUVPWJ; *semiusta* (*mius* in ras. Z^2) ZABRQE; *sed iusta* FC. To what can be inferred from the above examples, I add only 8.645 *sunt* MZU; *sint* Z^2F cett., where a correct reading in ζ is not found in F.

Appendix IV
Readings Originating in Z^2

Casual Errors of Z(M) Corrected by Z^2:

In this appendix, as in Appendix VI, to give a fuller notion of the work of the corrector, I list by line, corresponding to the apparatus criticus of Hosius, those casual errors which neither stem from traditional variants nor, because of their immediate correction, affect the tradition in later transmissions. If an unrelated manuscript should chance to share an error, it is listed. If there is more than one citation in Hosius for a line, the relevant entry involving Z is given suprascript. I cannot imagine that any reader will be interested in each detail of this listing. It does reflect the thoroughness of Z^2, however, and has as its other excuse for existence the possible convenience of collecting information which, because it does not affect the tradition, should be absent from future apparatuses. Where Hosius has two Z entries for a line and one has the subscript, it is to that one I refer. If Hosius has an entry like 3.625 *membris* MZ_1 and I do not cite it, it is because the corrector of Z is later than A. My information for that entry is *membris* MZABRYW.

Book 1: 13, 28, 37, 123 P, 176 WJ, 195 J, 225 agit, 258, 431, 451, 457, 460 P, 466 P, 497, 527 P, 550, 551, 572, 576, 587 Y, 600 W, 637 P, 638, 662 P, 677.

Book 2: 5, 6 U, 10, 14, 19 nullus P, 27, 31, 33 G(?), 47, 48, 49^2, 93, 116 P, 128, 172, 175^1, 179, 224, 231, 236, 264 R, 269, 272, 282 P, 293 P, 295, 300, 311, 316, 319, 327, 330, 356, 381, 388^1 Q, 397^2 Q, 401^1, 430, 439, 444, 446–448, 452^1, 459, 460, 463–464, 471, 480, 488, 496 P, 515 B, 527, 528, 534 P, 536, 540, 548, $554^{1,2}$, 565, 572, 594 G(?), 615^2, 641 C, 653, 658, 662, 667 bis, 675 bis, 694, 695, 716 B, 722 R.

Appendix IV

Book 3: 12, 18, 19², 46, 58, 63 A^v, 68 bis, 70¹, 76, 84 E, 90, 93 U, 95¹, 122, 124¹, 130, 134 accessus Z, 146, 156, 158¹, 161, 162, 177, 180, 189 bis, 190, 192, 206, 211, 215 bis, 217 P, 228 bis, 239 Q, 249 bis, 257, 263, 276, 279 bis, 281, 291, 293, 303, 314, 317, 322, 326, 328, 334, 339, 345, 346¹P, 346², 361 Q, 362, 363, 367 bis, 398, 404, 415, 417, 421¹ B, 425, 442, 456, 471, 479 RP, 480, 493, 494, 503 bis, 527, 533, 537, 543, 549 Y, 554, 570, 581 YE, 592, 600, 607¹ Y, 608, 612, 620, 629, 643, 647, 661, 679¹, 679² P, 683², 709, 718, 721, 738, 739, 752.

Book 4: 34 U, 42, 44, 59, 68, 90 Y, 97, 115, 119 Y, 122, 138, 139, 143, 151 paritur Z, 151 meles Z, 152, 188, 199 bis, 202, 213 PW, 219 P, 234¹ U, 234², 237 Y, 239, 242, 247, 249 P, 278 bis, 281, 288, 291, 296 prexetur Z, 311 B, 319, 337, 339 G, 353, 366, 370, 378, 382, 387, 391, 411, 412, 417, 423, 459, 463, 465, 477, 486 R, 491, 492, 496, 508, 509, 525, 528 bis, 531, 532, 535 P, 563, 564, 567 G, 571, 574, 578, 578² P, 584, 586, 588, 590 J, 593, 604, 605, 625 BR, 626, 627, 630, 634¹, 634² R, 637, 643, 647, 658, 662, 672 R, 679, 688, 693, 695, 708, 710 W, 722, 724, 734, 739, 741 summus Z, 746², 761, 764, 768, 785, 786, 788, 793 P, 797, 806, 815.

Book 5: 16 P, 19, 28 Y, 39, 52 bis, 53³, 54, 55¹, 62, 70, 72, 73, 78, 83, 86¹, 86² R, 88, 90, 94, 96², 114 YW, 115², 121, 124, 146, 148, 149, 150, 157, 160, 162, 163 Y, 187, 201, 211, 216, 227 bis, 233, 246 U, 268, 280, 283, 290, 322, 337, 341¹, 345, 346, 358, 374, 386, 404, 407 clausa Z, 410, 412, 413, 414, 416, 418, 419², 426 GC, 428 P, 434 P, 440 bis, 458, 469, 494 Y, 512, 512² W, 524, 525, 548, 552², 555, 564, 567 R, 568, 570, 580, 585, 588, 590, 608 Y, 618, 629, 635, 660 P, 715, 719, 720, 728, 731 bis, 737, 744, 745, 753, 756, 758, 759¹, 759³, 760, 763, 764, 769², 779 Q, 781 G, 785, 788, 808, 810.

Book 6: 12, 15, 16, 17, 18, 19, 22, 26, 31 bis, 40, 46, 54, 55², 62², 67, 69, 72, 82², 84, 90, 93, 101¹, 109, 111 P, 118, 125¹ J, 125 W, 131 P, 151 P, 155, 173, 182, 183, 195¹, 204, 206, 214¹, 226 bis, 232, 253² P(?), 263³, 267, 271, 285, 293, 294, 303, 305 G, 309, 322 bis, 332, 340, 350, 352 bis, 357, 361, 367 B, 373 Q, 382 E, 384 solum om. Z, 402 E, 404 E, 405, 408 discendi Z, 436, 437, 448, 458, 464, 479, 512 P, 521¹, 521 P, 530, 542², 543, 544 Y, 554 P, 556, 558, 559, 570, 575², 588, 589, 596¹ Q, 598, 599, 607, 610, 621 P, 632 P, 633, 638, 640, 645, 656 bis, 665 E, 670, 676, 678, 683 V, 691, 700, 702, 705 J, 714 W, 717 B, 720, 721 P, 722, 723, 732, 733 bis, 735 bis, 737, 742, 744 P, 746, 750, 761, 767 B, 771, 774, 775² P, 784, 795, 801, 806, 807, 810, 814, 815, 816 P, 822, 823, 825.

Readings Originating in Z^2

Book 7: 2, 8, 9, 25, 33 P, 34, 45, 64, 67, 69, 73, 80¹, 83 bis, 88 bis, 94 P(?), 110, 111, 126, 127, 136, 148, 150, 157, 163, 166 bis, 171, 174, 175, 179, 184 P, 197, 198, 199, 203 W, 209, 219, 220 B, 224 Pbis, 228, 232, 260 R, 261 B, 263, 271, 277 P, 279, 282, 301, 303, 309, 313, 317, 318, 323, 325, 330, 331¹, 340, 342, 349 P, 351², 354, 355, 362, 370 Y, 373 P, 379 W, 387, 390, 392 W, 400, 405, 413 bis, 416, 419², 430, 434, 442, 450, 454, 459, 463 P, 464 U, 466, 467, 475, 477, 482 P, 485, 486 P, 490 G, 494, 503, 504, 505, 508, 511, 514, 519 Y, 521 S, 526S, 530, 532, 533 W, 534, 539, 541, 546, 562, 564, 568, 574², 575 W, 578 bis, 580, 583, 593, 594, 604, 607, 608² PE, 611, 617 in pedis Z, 623, 626, 639, 641, 661, 676, 677, 682, 684, 688, 693, 695, 699, 712, 717, 725, 735, 738, 740, 749, 753 P, 757, 761, 766, 770, 779, 782 UP, 809, 812 R, 814, 825 W, 827, 830¹, 832, 835, 839, 841, 843, 845, 848, 849, 857, 867, 870.

Book 8: 3, 23, 26, 27 si, 43, 50, 58, 59*, 61 gato Z, 75, 78, 81, 82, 85, 103 ter, 108 lembos, 110, 115, 116, 118, 119, 123, 129, 132, 140, 144 similisto Z, 158, 160, 161, 170 bis, 173, 174, 178, 181, 195 U, 203, 221, 229, 233, 236, 239, 257, 264, 266³ Q, 268, 275², 293, 293 et om. Z, 293 nostro: non Z, 297 bis, 298, 300 B, 304, 326, 329 P, 330 dignas om. Z, 333, 334, 347 bis, 348, 354 R, 358, 360, 379, 380, 389, 390, 395, 397 W, 398, 407, 413, 423, 426, 428, 439, 441, 445, 455, 461 P, 462 bis, 465, 487, 488, 492², 499 CW, 522, 523, 526, 528, 531, 533, 534 W, 536, 538, 539, 540, 541, 545, 551, 552, 554, 555, 556 U, 560, 566, 569, 569² B, 571, 573, 575, 580 R, 582, 584, 587 R(?), 607 F, 610, 611 FP, 617 F, 624, 627 bis, 632, 633, 637, 640, 643, 647, 652, 653², 654, 658, 662, 663 bis, 671, 673, 686, 687, 696¹, 699, 707, 731 QPE, 734 P, 734², 753, 763 F, 766 C, 767, 771¹ B, 771², 778, 784, 785 bis, 787 F, 794 F, 796, 801 FB, 815 F, 818, 818² F, 826 FY, 830 F, 841 bis F, 842 F, 843² F, 847 F, 848 terra F, 852 en MZ, 862 F, 870² F.

Book 9: 3 RF, 4, 6² U(?), 9, 10, 28, 44² W, 52, 59, 72 W, 73 Non Z, 81², 85 RP(?), 86 F, 89 F, 92, 92² F, 105 FW, 140 Q, 142 U(?)P, 155², 156 P², 186, 231 P(?), 290² Q, 299, 343 W, 380 componientes Z, 399 BR(?), 417 R(?)P, 434², 575¹ R, 633 BR, 644, 653, 654, 655, 685 MP, 690 P, 706 U, 762 QVJ(?), 768 W 809 M, 811 PJ, 811 UE, 812 E², 821, 826, 837 QE, 878 P, 888 G, 905 U, 913 primam Z, 919 VE(?)J(?), 927 QE, 943, 1022 accipere B, 1026, 1045, 1087 P, 1100, 1101.

Book 10: 2, 15, 24 P, 29³ B, 40 BP, 43, 47, 137 M, 199 C, 206 M, 210², 241², 285, 320 bis, 370, 387, 403 bis, 422.

Appendix IV
Book 1

24	quot *Z²AB*	quod *MZRUVPEW*	quae *GJ*	*d. QY*
31	discindere *Z²ABGUVEWJ*	descendere *ZP*	discendere *MR*	*d. QY*
37	ipsa *Z²ABRGUVJ*	ista *MPEW*		*l.o. Z, d. QY*
40	mundo *Z²ABM*	munda *Z*rell.		*d. QY*
60	consulet *Z²ABRM(?)W*	consulat *ZGUVPEJ*		*d. QY*
198	latialis *Z²A²BR*cett.	latiaris *M(?)ZP* (latialaris *A*)		*d. Y*
209	iubas et uasto *Z²UVWM(?)* iubas et uasto graue *PE*	iubam et uasto graue *A²BRZQGJ* iubam et uasto *A*		*d Y*
277	at *Z²ABUVPEW* et ad *MZ*	sed *QGA*ᵛ		*d. R*
281	paratas *Z²AB*	paratis *rell.*		*d. R*
313	catonis *Z²ABCGWJ* catones *MZQYUVPA*ᵛ	catonum *RE*		
335	saltim *Z²ABRMEW*	saltem *ZQYGUVPJ*		
341	saltim *Z²ABRME*	saltem *ZQYGUVPWJ*		
414	aestuet *Z²ABR*cett.	aestuat *MZEW*		
419	late tunc *Z²MQP* et latet tunc *A²B* et latunc *A* et laete tunc *Z*	lates tunc *R*rell.		
420	saturi *Z²ABR*cett.*A*ᵛ et atyri *M*	saturis *ZCP* et aturis *G*		
423	biturix *Z²ABRMVPE*	bituris *ZCYGA*ᵛ et bitures *U*	bituri *QWJ*	
433	raptim *Z²ABRY*	raptum *rell.*		
435	pendenti *Z²ABRYE*	pendentes *rell.*		
442	tonsa *Z²AB*	tonse *rell. A*ᵛ (tonsas *Z*)		
448	demittitis *Z²ABR* et demittis *P*	dimittitis *rell.* et dimittis *Z*		
481	alpesque *Z²ABRCEW*	alpemque *MZQYGUVPJ*		
534	e *Z²ABR*cett.	de *MZEWA*ᵛ		
567	sanguinei *Z²ABRYGUPE*	sanguineum *MZCQVWJ*		
590	sterelesque *Z²ABR*	sterilique *rell. A*ᵛ et sterelique *Z*		
637	omina *Z²ABRGUPEWJ*	omnia *MZQYVA*ᵛ		
642	sine *Z²A²R*cett.*C*	cum *MZVA*ᵛ (sine cum *A*)		*n.l. B*
689	aeria *Z²ABR*	aeriam *MZYGUVEWJA*ᵛ	aeream *C* (erant *P*)	

Book 2

5	uisu *Z²AB*	uisum *rell.*

Readings Originating in Z^2

13	habent Z^2ABRcett.	habet MZ	
17	orbem Z^2ABR	urbem rell.A^v	
27	sed Z^2ABRcett.	nec MZ	
31	adfixere Z^2ABRcett.	afflixere UPE	l.o. Z
49	achimeniis Z^2ABRMC	achaemeniis rell.	n.l. J
54	hiberus Z^2ABRM et hiberos Z	hiberis rell.A^v	
57	collapsus Z^2ABRcett.	collatus $MZCP$	
120	carpentes Z^2AB	carpentis rell.	
133	paterent Z^2ABcett. et parerent MZ	pararent RV	
134	quot Z^2ABRcett.	quod $MZQYPA^v$ (quo J)	
135	quot Z^2ABcett.	quod $MZRCPA^v$	
181	exectaque Z^2A	exsectaque MZA^2BRrell.	
209	piguit $Z^2A^2BRYUEWJ$ et pinguit A	timuit $MZQGVPA^v$	
213	aquis $Z^2ABRQGJ$ et aqui U	aquae $MYVPE$ et aqua ZC et aques W	
253	famis Z^2ABM	fames rell.	
256	durasse $Z^2ABRVEWJ$	durare $MZYUP$ (dure Q)	n.l. G
284	fatus Z^2ABRUE	fatur rell.	
361	flamina Z^2A^2M et flumina B	flammea ZRrell.A^v (flammina A)	n.l. Z
370	colere Z^2AM et colore Z	coiere A^2Brell. et cogere R	
392	discedens Z^2ABRcett.	discendens $MZCJ$	
397	nulloque Z^2ABRcett. et nullo Z	nullo qua UVP	n.l. M
398	propiusque Z^2ABcett.	propriusque $MZRCW$	
406	rapax Z^2ABRcett.	capax MZC	
429	aspicit $Z^2ABRYUVPWJ$	excipit $MZQGE$	
431	omnem Z^2AB	omnis rell. et omnes A^v et hominis M	
474	nec pridem Z^2ABRWadn.^{v}	iam pridem rell.	
484	undique Z^2ABR	undaeque rell.	
503	uacante Z^2AB et uocante MZ	uacantem rell. A^v	
553	aruis $Z^2ABRYUVPE$	oris $ZMCQGWJ$	
558	disces $Z^2ABRYVEJ$ discet $CUPW$	discent $MZQG$ et discant A^vB^v	
567	omina Z^2A	omnia BErell.	
613	hac Z^2AB hanc $MZRCQYGPWJ$	hinc UVE	
618	laxsasque Z^2AW et laxasque $A^2BRYGVEJ$	lassasque $MZQUP$	
636	parthos $Z^2ABROYEW$	parios $MZGUVPJ$	

Appendix IV

642	sed $Z^2ABREWJ$		et $MZQYGUVP$	
650	pacis $Z^2ABRYUEWJ$		segnis $MZQGVPA^v$	
672	xerxen $Z^2ABRGEW$	xerxem QY et xersem UV	sersen ZMC (persem P)	
677	defert Z^2AB	deferret $QGVEJ$	differet MZA^v et differret $RYUPW$	
682	referet Z^2AB et referat Z et referret Q		reseret rell. A^v et reserat M	n.l. W
690	permonitus Z^2A et termonitus MZ	permonitos $A^2BRQYVPEW$	praemonitos GUJ	
707	classes Z^2ABRcett.	classis ZGP	classi M	
712	ad litora Z^2ARWJ	in litora $QGVPE$	in litore $MZYUA^v$ (in littore ad littora B)	
722	flexo iam Z^2A^2BREW et flexum iam A		flexi iam rell.A^v (flexum Z)	
726	aequora Z^2ABRcett.		aequore MGP (aequoris Z)	

Book 3

33	pignera Z^2AB		pignora rell.	
68	superant $Z^2ABM(?)Y$		superat rell.	
71	uictor $Z^2ABRQVEW$		ductor $MZGUPJ$	
73	ad Z^2ABRE		in rell.A^v	
95	getas Z^2ABR et getus P		getes $QYGUVEWJ$ et getis MZ	
108	uoces Z^2ABP		uocis rell.	
113	possint $Z^2ABQGVE$	possit MZY	possent $RUPJ$	n.l. W
127	uouere in Z^2		uouerunt rell. (uouererunt in A)	
135	polluet Z^2ABcett.		polluit $MZRE$	
137	honos Z^2ABRGE		honor $MZQYUVPWJ$	
149	nil iam Z^2ABRcett.	non iam MZ	nullam adn.	
171	gratia Z^2ABRW		graecia rell.	
176	populis Z^2A et populos Z		populisque A^2BRrell. et populosque M	
177	linquit $Z^2ABRUPEJ$		liquit $MZQYGVW$	
183	salmina Z^2A et silmina MZ		salamina A^2BRrell. et solamina U	
197	hemmus Z^2ABR		hemus rell.A^v	
211	post 193 Z^2ABRW			
254	et in proprio loco et post 243 Z^2AB			

Readings Originating in Z^2

256	trigride Z^2ABRM et trigrine Z	tigride *rell.*	
263	pelago Z^2A	pelagi *rell.*	
	undis $Z^2ABQGUVPJ$	undas $MZRYEW$	
276	huc Z^2ABRcett.	hunc $MZCV$	
305	pacifero Z^2ABRcett	pacifico $MZVPA^v$	
308	fama Z^2AB	fata *rell.*	
328	illis $Z^2ABQUVEWJ$	ullis $MZRYGP$	
347	si *om.* Z^2A		
350	quod $Z^2ABRUVEJ$	quae $ZMYGPW$	
352	mittantur Z^2ABR	mittentur *rell.*	
359	in Z^2A^2BRYEW	ad *rell.*A^v (adind A)	
382	diuersos uastos Z^2AB	diuerso uastos $RC(?)QYUVPEWJ$	diuersos uasto MZG
410	nullis Z^2AP et nuli Z	ullis A^2BRrell. et ulli M	
432	terrore Z^2ABRG	torpore *rell.* et torpere Z	
433	uidet Z^2A	uidit A^2BRrell.	
	librare Z^2A^2BRcett.	uibrare $MZQWA^v$ (libra** A)	
435	et fatur $Z^2ABRQYG$	effatur $MZUVPEW$	affatur J
456	aequantis $Z^2ABGUVPE$ et aequatis MZ	aequantes $RQYWJ$	
495	crates Z^2ABRcett.	grates $MZQP$	
499	nocturni Z^2ABRcett.	nocturnis $MZUP$	
531	aequore $Z^2ABRYGUVP$	aequora $MZQEWJ$	
549	eurisque Z^2ABRcett. eurusque MZY	eurisue GJ	
553	capessere Z^2ABRcett.	lacessere MZ	
564	percussa et $Z^2ABRUVEWJ$	percussae $MZQY$ et percussa est P	percussaque G
575	conserta $Z^2ABRMQYUWJ$	conferta $ZGVPE$	
586	tagus $Z^2ABRYEW$ et lagus JG^2	catus $MZQUPA^v$ et cagus V	satus C n.l. G
593	pelago Z^2ABcett.	pelagi MZP	pelagus $R(?)Y$
600	erumpere Z^2ABRcett.	erepere MZ et et repere U et eripere P	n.l. J
636	licida inmersus Z^2ABRY	licidan mersus *rell.*	
648	reliquit $Z^2ABRGUVEW$	relinquit $MZQYJ$	l.o. P
659	remos Z^2ABRCcett.	remis MZV et remi J	
	reducunt Z^2ABRcett.	recedunt $MZQYEWJ$	

Appendix IV

670	fusis *Z²ABRcett.*	fusus *ZG(?)U*	
673	excusso *Z²ABREW*	expulso *rell.*	
679	hastem *Z²ABR*	hostem *MZP*	hastam *rell.A*ᵛ
690	nec *Z²ABRcett.*	ne *MZYP*	
717	miciendis *Z²ABR*	mittendis *rell.A*ᵛ	
724	discendit *Z²A*	descendit *A²BRUPEWJ* discedit *MZQYGV*	
748	missi *Z²ABRQVEWJ*	missum *MZY*	mersi *GUP*

Book 4

40	librare *Z²ABRE*	uibrare *rell.A*ᵛ	
70	nimbos *Z²ABRcett.*	nimbi *MZ*	
92	occultos ... agros *Z²ABRE*	occultis ... agris *rell.*	
104	subtecta *Z²ABRQYUEWJ*	subtexta *MZP*	subiecta *GV*
171	*post* 177 *Z²ABRE*	*post* 170 *QGUVPWJ*	*om. MZY*
172	est *om. Z²ABE*	habent *rell.*	
202	iectant *Z²AB*	iactant *rell. A*ᵛ *et* luctant *MZ*	
242	ora *Z²A²BRQEWJ*	ira *MZYGUVPA*ᵛ (iora *A*)	
244	in nocte *Z²ABRQYVEWJ*	nocte *MZRGUPA*ᵛ	
279	omnes *Z²ABRE et* omnis *WJ*	amens *rell.A*ᵛ	
295	puteusque *Z²Acett.*	puteosque *A²BR*	tutelisque *MZ*
296	fastigia *Z²Acett.*	fastidia *MZA²BR(?)*	
299	tectis *Z²ABRYUVP et* lectis *MZ*	tecti *QGEWJ*	
303	sic *Z²ABRJ*	tunc *rell.*	
335	sicorim *Z²AQYGUVEWJ*	sicorum *MZBRP*	
346	causa ... magna *Z²ABR*	causa ... sola *MZQYGVJ*	sola ... causa *UPWA*ᵛ (causa ... causa *E*)
348	partes *Z²ABR*	partis *rell.*	
357	inermem *Z²ABRYGEWJ*	inermis *MZA*ᵛ *et* inermes *QUVP*	
364	usum *Z²ABRCQYGE*	usus *MZUVPWJ*	
372	poscit *Z²ABRYEJ*	coepit *MZCQGVPW*	
388	usi *Z²ABR*	usus *rell.*	
425	ferit hac *Z²A et* ferit ac *A²BRE*	ferit et *rell.A*ᵛ (feriet *Z*)	
427	decliuibus *Z²ABRQYVEW*	declinibus *MZGPJ*	
439	et *Z²AE*	aut *rell.*	

Readings Originating in Z^2

447 impedit $Z^2A^2BRCQGEJ$ impetit $MZYUVPW$ (impendit A)
469 deprensa $Z^2cett.A^v$ depresa $ABRP$ (depresensa $M(?)Z$)
483 prodere Z^2ABR perdere rell. (reddere Z)
499 transibit $Z^2A^2BRYGUPEJ$ transisset $MZQVW$ (transisbitset A)
503 sors $Z^2ABRcett.$ fors $MZGUP$
     laudi $Z^2ABRcett.$ laudis $MZGUEW$
515 licent Z^2AM et lucent Z licet rell. et lucet BR
518 permissum est $Z^2ABRcett.$ permissum $MZGP$
     mortis Z^2ABR fati $ZQYEM^vA^v$ leti $GUPWJM^2$ n.l. M
530 maris Z^2ABRW mari rell.A^v
562 iugulis $Z^2ABRcett.$ iuguli MZP iugulos G
567 cruoris $Z^2ABRQGVEW$ cruorem $MZYPJ$ et cruore U
584 forti uelis $Z^2A^2BRcett.$ fortem leuis MZ (fortiem uelis A)
586 clipeam $Z^2ARQYEWJ$ et clipea   clepeam A^2BGUVP
     MZ
610 terram Z^2AB terras rell.A^v
612 proiecit $Z^2Rcett.$ proieiecit A^2B prolegit MZ (proleiecit A)
625 urgueri $Z^2Acett.$ urguere $MZBR$
627 complet Z^2A compressis rell.
634 undis $Z^2ABcett.$ aruis $MZRC(?)A^v$
665 feros $Z^2ABRcett.$ ferox YW ferus MZ
671 quae Z^2ABRV qua rell.
672 atlans Z^2ACP et athlans A^2BR atlas rell.
677 autololes Z^2G autolopes $ZA^2BRrell.$ et autolobes A
     autdolopes P audolopes Y n.l. M
677b–678a   semper ... equo habent   om. $MZQUP$
     $Z^2ABRYGVEWJ$
705 pugnae Z^2ARY pugna $A^2Brell.$
719 ex Z^2ABR ab $MZCrell.$
     timeri $Z^2ABRcett.$ uideri MZE
726 obliquumque   obliquatque UP obliquusque $MZQGVW$
     $Z^2ABRYEJ$ et -osque A^v
745 medios Z^2ABRUW mersos rell.A^v n.l. Y
     proiecit Z^2AB deiecit rell.A^v
749 petiere $Z^2Acett.$ et patiere BR periere MZP
763 hostem Z^2AGUP hostes $A^2QYVEWJ$ et   aures BR
     hostis MZ

Appendix IV

769	uere *Z²ABR*		uero *rell.*	
805	urbis *Z²AB*	urbes *MZ*	urbi *rell.A*ᵛ	
811	sileri *Z²AB*		silere *rell.*	
821	iugulos *Z²ABRcett.*	iugulo *G*	iugulis *MZ*	
	nostros *Z²ABRYUVJ et* nostro *GW*		nostris *M et* nostri *ZQPE*	
	ensis *Z²ABRcett.*		enses *MZJ et* ense *W*	

Book 5

26	sequentur *Z²ABG*		sequetur *rell.* (sequantur *P*)	
39	libyes *Z²ABRYGUPJ*		libyae *QVEW* (libaeos *MZ*)	
44	exhausto *Z²ABRcett.*		exacto *N* (exhaucto *Z*)	
52	taugeti *Z²ABR*	taygete *MZW*	taygeti *rell.*	
	fama *Z²ABRcett.*		famae *MZ*	
55	thrasc- *Z²AMCUV*	rhasc- *ZA²BRQYGEWJ*		rascr★★★polin *P*
61	permissum est *Z²ABRCUJ*		permissum *MZQYGVPEW*	
91	contactumque *Z²ABRYUVPWJ*	contactusque *QGE*	contractumque *C*	
	et contactum *MZ*			
111	non nullo *Z²AB et* non nulla *MZ*	non ullo *rell. et* non ulla *E*		n.l. *P*
130	paret *Z²AB*		patat *rell.*	
131	parnasos *Z²ABR*		parnasus *rell. et* parnasas *MZ*	
133	in debita *Z²ABM et* indubita *Z*	in deuia *rell.A*ᵛ		
143	uitta *Z²ABRQGUVEJ*		uita *MZYGW*	
149	confusae *Z²Rcett. et* confussae *AB*	confessae *MZ*		
157	tripodas *Z²Rcett. et* tripidas *AB*		trepidos *MZ*	
158	impia *Z²ABRQUVPEJ*		improba *MZYGW*	
159	fingis *Z²ARcett.*	finges *MZ*	fingit *BP* (fugis *U*)	
173	igni *Z²ABRP*		igne *rell.*	
177	unum *Z²ABRQYU*		unam *MZGVPEWJ*	
209	exclusasque *Z²A*	exclusaque *A²BRY*	expulsaque *rell. NA*ᵛ	
210	restat *Z²ABR*		perstat *rell. NA*ᵛ	
233	ramnus *Z²AGVEJ*	rannis *A²R et* annis *BQY*	ramnos *UP* (ramnum *M(?)Z*)	
250	nonne *Z²AB*		non e *rell.* (non *MZ*)	

Readings Originating in Z^2

277	demitte senes Z^2ABR	dimitte senes *rell.* (demitti senis Z)		
293	sciat Z^2Acett. scias MZ	sciet BR		
311	tuis $Z^2AUVEWJA^v$	suis $MZA^2BRQYGP$		
328	sequentur $Z^2ABRQGUVEJ$	sequuntur $MZYPW$		
341	premit Z^2ABRcett.	premet $MZGJ$		
350	nec Z^2ABGEW	non $MZRQYUVPJ$		
379	dalmatico $Z^2ABGVEJ$	delmatico $MZRQYUPW$		
383	summo...honore $Z^2ABQGVE$	summo...honori MZP	summum...honorem $RYUWJN$	
399	faustus Z^2AR et fastus ZQA^v	fastos $MBYUVPEW$	fastis GJ	
419	furens Z^2ABRcett.	ferens $MZYG(?)J$		
421	iactantes $Z^2ABQGPE$ et ictantis MZ	iactatis $RYVWJA^vU^2$		*n.l.* U
	remis $Z^2ABRYVEWJ$	remi $MZQP$ et remo U	mali G	
431	mox $Z^2ABRQYGVEWJ$	et $MZCUP$		
444	naturae Z^2ABR	natura *rell.*		
449	hinc $Z^2ABYUVEW$	hic $MZRQGPJ$		
	profundo $Z^2ABR(?)$	profundi *rell.*		
456	dies $Z^2ABRYUP$ et diis MZ	diem $QGVEJW^2$		*n.l.* W
465	soluta $Z^2(A)BR$	solutae *rell.*		
474	nepotis $Z^2(A)BRYGJ$	nepotum $MZCQUVPEW$		
481	malorum $Z^2(A)BRCGWJN$	laborum $MZQYUVPE$		
518	inuerso $Z^2(A)BRYGE$	inuersa $MZQUVPWJ$		
541	rutilos $Z^2(A)B$	rutilas *rell.* et rutilans G		
552	qua Z^2AB qui R*rell.* et quid MZ	quod Q		
575	puppe Z^2ABRcett.	puppi MZ		
583	perrumpe Z^2ABRcett.	perrumpere $MZQP$		
608	atrum Z^2ABRcett.	atris MZY		
633	mutaque Z^2AB et mataque Z	motaque *rell.*		
665	nec sciet $Z^2ABRQEJ$	nesciet $ZCYGUVPW$		*d. M*
677	iacta Z^2AB	tacta *rell.*		*d. M*
769	non Z^2A^2BRcett.	nos $MZYW$ (nonos A)		
781	ferat $Z^2ABRQGE$	feret $MZUPWJ$	ferent YVA^v	
781	timebo Z^2ABcett.	tenebo MZG		
802	relinquit Z^2ABRJ	reliquit *rell.*		

Appendix IV
Book 6

7	cassum Z^2ABCY	casum *rell.*	casus MZ
24	scopulisque mouentibus Z^2ABRY	scopulis remouentibus $QUVPEW$	
	scopulisque uomentibus $GJSA^vM^2$	scopulis reuomentibus M	l.o. Z
29	huc Z^2ABUY^2	hic $MZCQGEWJP^2$	n.l. YP l.o. RS
		et hinc V	
41	tescua Z^2ARcett. *et* tescita B	testa MZ (pascua S)	
51	et $Z^2ABRUVPW$ en $MZEJ$	in $CQGA^v$ *et*]n S	
55	adiungere Z^2ABR	aut iungere *rell. et* aut rigere S	
62	Hic et Z^2ABRcett.	Illic $MZYW$	
76	ad moenia Z^2AB	moenia *rell.*	
77	descendat $Z^2ABRUVPE$	descendit $ZRQYGWJ$ *et* discendit $M(?)$	
80	duces $Z^2ABGUPEW$	ducis $MZRQYVJ$	
81	pabula Z^2AB	gramina *rell.* A^v	
94	pati $Z^2RQGUVPEJA^v$	patens MZA^2BYW (patiens A)	
100	perempta Z^2ABR	cadentum *rell.*	
101	manent Z^2ABR	iacent *rell.*	
112	minantes Z^2ABR	minantis *rell.*A^v	
114	rumpere rictu Z^2A	frangere morsu A^2BR*rell.*	
116	hac Z^2AJ	hoc A^2BR*rell.*	
128	ad $Z^2ABRQVPEW$	in $MZCYGUJA^v$	
134	nimbusque agens Z^2A	nimbusque ferens A^2BRQE	et nimbus agens $MZYGUVPWJ$
135	inmissae Z^2ABRcett.	emissae $MZUE$	
141	aut ferret Z^2AB	auferret *rell. et* auferre MZ	
144	implere Z^2AB	in plebe *rell.*	
147	in omne Z^2A^2BR	ad omne *rell.* (adimne A)	
150	abegit Z^2ABRcett.	adegit $MZQE$	
158	iste Z^2ABRcett.	ista MZY	
161	incursu Z^2ABRcett.	impulsu $MZYE$	
178	crinemque Z^2AB	crinesque *rell.*	
195	ossibus $Z^2AQYGUVEWJ$	hostibus MZA^2BRP	
196	leuibusque $Z^2ABRYGVEJ$	leuibusue $MZQUPJ$	
200	torta Z^2ABRV	portae *rell.*	
207	habent $Z^2ABRGEWJ$	om. $QYUVPMZ$	

Readings Originating in Z^2

208	getulus Z^2ABRYW		sic libycus rell.A^v		
214	gortinis Z^2ABRP		cortinis $QYGUVEWJ$ (cortinus MZ)		
226	e $Z^2AQGUVPEWJA^v$		et MZA^2BRY		
230	hunc Z^2ABR		hinc rell.A^v		
244	putastis Z^2AE		putatis BRrell.		
253	ueluti Z^2ABRW		uelut rell.		
263	nec Z^2ABRcett.N		non MZW		n.l. S
	ac Z^2ABRM		hac rell.NS		u.o. Z
275	cum Z^2ABRY		tunc (uel tum) rell.NS		
276	aperit Z^2A^2Rcett. et	aperto Z		aperi B	
	aperi A				
281	et $Z^2A^2BMQYGUPEJ$		ut $ZRCVWA^v$ (ut et A)		
286	trementi	tremente $BRQVJ$		premente MZE	
	Z^2AGUPW				
291	emisit $Z^2ABRQGEJ$		inmisit $YUVPW$ (misit MZ)		
	agmen Z^2ABREW		arma $MQYGUVPW$		u.o. Z
312	malorum $Z^2ABRCQYGVEJ$		laborum $MZUPW$		
313	e Z^2ABRcett.		e om. ZCP		
339	auersos	aduersos $MZYVE$		auersus GU	n.l. WJ
	$Z^2ABRQPJ^2$				
366	euenos Z^2ABEW et	euhenus V et euenus P		euuenos $RMZYGU$	
	euneos QJ			et ehuuenos A^v	
372	it $Z^2ABRYEWJ$		et $MZQGUVP$		
375	undae Z^2A^2BRcett.		undas MZ et undes A		
384	fregere $Z^2(A)BRQGEW$ et		rupere $YUVPM^2$		n.l. M
	regere Z				
401	terrenumque nouas $Z^2(A)BEW$		terrenum ignotas rell.		n.l. R
408	antra $Z^2(A)BRYUVPWJ$		arua $MZQGE$		
425	delphi Z^2	defili A^2BE		deli rell.	
	cynthia $Z^2(A)RUPE$ et cythia Z		pythia $QYGVJM^2$ et pinthia		n.l. M
			BW		
437	transierat $Z^2(A)BRYVPEWJ$		transierit $MZGU$		
445	uana $Z^2(A)BR$		una rell.		
465	tunc $Z^2(A)B$		nunc rell.		
474	non extulit $Z^2QYGUVPJ$		non expulit $(A)BREWG^v$		
	non explit (non ex in ras. Z^2)Z		non extulit (tulit in ras. M^2)M		
480	haemonidum $Z^2(A)BRUEW$		haemonium $MZQYGVPJ$		

Appendix IV

481	axes $Z^2(A)$BGEWJ · axem YUVP		agger Q	
	et axis MZR			
488	fouet $Z^2(A)$BRCGJ	fouent MZQYUVPEW		
506	propior Z^2AQGUVEJ	proprior MZBRYPW		
514	domos Z^2ABRcett.	domus ZQGE		
520	fulgura Z^2ABR	fulmina *rell.* et flumina P		
529	regentis Z^2ABRGUP et ri-MZ	regentes QYVEWJ		
532	lectum Z^2ABcett.V^2 lecto MZ	loetum RYJ		*n.l.* V
541	immersitque Z^2ABRW	immergitque *rell.*A^v		
562	e corpore Z^2ABRYGJ	corpore MUVPEW		*l.o.* Z
574	uagatis Z^2ABR	uagati *rell.* et uaganti A^v		
582	compressus conspersos	conspergos MZ		
	Z^2ABREJ CQYGUVPWA^v			
585	auellere Z^2A^2BR et auerrere MZ et auerre auertere			
	uellere A U QYGVPEWJA^v			
610	adrumpere Z^2ABRcett.	praerumpere MZW		
629	letos Z^2AB et leta Z	leto R*rell.* (lit★s A^v)		
646	antros Z^2ABR	antris *rell.*A^v		
648	tenareis Z^2ABRcett.	tenariis MZY		
650	emittere Z^2ABRcett.	admittere MZV		
652	illic Z^2ABRW illum MZ	illuc QYGUVPEJ		
674	puppem Z^2ABRVP	puppim MZQYGUEWJ		
679	libyce Z^2ABR	libyci *rell.*		
683	herbis Z^2ABQUPEWN	herbas MZRYGVJ		
688	gemitumgue Z^2ABR	gemitusque *rell.*		
690	strident Z^2ABRcett.	stridunt MZQE		
700	hecate hecates YGPJ	hicatis MZ		*n.l.* R
	Z^2ABQUVEW			
709	dedi et dedi MCGUPEW	deo Q		*n.l.* V
	Z^2ABRJV^2 et			
	dedit Z			
711	arepte praecanti Z^2AB	parete precante *rell.* et parate		
		peccanti Z		
725	erecto Z^2ABQUPE et electo MZ	ericto RYGVWJ		
730	tisiphone Z^2ABRQGPW	tesiphone YUVEJ (tesiphones MZ)		
745	uocata Z^2ABR	uocato *rell.* et uocatos Z		
746	non Z^2ARcett.	nox MZB		

Readings Originating in Z^2

747	erynae Z^2AB	erynen rell.
752	percussae Z^2ABRcett.	percusso ZQP
776	flatu Z^2AB et flacto Z	fletu rell.A^v et flectu M
778	tacitae $Z^2ABRGVEWJ$	tactae $MZQUP$
782	aliis Z^2A	alii rell. et alti MZ
797	calybum Z^2ABRY	calybis rell.A^v
802	refert Z^2ABRW	refer rell.
805	pompeio pompei BRW et	pompeius MZP et l.o. A
	Z^2A^2YGVEJ pompeii Q	pompeiis U
826	erecto Z^2ABQUE et erec*to Z	ericto $RYGVWJ$ n.l. MP
828	it $Z^2AGUVPEJ$ et id BR	et MZW

Book 7

3	currumque $Z^2ARYGEJ$	cursumque $MZBQUVPW$	
16	fuga fugas MZ	fugax A^2UJ et fuga	
	$Z^2AQYGVPEW$	ex BR	
19	bellorum Z^2A	bonorum rell.	
22	omina $Z^2ABRQYGUV$	omnia $MZCPEWJA^2$	
32	caperetis $Z^2ABRQYVPWJ$	raperetis GU et raparatis MZ	
50	admonet Z^2ABRGW	admouet rell.A^v	
52	uocatus Z^2ABR	uocatur rell.	
80	uelim $Z^2ABRQYGUEJ$	uelint $MZVPW$	
84	hauet Z^2ABRW et habet MZ	cupit A^v	
	auet rell.		
100	streni Z^2AB	sterni rell. et sternit MZ	
101	meis Z^2A^2BRcett.	malis MZ (meis malis A)	
106	instent $Z^2ABRQYGVPJ$	instet $M(?)ZUEW$	
130	mortis uenturae Z^2A^2BRYUW	et mors uentura est $MZQGVPEJA^v$	
		(et mortis uenturae A)	
139	cotibus Z^2ABW	cautibus rell.	
145	gigantes $Z^2ABRQYGE$	gigantas $MZUVPW$	l.o. J
154	habent Z^2ABRcett.	om. $MZU(?)PJ$	
157	fulgore fulgure $GVPW$	fulmine QE	l.o. J
	$Z^2ABRMYU$ et		
	fulgere Z		
163	signiferi Z^2ARcett.	signiferi Z^2AB	l.o. J

Appendix IV

166	eiecit $Z^2ABRQPE$		se iecit $YGUVWA^v$ (selegit MZ)	l.o. J
183	tumultus Z^2ARWM^2 et tumultis Z		tumultum $QYGVPE$ et tumultu $BCUA^v$	l.o. J, n.l. M
191	q. p. nescit in $Z^2ABRCQYEU^2$	q. p. nescius MZW	nescit q. p. in GVP	l.o. J, n.l. U
206	uacabit Z^2AB et uocabit Z	uacauit $RYGUVPM^2$	uacabat QEW	n.l. MJ
211	monebunt Z^2AB et manebunt U		mouebunt $MZRrell. A^v$ et uouebunt Y	
213	auebis Z^2A et fauebis MZA^v		fauebunt $A^2BRrell.$	
226	siccis et Z^2ABRP		sicci sed $QYGUVEWJ$ et siccis sed	MZ
240	mundi Z^2AB		regni $rell.A^v$ (regnum M)	
262	culpa $Z^2ABRQPEW$ et culpae MZ		culpam $YGVJ$ (culpas U)	
270	gragiis Z^2ABRY et gracus MZ		grais $rell.$ et grahis P	
272	et Z^2ABWJ		aut $rell.A^v$	
280	gentis Z^2ABGV		gentes $rell.$	
286	quarum $Z^2ABCQUPE$		quorum $MZRYGVWJ$	
295	bella Z^2ABRQE		tela $MZYGUVPWJ$	
303	paratur $Z^2ABRcett.$		parata $MQVP$ et parare Z	
310	respexerat Z^2ABM et resperat Z		respexerit $rell.$	
319	hosti Z^2ABRW		hostis $rell.A^v$	
324	uiolauit Z^2ABRP	uiolarit $MUVW$	uiolabit $QYEJ$	n.l. Z
328	tentetis Z^2ABR	tenditis MZA^v	tendetis $QYGVPEJ$ et tendentis U	
331	uires Z^2AB	uiris $QYGUVPJA^v$	uiri MEW	n.l. R, l.o. Z
364	aut Z^2ABRW		et $rell.A^v$	
388	annus Z^2A		annis $A^2BRrell.A^v$	
397	carpit Z^2ABRW		carpsit $rell.A^v$ et carsit ZE	
409	allia $Z^2Acett.$	alia $MZQP$	alea A^2BR	
411	quod Z^2ABREW	quo $MZYGPA^vQ^2U^2$	pro VJ	n.l. QU
415	hi $Z^2ABRcett.$ et hii C possent $Z^2ABRCUW$	possint M	hic $MZY(?)$ possunt $QYGVPEJ$ et poscunt Z	
416	longi $Z^2ABRcett.$	longe MP	mundi Z	
419	quae $Z^2ABcett.$	qua MR	quo Z	

Readings Originating in Z^2

421	annis $Z^2ABMYGVPJ$		armis $ZRQUEWA^v$	
437	add. post 428 Z^2A			
429	dahas $Z^2ABRQYPW$	dacas GVE et dachas UJ	das MZ	
440	regum Z^2ABG		legum $rell.A^v$	
450	minantis Z^2BRcett.	minantes YVJ et manantes U	manus MZ	
462	uultusque agnoscere quaerunt Z^2ABUW		tempus quo noscere possent ZR $rell.A^v$	
	VVLTVSQVONO S			n.l. M
478	inrupit $Z^2ABRQYVWJS$		inrumpit $MZGUPE$	
487	puras Z^2ABRcett.		pura $MZPS$	
	488, 510–519, 489–509, 520 Z^2ABW		488, 510–520, 489–509 U	
	488, 514–520, 489–503, 521 $C(?)$		488–521 rell.	n.l. R
489	hominum Z^2ABW		cladis $QYUVPEJ$ et cladiis MZ et gladiis S	n.l. R
493	uinxerat Z^2AB et uixerat MZW		iunxerat $rell.A^v$	n.l. R
502	partitur Z^2A		patitur A^2Brell.	n.l. R
506	deduxit $Z^2ABQUPW$		diduxit $MZYGVE$	d. J, n.l. R
514	mediique Z^2APS		medique rell.	d. J, n.l. R
536	cruor Z^2ABRcett.		cruoris $M(?)Z$	d. J
	iste Z^2A^2BRcett.		ipse MZ (ipte A)	d. J
	fundent Z^2ABYUP et fundet Z		fundunt $RQGVEWSM^2$	n.l. M, d. J
557	furoris Z^2ABR		furorum rell.	n.l. Q, d. J
563	contempta Z^2ABRM		contenta rell.	d. J
571	et Z^2AB		est rell.	d. J
600	pugnaces Z^2A		pugnacis rell. A^v	d. J
601	ullo Z^2AB		illo $rell.A^v$ et ille U	d. J
611	generique Z^2AB		generoque rell.	d. J
612	patrias Z^2ABR		stygias rell. A^v	d. J
623	quis Z^2ABR		qui rell.	d. J
	quis Z^2ABQE		qui rell.	d. J
624	transmittat Z^2AQPE		transmittant A^2BRrell.	d. J
634	quot $Z^2ABE(?)$		quod $rell.A^v$	
635	tibi Z^2A	ubi A^2RBYWJ	ibi $MZGVPEA^v$ et sibi U	
660	mundos Z^2A		mundo A^2rell.	
664	obruet $Z^2ABRQEW$		obruit $MZYGUVPJ$	

Appendix IV

687	habis Z^2A et abhis P et abis $A^2BRQYGVEWJ$		abit U et habit MZ	
696	erunt Z^2ABRcett.		erit MZA^v	
739	nec $Z^2ABRQYGEJ$		neque $MZUVPW$	
	uacabo	uocabo $YGPJ$	uacabant Z^{2a}	n.l. MZ
	$Z^{2b}ABRQUVEW$			
746	nec plura locutus $Z^2ABRUVEW$		sic milite iusso $MZQYGPJA^v$	
747	habent $Z^2ABRQGEWJ$		om. $MZYUVP$	
751	uolunt Z^2ABRcett.		ruunt $MZYUPJA^v$	
755	expuit $Z^2ABR(?)$	expulit rell.	extulit MPA^v et extulli Z	
767	mouet Z^2A	mouetur $MZYJ$	mouentur $A^2BRQGUVPEW$	
780	desisset Z^2ABRcett.	descisset UP et decisset J	dedisset MZ	
800	libycas Z^2A	libycis MZ	libyca A^2BRrell.	
	succensa Z^2ABRW		succensae rell.	
807	eruge Z^2A	erue A^v	erige A^2BRrell.	
815	locabit Z^2ABRW		uocabit rell. et uocauit CA^v et uocabat Q	
816	eunt Z^2ABUPW		sunt $MZRQYGVEJA^v$	
	ibit Z^2ABQVE		ibis $MZRYGUPWJA^v$	
817	latebis $Z^2ABRQYVW$		iacebis $MZGUPEJA^v$	
818	fortuna Z^2ABRcett.		fortunae $MZVJ(?)$	
820–822	habent $Z^2ABRUEWJ$		om. $MZQYGVP$	
826	labentque Z^2ABR		tabemque rell.	l.o. Z
828	ursi $Z^2ABRYGWJ$		ursae $MZQUVPE$	
842	ferus Z^2AB		feras rell.A^v	
	discerptus $Z^2ABRGPEWJ$		disceptus $MZQUV$	
844	degustantque Z^2ABRUW et digustantque		degustant $MQYGVPEJ$	
847	tanto Z^2ABCQE		tantum $MZRYGUVPWJ$	
852	romanus Z^2AA^v		romanos A^2BRrell.	
861	aratro $Z^2ABQVPEW$		arator $MZRYGUJ$	

Book 8

3	neganti $Z^{2b}ABM$	negantem rell.A^v et negante $Z^{2a}R(?)$	u.o. Z, n.l. Q

Readings Originating in Z^2

8	sui pretium Z^2ABRcett.	sui facinus UP	facinusui pretium M et sui facinus pretium Z	
11	quantum $Z^2ABRYGPJ$		quantam $MZQUVEW$	
27	pudet $Z^2ABRQVE$		piget $MZYGUPWJ$	
39	uector $Z^2ABRMYGEW$	uictor ZUP	rector QVJ	
46	cucurris Z^2A et curis A^2B et curris $YPJR^2$	currit MZ et cucurrit U	currens $QG(?)VEW^2$	n.l. RW
61	iacebam Z^2A	iacet rell.		
76	miserere gementes $Z^2ABR(?)$ et -tos Z et -tis MU et -tem P	miser erige mentem $QYGVEWJA^vR^2$		
99	rerum Z^2ABR	regum rell. et regnum MZ		
108	confundit Z^2ABPJ	confudit rell.		
120	bellum Z^2ABR	fatum rell. A^v		
133	ulla $Z^2AYGUVEJ$ et nulla P	ullo A^2BRQW et ullam MZ		
155	non Z^2A^2cett.	iam $MZUP$ (Ianōm A)		
157	turba Z^2ABR	turbae rell.		
158	coniuges Z^2A	coniuge rell.		
170	dirigat $Z^2ARYGUPJ$ et digerat B	dirigit $MZVW$	derigat QE	
181	tendet Z^2ABUEW et tendat Z	tendit $RMQYGVPJ$		
192	portus Z^2AB	portum rell.		
224	decurrere $Z^2AMQYGVE$	discurrere RPW	decurre $ZBUJ$	
238	ualet Z^2ARP	uolet $QYGUVEWJA^v$	uolit MZ (uidet B)	
240	famuli $Z^2QYGVEJ$	famulos MZ et famulis ABR et famulus W	famulo UPA^v	
	ruptos Z^2ARW et ruptis B	raptos $ZYUVEJM^2$ et raptus GPA^v	rapto Q	n.l. M
242	aeuo Z^2A	aeuum A^2BRrell.		
247	reliquit $Z^2ABRYGJ$	relinquit $MZQUVPEW$		
251	phaseli Z^2ABRV	phaselis rell.	faselo C	
260	silinis Z^2ABRE et selinis CGU	silinus $MZYW$ et selinus $VPJA^v$ (selicinis Q)		
274	iuuare $Z^2ABRYGUPJ$	tueri $MZVEW$		l.o. Q

Appendix IV

278	quem non Z^2ABR quemnam A^vMZJ et quaenam $YGUVE$		
	et quae non W quem nam P		
279	proceres Z^2ABR	uobis rell.A^v	l.o. Q
280	exponam $Z^2ABRYGEJ$	expromam $ZUVPW$	l.o. Q
		(expinam M)	
	uersant Z^2ABRW	uergant rell. A^v et uergam M^2	l.o. Q
311	fallunt $Z^2cett.C$	fallent MZc	l.o. Q
314	feci sat $Z^2ABRMUPW$	feci sed $QYGVEJ$ et feci set Z	
315	cruenta Z^2ABR	cruente rell.A^v et cruentur Z	
324	geras Z^2ABR cett. geris UP	geram $M(?)Z$	
327	crassos $Z^2Acett.$ et grassos MZ	crassu A^2B et crassum M^2	
	sensit $Z^2Acett.$	sentit $MZPA^v$	
351	qua Z^2AB	quam rell.	
360	lacessit Z^2ABCWJ	lacesset rell.	
370	arma Z^2ABR	arua rell. A^v	
377	illi Z^2AB	illis rell.A^v	
392	moriare $Z^2A^2BRcett.$	moria MZ (morire A)	
393	tegant et uilia Z^2ABR	tegant ac uilia rell. (togata ciuilia MZ)	
399	tabe Z^2ABR	taede rell.	
405	fratrum Z^2ABR	regum rell.A^v et regnum MZ	
415	sciet $Z^2ARcett.$ scient M et sciant Z scilicet B		
429	ea Z^2AB	eat $M(?)$rell.	
430	possim $Z^2cett.$ et possit MZ	possem A^v	
	possi A et poss B		
431	araxen $Z^2ARQUVPEW$	araxem A^2BYGJ (araxe MZ)	
448	dedita Z^2ABR et dedit Z	debita rell.A^v et debit M	
451	ueteris $Z^2ABRcett.$	ueteri $MZUW$	
	aulae $Z^2ABRcett.$	aula $MZUPW$	
455	habet $Z^2ABRcett.$	habes MZP	
475	coire Z^2ABRJ et colore MZW	coiere rell.	
492	gladii $Z^2ABRCQYGVPE$	gladiis $MZUWJA^v$	
498	neu te $Z^2ARcett.$ et neut B	neu nos UPA^v et neu nas Z	n.l. M
515	cadenti $Z^2AQYGUVPEJA^v$	cadendi MZA^2BRW	
537	liceret Z^2ABR et licere	iubere rell.	
	$WM^2B^2A^v$		
568	quo Z^2ABRQY	quod rell.	
580	e $Z^2ABRYUVPEW$ et a YJ	e om. $MZCG$	

Readings Originating in Z^2

587	alto $Z^2ABRFYGUPJ$	alio $MZQVEA^v$ et alios W	
595	parantem $Z^2ABRQUVPEWJ$	parentem $MFYG$ et parentum Z	
612	cum Z^2ABR	tum *rell.*	
618	at Z^2ABRG et ast Y	sed *rell.*A^v	
628	auctoremue Z^2ABRYP	auctoremque *rell.*A^v	
629	iacerentque Z^2ABR	lacerentque *rell.* et laceraque M	
642	cui ius $Z^2ARYUVPWJ$ et cui uis G	cuius $MZBQEA^v$	
645	sint Z^2ABRFcett.	sunt MZU	
688	sceleri $Z^2ABRUVPWJ$	sceleris $MZYQGE$	
693	sororis $Z^2AQYGVEJA^v$	sorori MZA^2BRFUW et soleri P	
715	cordus Z^2ABRE et cordis Z et cardis W	codrus $QYGUVPJM^2$	*n.l.* M
727	effudit Z^2ABRcett.	effundit MZP (infudit F)	
731	eoos $Z^2ABRYGUVWJ$ et eos Q	eous $MZPE$	
734	ignis Z^2AB ignes Rrell.A^v	ignem FE	*l.o.* Q
738	sordidus Z^2ABRcett.	sordibus $ZQGF$	
741	munere $Z^2ABRGUVP$	funere $MZQYEWJ$	
744	crementes Z^2AB	crementis Rrell.A^v	
749	relictum est $Z^2ABRQYGUEJ$	relictum FVP (relictus MZ)	
784	i $Z^2ABRMQYGVPEW$	in RZF et im P (sis U)	
786	semiusta Z^2ABRQE semusta $YGUVPWJ$	sed iusta $MZFC$	
791	religato fune moueret Z^2ARcett. (et remoneret BQ)	funere ligato remoueret $MZFW$	
809	sertoris Z^2ABRMF et sertor Z	sertori $QGUWA^v$ et sertorii $YVPEJ$	
824	inmerito $Z^2ACYUVPEJA^v$	merito $MZA^2BRFQGW$	
848	nimiis $Z^2ABRQYGVEW$	nimis $MZFUJ$ (nimbis P)	
852	imbrifera Z^2A^2BFcett. et umbrifera ZP	imbriferas $ARMCA^v$	
860	es Z^2ABRU	est $ZFYGVPWJM^2$	et QE
	numine Z^2ABRcett.	nomine $MZQG$	
865	sepulchri Z^2ABRW	futuris *rell.*FA^v	

Book 9

29	illa Z^2AB	ille $ZRFQUVPEW$	ipse $MYGJA^v$
39	clausus Z^2ABR	classis MZ	classi *rell.*A^vF

Appendix IV

42	nec Z^2ABR	neque *rell.*	
73	hic $Z^2AQYGVPJ$	hinc $A^2BRMFUEW$ *et* hin Z	
79	tenens Z^2A^2BRYWJ	terens $MZQGUVPEA^v$ (ternens A^v)	
87	*habent* $Z^2ABRYGVEWJ$	*om.* $MZFQUP$	
100	*habent* $Z^2ABRGUVPW$	*om.* $MZFQEJ$	
104	potuit $Z^2ABYGJA^v$	potui $MZFRQUVPEW$	
120	timori Z^2AB	timore *rell.*	
130	rura $Z^2ABRQYGEJ$	regna $MZUVPW$	
131	hospitii Z^2ABRMP	hospitiis $ZQYGUVEWJ$	
133	matris Z^2ABR	patris *rell. et* patres A^v	
138	deformia Z^2RW *et* deforma AB	sublimia *rell.* A^v	
150	nusquam $Z^2ARMYGUPWJ$	numquam ZA^2BVE *et* nuncquam Q	
155	tumulis Z^2ABR*cett.*	cumulis $MZUP$	
	euulsas Z^2ABR	euulsus *rell.* A^v	
206	et nunc et ficta Z^2A et nunc ficta A^2BR	nunc et ficta *rell. et*	
		nunc efficta Q	
241	coget Z^2AMCPW	cogit $A^2BRQYGUVEJ$ *et* cocyt Z	
251	romanis Z^2ABR romana MP	romanus *rell.* A^v	
253–254	*habent* $Z^2ABRUVEW$	*om.* $MZQYGPJ$	
271	philippos Z^2AB	philippis *rell.*	
288	tum si Z^2ABJ	phrygii *rell. et* phygii Z	
290	amore Z^2ABRJ	amorem *rell.*	
299	catoni Z^2AQWA^v catonis ZA^2BRYGE catonem $MUVPW$		
300	libyci $Z^0ABRQYGEWJ$	libycis $MZUVP$	
308	terra $Z^{2b}A$*cett.* terras Z^{2a}	terrae Z	
314	zona uicinae Z^2A zonae uicinae ZP	zonae uicina A^2BR*rell.*	
329	auerritur Z^2ABR	auertitur *rell.* A^v	
331	mari est Z^2ABR	mari *rell.*	
332	prementem Z^2ABR	frementem *rell.* A^v	
337	pendit Z^2ABRQ	pendet *rell.* (pendat Z)	
355	lethes Z^2ABRW	lethon *rell.* A^v *et* letho P	
361	graues $Z^2AMYGUVPJ$	grauis ZA^2BRQEW	
377	temperet Z^2ABR*cett.*	temperat $ZQVE$	*l.o.* P
386	uenient Z^2ABMP	ueniant *rell.*	*l.o.* Z
401	sub crimine $Z^2ABRMUPEWJ$	discrimine $ZQYGVA^v$	
406	calentes Z^2AB*cett.*	pauentes $ZRQU$	
421	imbres Z^2ABR	ullis *rell.*	

Readings Originating in Z^2

428 umbris $Z^2ABRYGUWJ$ umbra $ZQVEA^v$ austro MP

430 petimus Z^2A et petimus ab $ZA^2BR(?)CQW$ petemus ab MUP petiuimus $YGVEJ$

432 perusti Z^2ABRcett. et perustis Z peruste MP

440 rara Z^2AB rura rell.

459 uolitant $Z^2ABRYGJ$ uolitantque $MZQUVPEW$

461 licet Z^2ABRcett.   libet MP (leget Z)

462 tantum Z^2ABRcett.   tantus $MZUP$

471 qui Z^2AB quia rell.

477 demissa $Z^2AMQUEW$ et demassa B dimissa $RYGVJ$ l.o. ZP

487 *post* 484 Z^2ABR 485–487 om. MP ord. uulg. rell.

494 habent $Z^2ABRYGEWJ$ om. $MZQUVP$

499a–b habent Z^2ABRW om. rell.

499c = 606 humor Z^2ABRW unda (*in* 606) rell.

512 corniger Z^2ABRGJ sortiger $MZQYU(?)V(?)PEW$

513 uibrant Z^2ABR et uibrat Y uibrans $MZQUVPEW$ et uibras GJ

536 arens Z^2A^2BRGJ et urens A ardens rell.A^v

549 ortator Z^2A et orator Z hortator $QYGUVEJA^v$ et hortatos A^2B hortatur MP et hortatu RW

550 fors Z^2AYG et frons B sors rell.

551 ut Z^2ABR et rell.

557 superisque Z^2ABR sequerisque rell.A^v

562 replent Z^2ABR reple rell.A^v

595 nullo Z^2A ullo $A^2BRMUPWJ$ illo $ZQYGVE$

596 malorum Z^2A maiorum rell.

602 puderet Z^2ABR pudebit rell.A^v

604 es om. Z^2ABRQE habent rell. (est W)

634 subrectae Z^2ABRcett. et sueretie Z subrecta MYG

638 se Z^2ABRcett.   si ZGJ

647 caelo pelagoque Z^2A^2Bcett.   pelago caeloque QGE caeloque pelagoque AR (ceta pelago Z)

648 solitum Z^2ABRGU insolitum $M(?)ZQYVPEWJ$

653 gorgones Z^2ABRW gorgonos MZP gorgonis $QYGUVEJ$

Appendix IV

658	palladis Z^2A^2BR *et* pallades A	pallados *rell.*A^v		
662	praeceps Z^2ABRC	praepes *rell.*A^v (praepe Z)		
664	fuluo $Z^2ABRYWJ$ *et* fuso GA^v	*l.o.* $MZQUVPE$		
692	polum Z^2ABMUP	solum $ZRQYGVEWJA^v$		
708	aut Z^2ABR at $ZGEWJA^v$ *et* ad	an C		*n.l.* UV
	MQP *et* ast Y			
711	uias Z^2ABRQ	uia *rell.*		
719	amphisbaena $Z^2AMQYGVP$	amphisibaena $A^2BRUEWJ$		
		(amphybaena Z)		
721	paroeas Z^2ABRW parias	carias MP		
	$ZCQYGUVEJA^v$			
742	tabes Z^2ABR	tabe *rell.*		
752	uidens Z^2ABR	bibens *rell.*A^v		*l.o.* E
753	fatique $Z^2Acett.A^v$	fatisque A^2BRZW		
760	cruore $Z^2ABRCQYGVJ$	ueneno $MZUPEW$		
774	quantus $Z^2ABMQUVPE$	quantum $ZRYGWJ$		
793	miscens $Z^2A^2BRcett.$ *et*	miscet YGJ		
	miscent Z *et* (miscents A)			
795	tollente $Z^2ABRMPW$	pollente $QGUVEJA^v$ *et* pallente ZY		
798	exultat Z^2ABR	exundat *rell.*A^v (ebullet W)		
821	satae Z^2A *et* satei BR *et* sitae P	sabei $ZA^2QGUVEJ$		*n.l.* M
	et saitae CA^v	*et* subei Y		
822	saeuus $Z^2ABRcett.$ *et* saeuas Z	saeuo $CYVE$		
832	leti $Z^2ABRcett.$ *et* leto M	lati ZE		
845	torrente Z^2ABR *et* torrentes Z	torpente *rell.*A^v		
890	periclis Z^2AYGJ	periclo $MZA^2BRQUVPEW$		
902	ualido Z^2ABR	calido *rell.*		
913	qua $Z^2ABRMPEW$	quas $ZYGUVJ$		*l.o.* Q
914	expurgat Z^2AMYVW *et*	expurgant $ZGUEJA^v$ *et*		*l.o.* Q
	expugnat P	expugant BR		
916	stridet $Z^2ABRGVEW$	stridit $MZQYUPJ$		
917	tramarix Z^2A *et* tamarix $A^2BRrell.$	cataris P *et* catatrix M		
	tamatrix Z			
	comis $Z^2ABRYGUVWJ$	comas $MQPE$ *et* commas Z		
924	habent $Z^2ABRQYGUJ$	*om.* $MZUPEW$		
931	fuit Z^2A	fugit $A^2BRrell.$		*l.o.* Z
942	illic $Z^2ABRcett.$	illis YJ (illi Z)		*n.l.* G

Readings Originating in Z^2

945	non culta $Z^2ABRQYGEJ$ et culta Z	nunc uisa $MUPW$ et tunc uisa V	
948	quieta $Z^2AMPEWJ$	quietam $A^2BRZQYGUV$	
956	pelago Z^2ABRGW	pelagi $MZQYUVPEJ$	
984	smyrnaei $Z^2ABRYGVJ$ et smyrne Z	zmyrnaei $MQUPEW$	
1080	nec Z^2ZBRW	ne rell.A^v	
1091	tura Z^2Acett. et dura P	iura A^2BRZ	
1100	sate Z^2A	a te A^2Mrell. et ad te BR	abs te QVE (ata Z)
	ueteres Z^2ARcett. et ueteras B	ueteris UP et uetares Z	

Book 10

8	habent Z^2ABRQJ (post 6 Q)	om. rell.	
	nec Z^2ABR	ne QJ	
	habebit Z^2	amaret Q	u.o. $ABRJ$
47	propius Z^2ABcett. proprius RZ	propeius P et propeus M	
56	biremis Z^2ABY et biremus Z	biremi rell.A^v et triremi J	
80	dependit Z^2ABRcett.	dependet $MZUE$ (deprendat P)	
97	inire peto Z^2Acett.A^v ni repeto A^2BR	habere peto YGJ (intrepedo Z)	
106	iudice Z^2ABRcett.	caesare $ZUVE$	n.l. G
		post 107 desinit P	
122	fulget $Z^2ABMGUWJ$	fulcit $ZQYVE$	n.l. R
	toris Z^2ABcett.	toros QVE (torios Z)	n.l. R
128	hoc Z^2ABR	hos rell.A^v	
143	coluit Z^2A	soluit A^2BRrell.	
	ex denso Z^2ABR	extenso rell.	
145	qualis Z^2ABR	quales rell.	
160	hiemeque Z^2A	gemmaeque rell.	
187	fatibus Z^2A et factibus M	fastibus rell.	
261	refundunt Z^2A^2BRcett. et refendunt Z	profundunt MU	n.l. A
272	quos $Z^2AM(?)QGVE$	quem $ZA^2BRYUWJ$	
290	flexus Z^2ABRcett.	flexu $ZQVE$	
312	populis Z^2ABRW	populos rell.A^v	

Appendix IV

316	moturus Z^2AB	moturum *rell. et* moturam Z *l.o.* M
329	tacens $Z^2ABRMUW$	iacens $ZCQYGVEJA^v$
335	nil $Z^2ABRQVE$	nihil $MZYGUW$
341	fama Z^2ABR	fata *rell.*A^v
369	credit Z^2ABRV	credet *rell.*
383	populorum $Z^2ABRcett.$	populo ZUV
385	nobis Z^2ABRW	uenit *rell.*A^v
391	peraget $Z^2ABRcett.$	peragit $ZYGU$
421	uincent $Z^2ABRcett.$	uincunt ZQV
426	manu $Z^2ABMYUEJ$	manus $ZRQGVW$
435	cadentem Z^2ABR	calentem *rell.*A^v
451	uetantem $Z^2ABRYGU$ *et* uitantem Z	uetante $MCVEWJ$ *et* betante Q
455	mauros Z^2ABR *et* maros Z	maurus *rell.*

post 475 *desinit* A

Appendix V
Readings Originating in A

Book 1

129	coire *ABJ*	cogere *MZPE*	coiere *RGUVW*	d. *QY*
131	dedicit *AMP*	dedidicit *rell.*		d. *QY*
198	latialaris *A*	latiaris *M(?)ZP*	latiatis $Z^2A^2BRrell.$	d. *Y*
	ippiter *AB*	iuppiter *rell.*		d. *Y*
209	iubam et uasto *A*	iubam et uasto graue $A^2BRZQGJ$		
	iubas et uasto *M(?)Z^2UVW*	iubas et uasto graue *PE*		d. *Y*
419	latunc *A et* laete tunc *Z et* late tunc *MZ^2QP et* latet tunc A^2B	lates tunc *Rrell.*		
446	et tarani *AB et* taranis *rell.*	et caranis *G* (et terranis *P*)		
	ora AP^2	ara *rell.*		
468	complent *ABR*	complet *rell.A^v*		
624	rimes *ABRMP*	rimas *rell.*		
642	sine cum *A*	cum *MZVA^v*	sine $Z^2A^2RCrell.$	n.l. *B*
679	terram *ABME*	terra *rell.*		

Book 2

27	sed nec tam *A*	sed iam $Z^2A^2BRrell.$	nec tam *MZ*
48	armis *ABRQ*	arma *rell.*	
51	fundet *AM*	fundat *rell.*	
58	decidit *A*	decidat $Z^2A^2BRrell.$	decedat *MZ*
71	laxere *AB*	laxaeque *rell.A^v*	

Appendix V

138	uulnerae *A*	uulnere *Z*		uulnera *Z²A²BRrell.*
151	fratris *ABY*	fratres *rell.*		
209	pinguit *A*	piguit *Z²A²BRYUEWJ*		timuit *MZQGVPAᵛ*
235	pauida *ABR*	pauidi *rell.*		
269	fulluminibus *A*	fulminibus *Z²A²BRrell.*		fluminibus *Z*
270	imanque *A*	imaque *Z²A²BRrell.*		inque *MZ*
332	gemina geminas et *A*	geminas et *Z²A²BRrell.*		gemina sit *Z*
361	flammina *A et* flamina *Z²A²M*	flammea *rell.Aᵛ*		n.l. *Z*
	et flumina *B*			
426	culta *ABREWJM²U²*	tecta *rell.Aᵛ et* dexta *P et* tuta *Y*		
468	arca *AB*	arce *rell. et* archte *R*		
554	hosts *A*	hostis *Z²A²BRrell.Aᵛ*		hosti *MZ*
620	copomposuit *A*	opposuit *Z²A²BRrell.*		composuit *MZ*
655	*om. AB*			
675	*om. A*			

Book 3

8	cessarunt *AB*	cesserunt *rell.*	
127	uouerunt in *A*	uouere in *Z²*	uouerunt *rell.*
177	alpheus *ABREWJ*	alpheos *rell.*	
242	repletis *ABR*	repletos *rell.*	
302	grata *ABR*	graia *rell.Aᵛ*	
359	adind *A*	ad *MZQGUVPJAᵛ*	in *Z²A²BRYEW*
373–374	*om. A*	habent *rell.*	374 *om. B*
414	ipsere *A et* pere *Z*	ipse *Z²A²rell.*	
417	fame *AB*	fama *rell.*	
433	libra** *A*	librare *Z²A²BRrell.*	uibrare *MZQWAᵛ*
456	turres *ABYGUVEWJ* (turbes *R*)	turris *MZQP*	
683	ac *ABRY*	at *rell. et* ad *Aᵛ*	
747	semianimesque *ABRMP*	semianimisque *rell.*	

Book 4

46	facilis *A*	facili *rell.*	
57	partitor *AAᵛ*	portitor *rell.*	
242	iora *A*	ira *MZYGUVPAᵛ*	ora *Z²A²BRQEWJ*

Readings Originating in A

246	complexus *AB*		complexu *rell.*	
296	rigui *A*	exigui *A^v*	inrigui *rell.*	
317	quis *AB M(?)*		quos *rell.A^{v}M^2*	
349	non *AB*		nos *rell.*	
378	egerit *ABR*		erigit *rell. A^v.*	
405	ader *ABR*		iader *rell.*	
447	impendit *A*	impedit *Z^{2}A^{2}BRCQGEJ*	impetit *MZYUVPW*	
452	illa *Acett.*		illam *MZBR*	
455	impendant *ABR*		impendent *rell.*	
462	opeterginis *ABR*		opiterginis *rell.*	
469	depresa *ABRP*	depresensa *M(?)Z*	deprensa *Z^{2}rell.A^v*	
499	transisbitset *A*	transibit *Z^{2}A^{2}BRYGUPEJ*	transisset *MZQVW*	
502	obsessu *AB*		obsessis *rell.*	
565	ex *A*	exegre (g *in ras. Z^2*)*Z* et exegere *A^{2}Brell.*	egere *R*	*u. in ras. M^2*
584	fortiem uelis *A*	forti uelis *Z^{2}A^{2}BRrell.*	fortem leuis *MZ*	
612	proleiecit *A*	proieiecit *A^{2}B*	proiecit *Z^{2}Rrell.* et prolegit *M(?)Z*	
636	conflexere *AB* uiribus igne ille *A*		conflixere *rell.* et confixere *M* uiribus ille *rell.*	
677	autolobes *A et* autolopes *ZA^{2}BRrell. et* autdolopes *P et* audolopes *Y*		autololes *Z^{2}G*	*n.l. M*
781	constrixit *AYU et* constricxit *B*		constrinxit *rell.*	

Book 5

100	uaporant *AB*	uaporat *rell.*
149	confussae *AB et* confessae *ZM*	confusae *Z^{2}rell.*
157	tripidas *AB et* trepidos *MZ*	tripodas *Z^{2}rell.*
261	effundere *AB*	effudere *rell.*
284	ignaras *AB*	ignaros *rell.*
312	omnem *ABJ*	omne *rell.*
355	dextris *AB*	dextras *rell.A^v et* dextra *R*
407	brundisi *AB*	brundisii *rell.*

Appendix V

420 om. *A*
432 om. *A*
462–543 see Appendix I

608	ure *A*	ere *Z*	euri *Z²A²BR rell.*	
625	astra *Acett.*	anstra *Z²*	anstre *M(?)Z*	
708	consorti *A*	consortes *B et* consortis *Z²A*	consertis *rell.*	d. *M*
769	nonos *A*	nos *MZYW*	non *Z²A²BR rell.*	

Book 6

48	attollit *AB*		attollat *rell.A*ᵛ
62	libiaeque *AB*		libycaeque *rell.*
68	unde *ABM*		unda *rell.*
94	patiens *A*	patens *MZA²BYW*	pati *Z²RQGUVPEJA*ᵛ
134	peribant *AB*		peribat *rell.*
147	adimne *A*	in omne *Z²A²BR*	ad omne *rell.*
276	aperi *A et* aperti *B*	aperto *Z*	aperit *Z²A²rell.*
281	ut et *A*	ut *ZRCVWA*ᵛ	et *Z²A²BMQYGUPEJ*
375	undes *A et* undas *MZ*		undae *Z²A²BR rell.*

376–488 see Appendix I

585	uellere *A et* auellere *Z²A²BR*	auerrere *MZ et* auerre *U*	auertere *rell.A*ᵛ
740	hentnea *A*	etnea *CUJ*	hennaea *rell.*
798	constrictas *ABRW*		constrictae *rell.A*ᵛ *et* constructae *P*
808	descendere *ABR*		descendite *rell.*

Book 7

13	populis *ABR*		populi *rell.*	
32	fractum *A*		fructum *rell.A*ᵛ	
101	meis malis *A*	meis *Z²A²BR rell*	malis *MZ*	
116	qua *ABR*		quam *rell.*	
120	populus *AB*		populis *rell.*	
130	et mortis uenturae *A*	et mors uentura est *MZQGVPEJA*ᵛ	mortis uenturae *Z²A²BRYUW*	
145	rapidos *AY*		rabidos *rell.*	

141

Readings Originating in A

255	meminit *A et* eminit *B et* mini *R*	memini *rell.*A^v		
349	iuuet *AB*	iubet *rell.*		
402	iuncto *ABUVW*	uincto *rell. et* uicto *MZ*		
471	prae *ABR*	post *rell.* A^v		comp. super p *n.l.* Z
563	ipte *A*	iste Z^2A^2BR*rell.*	ipse *MZ*	d. *J*
589	tangi *ABRP*	tanti *rell.*		
590	temerarios *AMU*	temerarius *rell.*		
659	iam *ABRG(?)*	ait *rell.*G^2		
670	ducti *AB*	duci *rell. et* ducis *P*		
690	praestat *AB*	perstet *QUVEJ*	perstat *MZRYGPV*	
774	uidit *AUP*	uidet *rell.*		
851	infracta *AB*	infata *Z*	infecta Z^2*rell.*	
857	effundere *A*	effure *MZ*	effudere Z^2BR*rell.*	

Book 8

155	Ianōm *A*	iam *MZUP*	non Z^2A^2BR*rell.*	
184	rates *ABR*	ratis *rell.*		
254	famulis *ABR et* famulos *MZ et* famulus *W*	famuli $Z^2QYGVEJ$	famulo *UPA*^{v}	
268	ut nequam *A*	ut nequeam Z^2R*rell.*	ut nequem *MB et* unequem *Z*	
298	pelaeas *AB*	pellaeas *R*rell.	palaeas *MZ*	l.o. *Q*
312	uulgantis *AB et* uulgatis *MZ*	uulgati *rell.*A^v		l.o. *Q*
318	maeotidas *A et* maeotides *MZ*	maeotida Z^2A^2BR*rell.*		
392	morire *A*	moriare Z^2A^2BR*rell.*	moria *MZ*	
430	possi *A et* poss *B et* possit *MZ*	possim Z^2*rell. et* possem A^v		
466	ennuada *A*	in uada Z^2A^2BR*rell.*	ennua *Z*	
479	plebes *ABR*	phoebes Z^2*rell.* A^v *et* phoebe *MZW*		
512	ptolemaeo *ARM*	ptolomaeae A^2BZ*rell.*		
567	externis *ABJ*	externae *rell.*		
629	spargunt *AB*	spargant *rell.*		
772	buste *AB*	busto *FQE*	busti *rell.*	
788	restringuit *ABF*	restinguit *rell.*		
852	imbriferas *ARMCA*^{v}	imbrifera Z^2A^2BF*rell. et* umbrifera *ZP*		

Appendix V
Book 9

79	ternens *A*	terens *MZQGUVPEA*ᵛ	tenens *Z²A²BRYWJ*	
138	deforma *AB*	deformia *Z²RW*	sublimia *rell.A*ᵛ	
369	attingit *AB*	attigit *rell.*		
394	meliora *AB*	meliore *rell.*		
412	aut *ABE*	at *rell.*		
498	quae *ABR*	quem. *rell. et* quam *P*		
563	urens *A*	arens *Z²A²BRGJ*	ardens *rell.A*ᵛ	
644	uicerit *A*	uinceret *A²BRZ*	uinceret *rell.*	
647	caeloque pelagoque *AR*	caelo pelagoque *Z²A²Brell.*	pelago caeloque *QGE* (ceta pelago *Z*)	
658	pallades *A*	pallidis *Z²A²BR*	pallados *rell.A*ᵛ	
689	alas *ABR*	ales *rell. A*ᵛ		
751	pauidumque *A et* padumque *A²Rrell.*	panumque *BP*	pacumque *M*	
793	mincents *A et* mincent *Z*	miscens *Z²A²BRrell.*	miscet *YGJ*	
833	cuius *AB*	tutus *rell.*		
852	iniustus *A*	inustis *B*	inustus *rell.*	
881	exonerant *ABRE*	exonerat *rell.*		
915	medicatos *ABRP*	medicatus *rell. A*ᵛ		
934	exsiccat *ABR*	et siccat *rell.*		
1003	reliquid *A et* reliquit *YGUVJ*	relinquit *MZA²BRQPEW*		
1101	digneque *A et* digne *Z*	dignaque *Z²A²BRrell.*		

Book 10

8	habebit *Z²*	amaret *Q*	u.o. *ABR*	l.o. *rell.*
9	feretur *A*	fertur *rell.*		
22	sacratus *ABRQ*	sacratis *rell.*		
38	siticus *A*	syrticus *rell.*		
185	uestris *ABR*	uestri *rell.*		
229	hiberno *ABRW*	hibernis *rell.*		
245	fluctus *ABRMUVW*	fluctu *ZCYGEJ et* flatu *Qc*		
356	foras *AB*	pharos *rell.A*ᵛ		
463	neque *ABR*	nec *rell.*		

Appendix VI
Readings Originating in A^2

Casual errors of $(M)Z$, uncorrected by Z^2 and therefore in A, but corrected by A^2:

Book 1: 225^1, 507, 545, 607.
Book 2: 39, 122, 123, 175^2, 205, 227^2, 276, 279, 299, 345, 349 R, 350, 387, 402, 419^2, 431, 545, 554^3, 585^1, 624, 660.
Book 3: 19, 47, 128, 168, 350 sacyntum Q, 389, 410^2, 429, 510 A^v, 510^2, 623, 638, 722, 753 par ZA.
Book 4: 5 petreius (tre *in ras.* A^2Z^c), 67, 118, 143, 188, 270, 274, 346, 383, 394, 460, 523, 530, 544, 551, 584, 645, 667, 722, 770, 815.
Book 5: 17, 19, 123, 159^2, 199, 235, 236, 260, 262, 312, 363, 372 G, 441, 566, 584 P, 584^2, 606, 618, 625, 766, 776.
Book 6: 1, 4, 33, 84, 139 Y, 167, 170, 250 P, 255, 319, 354, 530, 575, 593, 596, 730, 778 P, 808 P.
Book 7: 64 P, 75, 190, 215, 268, 297^3, 311, 359, 364, 510, 521 S, 585, 608, 634, 653, 707, 708, 730, 744, 790, 827 R, 856.
Book 8: 18, 27, 52, 94, 195 U, 275, 318, 322, 323, 423, 427, 455, 467 P, 515 J, 569, 847 F.
Book 9: 11, 28 J, 157, 196^1, 196^2 R, 246, 287, 759, 937 P, 951, 971 C, 1006, 1016, 1076 *bis*, 1078, 1091^2.
Book 10: 86, 209, 223, 237, 309 R, 402.

Book 1

131   dedidicit *A^2BRcett.*   dedicit *AMP*   d. *Y*

Appendix VI

183	superauerat A^2BRcett.	superat A	d. Y
198	latialis Z^2A^2BRcett.	latiaris $M(?)ZP$ (latialaris A)	d. Y
206	libyae A^2B	libyes rell.	d. Y
209	iubam et uasto graue $A^2BRZQGJ$ iubam et uasto A	iubas et uasto $M(?)Z^2UVW$ iubas et uasto graue PE	d. Y
246	diriguere A^2BRcett.	deriguere $MZAQ$	d. Y
247	tacito mutos A^2BRMQU tacitos muto $GVPJ$	taciti mutos ZA (tactos mutos) E	l.o. W, d. Y
250	populis A^2B populos $MZAR$rell.	populo A^v	
419	latet tunc A^2B et late tunc Z^2MQP et laete tunc Z et latunc A	lates tunc $RYGUVEWJ$	
446	ara A^2BRcett.	ora AP^2	
534	e Z^2ABRcett.	de $MZEWA^v$	
637	omina $Z^2ABRGUPEWJ$	omnie $MZQYVA^v$	
639	at A^2BRcett. et ad PC	aut MZA	
642	sine Z^2A^2RCcett.	cum $MZVA^v$ (sine cum A)	n.l. B
660	gradiue A^2Rcett.	grauide $M(?)ZAP$ (grande B)	
667	confundent A^2BRY	confundet rell. et confundit G	

Book 2

27	sed iam Z^2A^2BRcett.	nec tam MZ (sed nec tam A)	
58	decidat Z^2A^2BRcett.	decedat MZ (decidit A)	
106	praecepisse $A^2BRYVPEJ$ praecipisse $MZAW$	praecipitasse QGU	
122	pendentia A^2BRcett.	prudentia $MZAA^v$	
126	uestae $A^2BRM(?)$	dextrae rell.CA^v	n.l. A, u.o. Z
138	uulnera Z^2A^2BRcett.	uulnere Z (uulnerae A)	
181	exsectaeque A^2BRcett.	exectaque Z^2A	
209	piguit $Z^2A^2BRYUEWJ$	timuit $MZQGVPA^v$ (pinguit A)	
269	fulminibus Z^2A^2BRcett.	fluminibus Z (fulluminibus A)	
270	imaque Z^2A^2BRcett.	inque MZ (imanque A)	
332	geminas et Z^2A^2BRcett.	gemina sit Z (gemina geminas et A)	
345	mutarin A^2R et mutari ZAA^v mutari et B	mutarim rell.	
349	propior A^2Bcett.	proprior $MZARA^v$	

Readings Originating in A^2

361 flamina Z^2A^2M B   flammina A et flumina   flammea rell.A^v n.l. Z
370 coiere A^2Bcett.   colere MZ^2A et colore Z et cogere R
417 libycas...harenas $A^2RCQYGWJ$ libycis...harenis MZAUVPE (libicias...harenias B)
469 aesculea $A^2BRUPEWA^v$(?)   asculea MZAQYVJ (exculea G)
506 subrepsit $A^2BRQEWJ$ subrepit MZAYGUVP
554 hostis Z^2A^2BRcett.A^v hosti MZ (hosts A)
618 laxasque $A^2BRYGVEJ$ et laxsasque Z^2AW lassasque MZQUP
620 opposuit Z^2A^2BRcett.   composuit MZ (copomposuit A)
645 signastis A^2BRYPW signatis MZAQGUVEJ
675 om. A, add. A^2
690 permonitos $A^2BRQYVPEW$ permonitus Z^2A et termonitus MZ   praemonitos GUJ
715 phasidos A^2cett.   phasidis MZA (phasidios BR)
722 flexo iam Z^2A^2BREW flexi iam $MQYGUVPJA^v$ flexum iam A et flexum Z

Book 3

127 uouerunt A^2BRcett.   uouere in Z^2 (uouererunt in A)
150 auertant A^2BYPW auertat rell.
167–168 post 165 A^2BR post 166 $QYGVWJ$ om. MZAUPE
176 populisque A^2BRcett. et populis Z^2A populosque M et populos Z
183 salamina A^2BRcett.   salmina Z^2A et silmina MZ   solamina U
186 cortina A^2Bcett.   coturna M(?)ZAY et corna R
263 pelagi A^2BRcett.   pelago Z^2A
277 maeotidas A^2BRYWJ maeotidos MZAQGUVPE
326 parente Z^2A^2BRcett.   parentis Z et parentes A
346 et effosam Z^2A^2Bcett. et et effonsam Z   effosam Z^2A
347 si habent A^2BRcett.   om. Z^2A
359 in Z^2A^2BRYEW ad $MZQGUVPJA^v$ (adind A)
363 occurrant $A^2BRQYUEWJ$ occurrunt MZAGVP
373–374 habent A^2Rcett.   om. A et 374 om. B

Appendix VI

392	tenentur A^2Rcett.	tentur B	tenetur $M(?)ZA$
410	ullis A^2BRcett. et ulli M	nullis Z^2AB et nuli Z	
433	uidit A^2BRcett.	uidet Z^2A	
	librare Z^2A^2BRcett.	uibrare $MZQWA^v$ (libra** A)	
466	haud A^2BRcett.	haud ZA	aut MC
479	parati $A^2BYUVWJ$	paratis $MZARQGPE$	
503	et A^2B et set M	nec rell. et ne RC et $\bar{n}$ Y	
516	stolchados A^2BR	stochados MZA	stoechados rell.
645	tibi A^2BRM	ibi rell.	
724	descendit $A^2BRUPEWJ$	discendit Z^2A	discedit $MZQYGV$
738	soluta est A^2BR et soluta M	solutas rell.	

Book 4

40	uacauit $A^2BRYUPWJ$	uacabit $MZAE$	uacabat QGV	
46	et $A^2BRMYG(?)W$	ex $ZAQUPEJ$		
	facili A^2BRcett.	facilis A		
61	in A^2BRcett.	ab QV		l.o. A
71	notus $A^2BRMQYUVPW$	notos $ZACGEJ$		
82	caelo diffusum $A^2BRQGUVEWJ$	caelo defusum CP	fusum de caelo $MZAY$	
100	absorbit A^2BRQ	absorpsit $Z^2AMYGEW$	absorsit $ZCUVP$	
166	fugientes Z^2A^2BRcett.	fulgentes MZW (fugigentes A)		
199	luxere foci A^2BRcett.	foci luxere MZA	duxere foci G	
239	si torrida A^2Bcett.	sit horrida $MZAR$		
242	ora $Z^2A^2BRQEWJ$	ira $MZYGUVPA^v$ (iora A)		
265	habet A^2BR et abet MC	auet rell.A^v (audet E)		
295	puteosque A^2BR	puteusque Z^2Arell.	tutelisque MZ	
296	fastidia $A^2BR(?)MZ$	fastigia Z^2Arell.		
	inrigui A^2BRcett. et rigui A	exigui A^v		
297	tam $A^2BRQYGVEWJ$	iam $MZAUP$		
425	ferit ac A^2BRE et ferit hac Z^2A	ferit et rell. (feriet Z)		
428	agat refluoque A^2BRcett.	agratifluoque ZA et agrat[A^v)		
439	aut A^2BRcett.	et Z^2AE		
447	impedit $Z^2A^2BRCQGEJ$	impetit $MZYUVPW$ (impendit A)		

Readings Originating in A^2

499	transibit $Z^2A^2BRYGUPEJ$	transisset $MZQVW$ (transisbitset A)		
565	exegere $A^2Bcett.$	exegre (g *in ras.* Z^2)Z	ex A	*u. in ras.* M
	et egere R			
584	forti uelis $Z^2A^2BRcett.$	fortem leuis MZ (fortiem uelis A)		
586	clepeam A^2BGUVP	clipeam $Z^2ARQYEWJ$ *et* clipea MZ		
612	proieiecit A^2B *et* proleiecit A	proiecit $Z^2Rrell.$ *et* prolegit MZ		
613	libyco A^2BQYEW libyci *rell.*	libyae U		
627	compressis $A^2BRcett.$	complet Z^2A		
636	uiribus ille $A^2BRcett.$	uiribus igne ille A		
659	ualli $A^2Rcett.$	uallis $M(?)ZA$ (uallo B)		
672	athlans A^2BR *et* atlans Z^2ACP	atlas *rell.*		
673	a $A^2BRcett.$ e AG	et UP		
677	autolopes $A^2BRZcett.$ *et*	autololes Z^2A *et* autolobes A *n.l.* M		
	autdolopes P *et* audolopes Y			
705	pugna $A^2Bcett.$	pugnae Z^2ARY		
763	hostes $A^2QYVEWJ$ hostem Z^2AGUP	aures BR		
	et hostis MZ			

Book 5

55	rhasc- thrasc- Z^2AMCUV	rascr**polyn P	
	$A^2BRZQYGEWJ$		
102	cunctis nullique $A^2BRcett.$	nulli cunctisque $MZAYW$	
209	exclusaque A^2BRY exclusasque Z^2A	expulsaque *rell.*NA^v	
233	rhannis A^2R *et*	rhamnus Z^2AGVEJ *et*	ramnum $M(?)Z$
	annis BQY	ramnos UP	
311	suis $A^2BRMZQYGP$	tuis $Z^2AUVEWJA^v$	
420	nec A^2BMZP	ne *rell.*	*l.o.* A
432	*om.* A, *add.* A^2		
569	in A^2BMZ	an *rell.*	*l.o.* A
608	euri $Z^2A^2BRcett.$ *et* ere Z	ure A	
650	sassona A^2BRCW	sasona *cett.*	*d.* M
670	desint $A^2Bcett.$ desinit R	desit MZA	
708	consortis A^2Z *et* consorti A	consertis *rell.*	
	consortes B		
715	confusos $A^2BRcett.$ cfusos A	c'fusos Z	
769	non $Z^2A^2BRcett.$	nos $MZYW$ (nonos A)	
779	uentus A^2B	euentus *rell.*	
785	opposita A^2BRY	posita *rell.*	

Appendix VI
Book 6

1 propinquis *A²BRMYPEW*   propinqui *QGUVJ*   propinquos *ZA*
7 ali *A²B*   alia *MZAP*   alea *rell.*   *n.l. R*
49 circumdata *A²BRcett.*   circumdata est *ZAQ*
63 harena *A²BRQYGUVWJ*   harenae *MZAPE*
94 patens *A²BMZYW*   pati *Z²RQGUVPEJA*ᵛ (patiens *A*)
112 morsu *A²BR*   morsus *MZAQE*   foliis *YGUVPWJ*
114 frangere morsu *A²BRcett.*   rumpere rictu *Z²A*
116 hoc *A²BRcett.*   hac *Z²AJ*
134 nimbusque ferens *A²BRQE*   et nimbus agens *MZYGUVPWJ*   nimbusque agens *Z²A*
137 impactu *A²BR*   impacti *rell.A*ᵛ
147 in omne *Z²A²BR*   ad omne *rell.* (adimne *A*)
150 pauor inquit *A²BRcett.*   inquit pauor *MZAYW*
195 hostibus *A²BRMZP*   ossibus *Z²AQYGUVEWJ*
226 et *A²BRMZY*   e *rell.A*ᵛ
276 aperit *Z²A²cett. et* aperi *A et* aperti *B*   aperto *Z*
281 et *Z²A²BMQYGUPEJ*   ut *ZRVCWA*ᵛ (ut et *A*)
375 undae *Z²A²BRcett.*   undas *MZ* (undes *A*)
416 proprius *A²BRMZP*   propius *rell.* (propitius *A*)
425 defili *A²BE*   delphi *Z*?   deli *rell.*
585 auellere *Z²A²BR et* auerrere *MZ et* auerre   auertere uellere *A*   *U*   *QYGVPEWJA*ᵛ
746 excussa *A²BRYGJ et* excussat *MZA*   concussa *QUVPEW*
782 alii *A²BRcett. et* alti *MZ*   aliis *Z²A*
805 pompeio   pompei *BRW et*   pompeius *MZP et* *Z²A²YGVEJ*   pompeii *Q*   pompeiis *U*   *l.o. A*
811 ducibus *A²BRcett.*   ducimus *MZAA*ᵛ

Book 7

16 fugax *A²UJ et* fuga ex *BR*   fuga *rell.*   fugas *MZ*

Readings Originating in A^2

19	bonorum A^2BRcett.	bellorum Z^2A	
28	somnos A^2BR	somnus rell.	
33	urbe A^2BRcett.	orbe $MZAPA^v$	
101	meis Z^2A^2BRcett.	malis MZ (meis malis A)	
122	fors feret A^2B feret fors MZA	sors feret rell.A^v	
130	mortis uenturae Z^2A^2BRYUW	et mors uentura est $MZQGVPEJA^v$	
		(et mortis uenturae A)	
145	rabidos A^2BRcett.	rapidos AY	l.o. J
163	signifieri A^2BZ	signiferi Z^2ARrell.	
213	fauebunt A^2BRcett.	fauebis MZA^v et auebis Z^2A	
221	at A^2BRcett.	ad $MZAGP$	
297	aut A^2BMZ et haut EW	haud rell.	
363	est limine A^2BRU	limine rell.	
388	annis A^2BRcett.A^v	annus Z^2A	
409	romanis A^2BRcett.	romanus ZA	
409	alea A^2BR alia $MZQP$	allia $Z^2AYGUVEWJ$	
437	add. post 428 Z^2A, corr. A^2		
463–462	$A^2BQGVPEJ$	462–463 $MZARYUW$	
502	patitur A^2Bcett.	partitur Z^2A	
514	medique A^2BRcett.	mediique Z^2APS	d. J, n.l. R
521	labaret A^2BRcett.	laboret MZA	d. J
536	iste Z^2A^2BRcett.	ipse MZ (ipte A)	d. J
541	orbis hiberi Z^2A^2BRcett.	orbi hibernus MZ	l.o. A, d. J
574	subigit $A^2BRQYGVE$ et subicit UP	subegit MZA (subiit W)	d. J
590	temerarius A^2BRcett.	temerarios AMU	d. J
600	pugnacis A^2BRcett.A^v	pugnaces Z^2A	d. J
607	domiti A^2BRcett.	domitis ZAA^v	d. J
618	sequentem A^2BRcett.	sequentis MZA et sequentes Z^cE	d. J
624	transmittant A^2BRcett.	transmittat Z^2AQPE	d. J
635	ubi A^2BRYWJ ibi rell.A^v et sibi U	tibi Z^2A	
660	mundo A^2BRcett.	mundos Z^2A	
687	abis A^2BRcett. et habis Z^2A et ab his P	habit MZ et abit U	
732	reuocet A^2B	reuocent rell.	
757	putabunt A^2BRcett.A^v	putabant $MZAE$	
767	mouentur A^2BRcett.	mouetur $MZYJ$ et mouet Z^2A	

Appendix VI

774	uidet A^2BRcett.	uidit AUP	
800	libyca A^2BRcett.	libycis MZ	libycas Z^2A
807	erige A^2BRcett.	eruge Z^2A	erue A^v
852	romanos A^2BRcett.		romanus Z^2AA^v

Book 8

46 curis A^2B et curris currit MZ et cucurrit U currens $QG(?)VEW^2$
   $YPJR^2$ et   n.l. RW
   cucurris Z^2A

48 uidens $A^2BRYPWJ$ uides $MZAG$ uidet $QUVE$
61 iacet A^2BRcett.   iacebam Z^2A
64 fato A^2RJ et fata A^v fatum rell. (ferro B)
113 dignare A^2BRUPW dignere $ZAQYGVEJ$ (degnere M)
117 uictores A^2BR uictoris rell.A^v
118 habet $A^2BRYGWA^v$ habent rell.
133 ullo A^2BRQW ulla $Z^2AYGUVEJ$ et ullam MZ et
                      nulla P
141 nunc quaerere certum est   nam quaerere certum MZA (nunc
    A^2Rcett.   quaestum est B)
153 quamuis $A^2BCQYGEWJA^v$ quam uix $MZARUVP$
155 non $Z^2A^2BRQYGVEWJ$ iam $MZUP$ (ianōm A)
158 coniuge A^2BRcett.   coniuges Z^2A
164 iacentem A^2BRW iacentis $MZAQ$rell.   iacentes GPJ
184 syrtim A^2BRcett. et syrti ZA syrtis GWJ et syrtes Y
195 sasinae A^2BGP asinae MZArell.
229 propior A^2BRcett.   proprior $MZACU$
242 aeuum A^2BRcett.   aeuo Z^2A
327 crassu A^2B crassos Z^2Arell. et   crassum M^2
                    grassos MZ
341 potest ex quem A^2BR potes te quem rell.
392 moriare Z^2A^2BRcett.   moria MZ (morire A)
431 araxem A^2BYGJ araxen $Z^2ARQUVPEW$ araxe MZ
449 quis $A^2BRYEWJ$ qui $MZAQGUVP$
466 in uada Z^2A^2BRcett.   ennua Z (ennuada A)
471 languent A^2Bcett. et langent U languit $ZA(?)$
    et langunt P

Readings Originating in A^2

475	acoreos A^2B	acureos $MZAP$	acoreus *rell*.	
506	*alt*. fugit $A^2BRcett$.	tonet $M(?)ZAA^v$		*u.o.* P
512	ptolemaeae A^2Bcett.	ptolemeo ARM		
515	cadendi A^2RBMZW	cadenti $Z^2Arell.A^v$		
564	celsa $A^2BRYGUPJ$	celsae $MZAQVEWA^v$		
597	remane $A^2Bcett.A^v$	remanet $MZAR$		
693	sorori $A^2BRMZFUW$	sororis $Z^2AQYGVEJA^v$ (soleri P)		
794	condi $A^2BRcett$.	condita $MZAF$ et condit W		*n.l.* J
803	si nullo $A^2BRcett$.	in nullo Z et in ullo	si in nullo W	
		Z^2AMA^v		
824	merito $A^2BRMZFQGW$	inmerito $Z^2ACYUVPEJA^v$		
852	imbrifera $Z^2A^2BFcett$. et	imbriferas $ARMCA^v$		
	umbrifera ZP			

Book 9

12	miratur A^2BQYGU	miratus $MZARFVEWJ$ et miratos P		
67	busta $A^2BRQYVEWJ$	iusta $MZAFGUP$		
71	non imis $A^2BRcett$.	nominis $ZAR(?)W$ (num imis Y)		
73	hinc $A^2BRMFUEW$ et hin Z	hic $Z^2AQYGVPJ$		
79	tenens Z^2A^2BRYWJ	terens $MZQGUVPEA^v$ (ternens A)		
92	uobis $Z^2A^2BRcett$.	nobis Z		*n.l.* A
150	numquam A^2BZQVE	nusquam $Z^2ARMYGUPWJ$		
206	et nunc ficta A^2BR	et nunc et ficta Z^2A	nunc et ficta *rell*. et	
			nunc efficta Q	
241	cogit $A^2BRcett$. et cocyt Z	coget Z^2AMCPW		
299	catonis $A^2BRZYGE$	catoni A^vZ^2AQW	catonem $MUVPW$	
314	zonae uicina	zona uicinae Z^2A	zonae uicinae P et	
	$A^2BRcett$.		zonae uitinae Z	
354	delecta A^2BR	dilecta *rell*.		
361	grauis $A^2BRZQEW$	graues $Z^2AMYGUVPJ$		
430	petimus ab	petemus ab MUP	petiuimus $YGVEJ$	
	$A^2BR(?)ZCQW$ et			
	petimus Z^2A			
464	nullusque $A^2BRYGWJ$	nullisque $MZAQUVPE$		
478	qua A^2B	quae *rell*.A^v		
528	sic A^2BR	hic *rell*.		

Appendix VI

549	hortatos A^2B et	hortator $QYGUVEJA^v$	hortatu RW	
	ortator Z^2A et	et hortatur MP		
	orator Z			
595	ullo $A^2BRMUPWJ$ et nullo Z^2A	illo $ZQYGVE$		
596	maiorum A^2BRcett.	malorum Z^2A		
604	nunc. $A^2BRMQYVPEJ$	hunc $ZAGUW$		
644	uincerit A^2BRZ et uicerit A	uinceret rell.		
647	caelo pelagoque	pelago caeloque QGE		
	$Z^2A^2BM(?)YUVPJ$			
	ceta pelago Z	caeloque pelagoque AR	n.l. W	
658	palladis Z^2A^2BR	pallados rell.A^v (pallades A)		
686	ascenderit A^2B et	scenderit ZA et	scanderet W et	
	ascenderet R	scinderit A^v	scinderet rell.	
719	amphisibaena $A^2BRUEWJ$	amphisbaena $Z^2AMQYGVP$		
		(amphybaena Z)		
751	padumque A^2Rcett. panumque BP	pacumque M		
	et pauidumque A			
753	fatisque A^2BRZW	fatique Z^2Arell.A^v		
759	sitim A^2Bcett.	situm ZAR		
793	miscens Z^2A^2BRcett. et miscents	miscet YGJ		
	A et miscent Z			
821	sabei	satei BR et saitae CA^v et	sagaei W et	n.l. M
	$A^2ZQGUVEJ$	satae Z^2A et site P	subei Y	
822	robore A^2BRcett.	robora ZAA^v		
826	uolarent A^2BRcett.A^v et uolaret P	uolare Z^2A		
867	poli sed $A^2BRQYGEWJ$	polis et $MZAUP$		n.l. V
890	periclo $A^2BRMZQUVPEW$	periclis Z^2AYGJ		
906	caessere A^2B caesare ZA	cessere rell.		
916	chalbana A^2BRZQ et chabana A	galbana rell.		
917	tamarix tramarix Z^2A et	catatrix M et		
	$A^2BRQYGUVEWJ$ tamatrix Z	catarix P		
919	sonans A^2BRWU^2 sonant MVP	sonat $ZAQYGEJ$	n.l. U	
929	haud A^2BR et haut ZA	aut rell.		
931	fugit A^2BRcett.	fuit Z^2A		l.o. Z
948	quietam $A^2BRZQYGUV$	quieta $Z^2AMPEWJ$		
960	ferens A^2BRcett.A^v	ferens ZA		
975	qui A^2BRcett.	quis ZAP		

Readings Originating in A^2

979	hectoreas $A^2BRZQYEJ$	herceas $MGUVPWA^v$	l.o. A
1003	relinquit $A^2BRMZQPEW$ et reliquid A	reliquit $YGUVJ$	
1083	hospitium et A^2B hospitium est RW	hospitium rell.	
1091	iura A^2BRZ	tura $Z^2Arell.$ et dura P	
1101	dignaque $Z^2A^2BRcett.$	digneque A et digne Z	

Book 10

29	pari A^2BR	patri rell.A^v et patro M apatri C	
97	ni repeto A^2BR	habere peto YGJ inire peto $Z^2Arell.$ (intrepedo Z)	
99	timores A^2BR	tumores rell.	
104	nequiquam $A^2BRMQGVPEWJ$	nequicquam $ZAYU$	
	post 107 desinit P		
112	extruit $A^2BRMYGUWJ^2$	extruet ZAE	extruat Vat. 3284 (exibuit Q)	n.l. J
143	soluit $A^2BRcett.$	coluit Z^2A	
160	crystallus $A^2BRQUVEWJ$ gemmaque $A^2BRcett.$	crystallos $MZAYGA^v$ hiemeque Z^2A	
187	fastibus $A^2BRcett.$	fatibus Z^2A et factibus M	
197	caelicolas $A^2Bcett.$ et caelicolos R	caelicolis $MZAU$	
213	aegogeron A^2BM	aegoceron rell.	
261	refundunt $Z^2A^2BRcett.$ et refendunt Z	profundunt MU	n.l. A
272	quem $A^2BRZYUWJ$	quos $Z^2AM(?)QGVE$	
289	es $A^2BM(?)$	is rell.	
357	nupsit A^2BRW et nubsit E	nubit rell. (nūsit A^v)	

Appendix VII
Readings of A^v

Book 1

40	funesta A^vcett.	funestam A^2	funesto M	d. QY
166	arcessitur A^vC	accersitur $ZABGUVPE$ et arcersitur RWJ	accessitur M	d. QY
179	fatalis $A^vMVBerol.f.35$	letalis rell.		d. Y
183	superauerat A^vcett.	superat A		d. Y
198	iuppiter A^vcett.	ippiter AB		d. Y
214	pumceus A^v	puniceus rell.		d. Y
246	alligat $A^vQG(?)J$	occupat rell.		d. Y
250	populo A^v	populis A^2B	populos rell.	
268	immota A^v	iam mota rell.		d. R
277	sed A^vQG	at rell. et ad MZ		d. R
313	catones $A^vMZQYUVP$	catonis $Z^2ABCGWJ$	catonum RE	
340	paruerit A^v	paruerim rell.		
381	castra A^vcett.	signa $ZABR$		
389	nubiferae A^vGVPWJ	piniferae $MZABRQYUE$		
397	fluminis A^v	uosegi $G^2U(?)$	uogesi rell.	
416	ducat A^vCVP	tollat rell.		
420	saturi A^vYJ et satyri $Z^2ABRQUVEW$	saturis ZCP	atyri M et aturis G	
420	n.l. A^v	ripas rell.		

Readings of A^v

423	bituris $A^vZ(?)CYG$ et bitures U	bituri QWJ	biturix $Z^2ABRMVPE$
	sassones A^vMP	saxones G	sessones $ZABRQYUEWJ$ et suessones V
427	latios A^vQVPJ	latio $MZABRE$	latiis $YGUW$
429	foedere A^vMGUEJ		sanguine $ZABRQYVPW$
442	tonse $A^vcett.$		tonsa Z^2AB et tonsas Z
463	caducos A^v		caycos rell.
466	immenso A^v		immensae rell.
468	complet $A^vcett.$		complent ABR
483	gentibus A^v	a gentibus cett.	agitantibus $MZAB$
492	longu A^v		longa rell.
507	n.l. A^v	limina MZA	limine A^2BRrell. et lumine P
517	munim- A^v (sic)		munimine rell.
534	de A^vMZEW		e Z^2ABRrell.
566	monet A^vGPJ		mouet rell.
579	aruis $A^vG^2E(?)$	umbris UVP	auris rell.
588	errantis $A^vQYGUVPE$		uolitantis $MZABRWJ$
590	sterili $A^vcett.$ et stereli Z		stereles Z^2ABR
604	attollens $A^vEadn.$	attollensque U	et tollens rell.
633	pectora $A^vQYUVPE$ et pectore $MZABRW$		uiscera GJ
637	omnia A^vMZQYV		omina $Z^2ABRGUPEWJ$
642	cum A^vMZV		sine Z^2A^2RCrell. (sine cum A) n.l. B
680	hemi $A^vcett.$		hiemi $M(?)ZABR$
681	quod A^vQG^2	quo GP	quae rell.
687	enyo A^vCQVP		erynis rell.
689	aeriam $A^vcett.$	aeream C	aeria Z^2ABR (erant P)

Book 2

17	urbem $A^vcett.$		orbem Z^2ABR
54	hiberis $A^vcett.$		hiberus Z^2ABRM et hiberos Z
71	laxaeque $A^vcett.$		laxere AB
82	dabet A^v		debet rell.
93	ibi $A^vcett.$ (libyca sibi legens A^v)		

Appendix VII

97	usum A^vcett.	usus $MZABRJ$	
106	nec A^vcett.	non $MZABR$	
121	discerpsisse $A^vQGUVPEW$	discessisse $MZABRCYJ$	
122	prudentia A^vMZA	pendentia A^2BRrell.	
126	dextrae $A^vCQYGUVPEWJ$	uestae $A^2BRM(?)$	n.l. A, u.o. Z
134	quod A^vMZQYP	quot $Z^2ABRGUVEW$ (quo J)	
135	quod A^vMZCRP	quot $Z^2ABQYGUVEWJ$	
156	mortemque A^v	mortisque rell.	
189	ponti A^vG^vadn.	trunci rell.	
209	timuit $A^vMZQGVP$	piguit $Z^2A^2BRYUEWJ$ (pinguit A)	
221	sulla A^v	his illa ZAB	his sulla Rrell.
292	compressas A^vcett.	complossas $MZABRW$	
299	tumulos A^vA^2BRcett.	tumulus MZA	
310	hastis A^vcett.	hostis $MZABRW$	
313	cernere mortes A^vB^v	perdere mores $ABRQGVE$	pendere mores $YUPW$ n.l. ZJ
	pendere mortes M	perdere mores in ras. man. tard. Z	
319	q̄ A^v	qui MZA	-que A^2BRrell.
345	mutari A^vZA	mutarin A^2R et mutari et B	mutarim rell.
349	proprior A^vMZAR	propior A^2Brell.	
360	timidum A^vcett.	tumidum $MZABR$	
361	flammea A^vcett.	flamina Z^2A^2M et flammina A n.l. Z et flumina B	
364	suppara A^vcett.	suppera ZAB	
367	obsita A^vcett.	obsuta $MZABR$	
383	toti A^vCQUVJ	toto $MZABRYGPEW$	
388	urbique A^vcett.	ubique $ZABR$	
426	tecta $A^vMZQGUV$ et dexta P	culta $ABREWJ$ (tuta Y)	
431	omnes A^v et omnis cett. et hominis M	omnem Z^2AB	
452	turribus A^vcett.	turbibus $MZABR$	
469	aesculea $A^v(?)A^2BRUPEW$	exculea G	asculea $MZAQYVJ$
470	auertitque A^v	diuertitque rell. (deuexitque C)	
503	uacantem A^vcett.	uacante Z^2AB	uocante MZ
525	munus A^vcett. et manus P	minas $MZAB$	

Readings of A^v

535	difunditur A^v	effunditur $QGUVEJ$ et ex- P	perfunditur $MZABRYW$	
541	cum $A^vQYGUPEWJ$		quod $MZABRV$	
554	hostis $A^vZ^2A^2$cett.		hosti MZ (hosts A)	
558	discant A^vB^v et discent $MZQG$	discet $CUPW$		disces $Z^2ABRYVEJ$
570	quos $A^vQGUVPEWJ$		quod $MZABRY$	
587	flectente syene A^vcett.		flectentis yenen $MZAB$	
613	in artu A^v		in artum rell.	
614	linguam $A^vQGUVPEJ$		sulcum $MZABRYW$	
650	segnis $A^vMZQGVP$		pacis $Z^2ABRYUEWJ$	
654	obsessae A^vEadn.	oppressae $MZABRQYGWJ$	infestae UVP	
655	l. add. in marg. A^v			
674	sest*nque A^v		sestonque rell.	
677	differet A^vMZ et differret $RYUPW$	defert Z^2AB	deferret $QGVEJ$	
682	reseret $A^vRCYGUVPEJ$ et referet Z^2AB	referat Z et reserat M	referret Q	n.l. W
712	in litore A^vMZYU	in litora $QGVPE$	ad litora Z^2ARWJ (in litore ad litora B)	
721	erigit A^vB		eripit rell.	
722	flexi iam $A^vMQYGUVPJ$	flexo iam Z^2A^2BREW	flexum Z et flexum iam A	

Book 3

2	tenuere A^vWJc	mouere rell.
57	signe A^v	segne rell.
63	montis A^vMZ	montes Z^2ABrell.
73	in A^vcett.	ad Z^2ABRE
84	arce A^v et arcem MZE	arces Z^2ABrell. (urbes J)
86	qua A^vcett.	quae $MZABR$
102	nec A^vQGadn.^{v}	non cett.
145	qua A^v	quem rell.
147	quicquid A^v	quidquid uel quicquid rell.

Appendix VII

154	apertas A^v		reclusas rell.	
158	philippi A^vcett.		philippo ZAB	
160	quo A^vcett.		quod MZABR	
165	regna A^v		regum rell.	
174	coire A^vRP	coluere MZAB	coiere rell.	
179	tesproti driopesque A^vcett.		tesprotridiotesque MZABRY	
197	hemus A^vcett.		hemmus Z^2ABR	
207	marsea A^v		marsia uel marsya rell.	
272	lagsus A^v (sic)		lapsus rell.	
290	mersura A^v		missura rell.	
291	et A^vcett.		sed uel set MZABRYW	
302	graia A^vcett.		grata ABR	
305	pacifico A^vMZVP		pacifero Z^2ABRQYGUEWJ	
320	tonantem A^vcett.		sonantem ZAB	
347	cernis A^v et cernes V		cerni rell.	
359	ad A^vMZQGUVPJ		in Z^2A^2BRYEW (adind A)	
373–374	om. A, add. in marg. inf. A^v			
389	aeternumque A^vcett.		alternumque MZABRYW	
433	uibrare A^vMZQW		librare Z^2A^2BRrell. (libra** A)	
441	dodonis A^vGJ		dodones rell.	
500	erumpit A^v		erupit rell.	
510	fortuna A^vMZA		fortunam A^2BRrell.	
535	a A^v		at rell.	
586	catus A^vMZQUP et satus C		tagus Z^2ABRYEW et cagus V et lagus JG^q	n.l. C
593	nullae A^v	nulla MZABRP	nullam rell.	
607	dolorem A^vcett. et dolorum G		dolore MZAB	
609	pectore A^vRQYVW		pectine MZABGUPEJ	
624	manebat A^vMQGUVJ et manebant E et manebit P		tenebat ZABRYW	
638	uulnere A^vcett.		uulnera ZABR	
669	truncus A^v		truncos rell.	
672	tortum A^vQVEW		totum rell.	
673	expulso A^vMZQYGUVPJ		excusso Z^2ABREW	
674	sidentia A^vcett.		sedentia MZAB	
678	dum A^vcett.		cum MZAB	
679	hastam A^vcett.	hastem Z^2ABR	hostem MZP	

Readings of A^v

683	ad A^v	at *rell.*	ac *ABRY*	
687	fauces A^vQGPV^2 et faces *E*	flammas *rell.* et flammis *M*		
693	exercunt A^v	exercent *rell.*		
705	iecerunt A^vcett.	legerunt *MZABRW*		*l.o. Y*
715	neruis A^vM^2	membris *rell.*		
717	mittendis A^vcett.	miciendis Z^2ABR		
731	cadens A^vcett.	cadis *MZAB*		
735	oculos A^vcett.	oculis *M(?)ZAB*		
753	pars A^vcett.(A^2B)	per *ZA*		
760	trunci A^vM^2	trunco *rell.*		

Book 4

39	in tergum A^vcett.	integrum *ZABPW*		
40	uibrare A^vcett.	librare Z^2ABRE		
45	perducere A^v	producere *ZABRQYGPWJ*	praeducere *MUV* (procedere *E*)	
	gyro A^vcett.	cyro *ZAB*		
57	partitor A^vA	portitor A^vBRrell.		
60	cum A^vM^v	quo *rell.*		
90	mers[A^v	mersis *P*	mersi *rell.*	
112	intendas A^vErl. *304*	impendas *rell.*		
133	superenatat A^vadn.^{v}	superemicat *rell.*		
161	emitti A^vcett.	emittit *MZABR*		
169	locant A^vcett.	locat *MZABRYW*		
171	parentes A^vW	patresque *rell.*		*u.o. MZY*
177	propinquum A^vMGEJ	propinqui *ZABRQYUVPW*		
188	amauit A^vM^2	amabit *rell.*		
202	iactant A^vcett.	iectant Z^2AB et luctant *MZ*		
228	nefando A^vcett.	nefandus *MZAB*		
232	foedera $A^vGP(?)$	funera *rell.*P^2		
242	ira $A^vMZYGUVP$	ora $Z^2A^2BRQEWJ$ (iora *A*)		
244	nocte A^vMZGUP	in nocte $Z^2ABRQYVEWJ$		
265	auet A^vcett. et abet *MC*	habet A^2BR (audet *E*)		
274	ullo A^vcett.(A^2B)	nullo *ZAG*		
276	sibi A^vcett.	si ZZ^2ABG		
279	amens $A^vMZQYGUVP$	omnes Z^2ABRE et omnis *WJ*		

Appendix VII

283	martis $A^vGUVPWJ$		mortis $MZABRQYE$	
296	exigui A^v		inrigui *rell.* et rigui A	
317	quos $A^vcett.M^2$		quis $ABM(?)$	
346	sola ... causa A^vUPW	causa ... magna Z^2ABR	causa ... sola $MZQYGVJ$ (causa ... causa E)	
352	aperimus $A^vcett.$		asperrimus MZA (asprimus B)	
357	inermis A^vMZ et inermes $QUVP$		inermem $Z^2ABRYGEWJ$	
374	paratu A^vWJ	paratus Y	paratis *rell.*	
378	eregit $A^vcett.$		egerit ABR	
399	pauor $A^vC(?)V$		fauor *rell.*	
405	molles $A^vcett.$		moles $ZABR$	
419	molibus $A^vcett.$		mollibus $ZABR$	n.l. M
416	*l. om.* A, *add. in marg. inf.* A^v			
422	n.l. A^v			
424	ratibus A^v		tradibus *rell.*	
425	ferit et $A^vcett.$		ferit hac Z^2A et ferit ac A^2BRE (feriet Z)	
428	agrat[A^v	agratifluoque ZA	agat refluoque *rell.*	
431	cunctas $A^vcett.$		cuncta $ZABRY$	
458	caecisque $A^vcett.$		caesisque $ZABR$ et cessisque C	
469	deprensa $A^vZ^2cett.$		depresa $ABRP$ (depresensa $M(?)Z$)	
482	ann[A^v		annos *rell.*	
518	fati $A^vZQYVEM^v$	leti $GUPWJM^2$	mortis Z^2ABR	n.l. M
530	mari $A^vcett.$		maris Z^2ABRW	
573	tantis A^v		tanti *rell.*	
577	manu $A^vcett.$		manus $MZABQ$	
590	qua A^v	quas MZJ	quae Z^2ABR*rell.*	
595	python $A^vVadn.$		typhon *rell.*	
610	terras $A^vcett.$		terram Z^2AB	
634	aruis $A^vMZRC(?)$		undis Z^2AB*rell.*	
644	fato A^v	uiro *rell.* et uero U	uiro *om.* $ZABR$	
645	tactae $A^vYUVPEWJ$ et tacitae QG		factae $MZAB$ (tactae factae R)	
659	n.l. A^v			
673	ad A^v	a $ZABRQVEW$	et $YUPJ$ et e G	
692	regni A^v		regnum *rell.*	

Readings of A^v

707	pendere A^vcett.	prendere MZABR		
726	obliquosque A^v et obliquusque MZQGVW	obliquumque Z^2ABRYEJ et obliquatque UP		
736	et A^v	ut rell.		
745	mersos A^vcett.	medios Z^2ABRUW		n.l. Y
	deiecit A^vcett.	proiecit Z^2AB		
762	ulli A^v et illi ZABRYG	illis QVEWJ	ille MUP	
801	prodita iura A^vcett.	proditura MZABRY		
805	urbi A^vcett.	urbis Z^2AB et urbes MZ		
816	nunc A^vP	tunc rell.		
819	multatus A^v	mutatus rell.		

Book 5

37	en A^vcett.N	et M(?)ZABY(?)		
74	fatidicae A^v et fatidici B	thebanae rell.N et thebani C		
89	alterni A^v	aeterni rell.N		
96	conexa A^vcett.	conuexa MZABW		
101	inarimis A^v	inarimes rell.		
103	n.l. A^v			
114	ac A^v	et rell.		
118	quippe A^vcett.	quique MZAB		
	stimulo A^vcett.	stimulos MZABR		
123	iussu A^v	iussus rell.		
133	in deuia A^vcett.	in debita Z^2ABM (indubita Z)		
157	prodiderat A^vRQGEN	prodiderant rell.		
206	furoris A^vE$V^2$$M^2$$G^v$	furorum rell.N		
209	expulsaque A^vcett.N	exclusaque A^2BRY	exclusasque Z^2A	
210	perstat A^vcett.N	restat Z^2ABR		
219	uidit A^vcett.	uadit MZAB		
246	expulerant A^vZU	expulerat Z^2ABRrell.		
248	etiamnunc A^vcett.	etiamnum M(?)ZABR		
252	truncus A^vcett.	truncos ZABR		
284	paremus A^v	paremur rell.N		
297	eat o A^vQVE(?) JNU^2	fato MZABRY et fas o P	placeat GW	n.l. U

Appendix VII

311	tuis $A^v Z^2 AUVEWJ$		suis $MZA^2BRQYGP$	
314	sibi $A^v U(?)VP$		tibi *rell.*	
355	*n.l.* A^v		amolitur *rell.*	
	dextras A^v*cett. et* dextra R		dextris AB	
368	dextraeque A^v*cett.N*		dextraque $ZABR$	
374	hinc A^v*adn.*^{v}		hanc *rell.N*	
377	siphys A^v *et* siphus M^2 *et* sifus C		silphus U *et* silppus P	
	sippus $QGVEJ$ *et* sipus		EIBVS N	
	$M(?)ZABRYW$			
390	imperii A^v*cett.N*		imperio $MZAB$	
399	fastus $A^v ZQ$	fastis GJ	faustus Z^2AR *et* fastos	
			$BMYUVPEW$	
419	perfert A^v	perstet MZ	perflet Z^2ABR*rell.*	
420	*l.o. A add.* A^v			
421	iactatis $A^v RYVWJU^2$		iactantes $Z^2ABQGPE$ *et* ictantis MZ	
			n.l. U	
434	ligatae $A^v Y$ adn^v	ligato $M(?)ZABRQ$	ligata $GUVPEWJ$	
448	illinc $A^v CYUVE$		illic $MZABRQGPWJ$	
462–545	*habet A in manu tard. sine corr.*			
543	uocabant $A^v M$		uocabat *rell. et* uacabat P	
546–547	*ll. o. A, add.* A^v			
561	ad A^v*cett.*		at ZAB	
580	ac $A^v MZ$ *et* hac Y		haec *rell.*	
593	quid $A^v YVEJ$		quod $MZABRQGUPW$	
595	*l.o. A add.* A^v			
609	latuisse $A^v M^2$		iacuisse *rell.*	
660	peregit A^v		peregi *rell.N*	*d. M*
682	quo A^v*cett.*		quod ZAB	*d. M*
691	committere $A^v YGVEWJ$		quod mittere $ZABRQUP$	*d. M*
724	deponere A^v		seponere *rell.*	
728	magni A^v *et* magnis MZ		magne Z^2ABR*rell.*	
740	leto A^v*cett.*		lecto $MZABR$	
751	quaterent	quatient $MZAB$	quatiunt $QYGUEJ$ *n.l.* W	
	$A^v RVPW^2$			
759	uelim A^v*cett.*		uelint $MZAB$	
771	praebere $A^v M^2$		praestare *rell.*	
781	ferent $A^v YV$	ferat $Z^2 ABRQGE$	feret $MZUPWJ$	

Readings of A^v

782	belli A^vRPWErl. 304	bella rell.	n.l. Q
794	fructus A^vcett.	fluctus MZABR	

Book 6

22	habent A^v	habet Z^2rell.S	l.o. Z
24	scopulisque uomentibus A^vGJSM^2	scopulisque mouentibus Z^2ABRY	
	scopulis remouentibus QUVPEW	scopulis reuomentibus M	l.o. Z
48	attollat A^vcett.S	attollit AB	
51	in A^vCQG	en MZEJ	et $Z^2ABRYUVPW$ (]n S)
57	latis A^vcett.S	latus MZAB	
65	mediae $A^vYGUPEWJ$	medium MR et medio ZAB	mediis V et medies Q
81	gramina A^vcett.	pabula Z^2AB	
94	pati $A^vZ^2RQGUVPEJ$	patens MZA^2BYW (patiens A)	
100	cadentum A^vcett.	perempta Z^2ABR	
112	minantis A^vcett.	minantes Z^2ABR	
118	claustris A^vcett.	castris MZABYW (caustris P)	
122	dedignantur A^v	dedignatur rell.	
128	in $A^vMZCYGUJ$	ad $Z^2ABRQVPEW$	
131	attonitus A^v	attonitos rell.	
137	impacti A^vcett.	impactu A^2BR	
146	promotis $A^v(?)$	promotus rell.	
157	nos A^vcett.	non MZABC	
181	expulit A^v	extulit rell.	
201	summoueat A^v	promoueat rell.	
208	sic libycis A^vcett.	getulus Z^2ABRYW	
221	admentauit A^vPN	amentauit rell.	
226	e A^vZ^2Acett.	et MZA^2BRY	
228	dolorem A^vG^v	furorem rell.N	
230	hinc A^vcett.	hunc Z^2ABR	
262	tyrannum A^v	dominum rell.	
281	ut A^vZRCVW	et $Z^2A^2BMQYGUPEJ$ (ut et A)	
289	deponeret A^v	disponeret rell.	
291	superi A^v	super rell.	

Appendix VII

292	obsessum A^vVU^2	obsaeptum rell.		
301	rerum A^vG^vadn.	legum rell. et regum U		
330	phoebeus A^v	phoebeos rell.		
341	ibi A^v	imi rell.		
346	pelago $A^vYV^2Erl.$ 304	pelagi rell. et pelagis M		
350	emathis A^vcett.	emathiis ZABE et ematheis Y		
	aequoreis A^v	aequorei rell.		
366	ehuuenos A^v et	euneos QJ et euenos	euhenus V et euenus P	
	euuenos MZRYGU	Z^2ABEW		
368	amphry[A^v	amphrysus MYVW	amphrysos rell.	
374	phenisque A^v	phoenixque rell.		
376–488	habet A in manu tard. sine corr.			
493	spernendisque A^v	spernendique rell.		
520	captat A^vcett.	cartat Z^2B (carptat A)		
541	immergitque A^vcett.	immersitque Z^2ABRW		
552	ferarum A^vN	luporum rell.		
555	erumpant A^v et erumpam Z	erumpat Z^2ABRrell.		
574	uaganti A^v	uagatis Z^2ABR	uagati rell.	
579	urbem A^v	orbem rell.		
581	pollutus A^v	pollutos rell.	polluto VP	
582	conspersos A^vcett.	conspergos MZ	compressus Z^2ABREJ	
585	auertere	uellere A et auellere	auerrere MZ et auerre U	
	$A^vQYGVPEWJ$	Z^2A^2BR		
601	sibi A^v	tibi ZABRQYGEWJ	mihi MUVP	
629	lit*s $A^v(?)$	letos Z^2AB	leto rell. et leta Z	
646	antris A^vcett.	antros Z^2ABR		
653	discendit ad A^v	descendit ad G^vV^2	descenderit rell.	
756	terraeque A^vV	terraque rell.		
757	rectu A^v	rictu rell.		
771	tenet $A^vYEWErl.$ 304	decet rell.		
772	duraeque A^vcett.	duraque ZABQ		
776	fletu A^vcett. et flectu M	flatu Z^2AB et flactu Z		
787	curios A^vcett.	curio ZABR		
797	calybis A^vcett.	calybum Z^2ABRY		
798	constrictae A^vcett.	constrictas A^2BRW (constructae P)		
811	ducimus A^vMZA	ducibus A^2BRrell.		
820	tutius A^vcett.	totius ZABR		

Readings of A^v
Book 7

14	dum A^v		cum *rell.*	
18	ornante A^v*cett.*		ornante *in ras.* A^2	
22	omnia $A^vMZCPEWJ$		omina $Z^2ABRQYGUV$	
23	sides A^v		sedes *rell.*	
28	somnus A^v*cett.*		somnos A^2BR	
32	fructum A^v*cett.*		fractum A	
33	uel A^v		uelut *rell.*	
	orbe A^vMZAP		urbe A^2BR*rell.*	
50	admouet A^v*cett.*		admonet Z^2ABRGW	
84	si(natus)A^v (*sic*)		senatus *rell.*	
	cupit A^v	habet MZ	hauet Z^2ABRW *et* auet *rell.*	
88	nil A^vQUVPE	nihil GJ	non $MZABRYW$	
111	tuere A^v*cett.*		tueri $MZABR$	
115	quot A^v*cett.*		quod $MZABP$	
118	ruinae A^v		ruina *rell.*	
122	sors feret A^v*cett.*	fors feret A^2BR	feret fors MZA	
130	et mors uentura est $A^vMZQGVPEJ$		mortis uenturae Z^2A^2BRYUW (et mortis uenturae A)	
166	se iecit A^vYGUVW	eiecit $Z^2ABRQPE$	selegit MZ	*d. J*
168	quo A^v		quos *rell.*	*d. J*
169	nomina A^v		numina *rell.*	*d. J*
176	oesseam A^v		osseam *rell.*	*d. J*
177	miratus A^v		miranur *rell.*	*d. J*
183	tumultu A^vBCU *et* tumultum $QYGVPE$		tumultus Z^2ARWM^2 *et* tumultis Z	*n.l. M, d. J*
192	euganeo A^v*cett.*		euganeos $MZAB$	*d. J*
205	sumnos A^v (*sic*)	summos *rell.*	summus $MZAB$	
211	mouebunt A^v*cett. et* uouebunt Y		monebunt Z^2AB *et* manebunt U	
213	fauebis A^vMZ *et* auebis Z^2A		fauebunt A^2BR*rell.*	
215	discindens A^vM		descendens *rell.*	
221	dessant A^v		densant *rell.*	
225	habenis A^vBRWJ	habena QE	habenae $MZAYGUVP$	
230	iter eis A^v		itireis *rell.*	
231	prodistis A^v*cett.*		proditis $MZABR$	
232	cedras A^v		caetras *rell.* (ceteras MZ)	

Appendix VII

240	regni A^vcett. et regnum M		mundi Z^2AB		
248	magnis A^v		magni rell.		
255	memini A^vcett		meminit A et eminit B et mini R		
272	aut A^vcett.		et Z^2ABWJ		
279	urbem A^v		orbem rell.		
280	triumphum $A^vRQYGEW$		triumphi $MZABUVPJ$		
290	quo se A^v		quod si rell.		
309	mors A^v		sors rell.		
319	hostis A^vcett.		hosti Z^2ABRW		
328	tenditis A^vMZ	tendetis $QYGVPEJ$ et		tentetis Z^2ABR	
		tendentis U		(tendatis W)	
331	cerisque A^v		ceresque rell. et geresque MZ		
	uiris $A^vQYGUVPJ$	uires Z^2AB		uiri MEW	l.o. Z, n.l. R
335	locassent A^vP		locasset rell.		
345	gentes A^v		gentis rell.		
349	iubet A^vcett.		iuuet AB		
364	et A^vcett.		aut Z^2ABRW		
387	heae (sic) A^vR et	ne P		haec $MZABQYW$	
	hae $GUVEJ$				
388	annis A^vcett.		annus Z^2A		
396	que*etusque A^v		questusque rell.		
397	carpsit A^vcett.		carpit Z^2ABRW (carsit ZE)		
402	uincto $A^vZ^2RQYGPEJ$		iuncto $ABUVW$ (uicto MZ)		
404	frequente A^vZ^2A		frequentem A^2BRMZrell.		
411	quo	quod Z^2ABREW		pro VJ	n.l. QU
	$A^vMZYGPQ^2U^2$				
419	urbem A^vC		orbem rell.		
421	armis $A^vZRQUEW$		annis $Z^2ABMYGVPJ$		
440	legum A^vcett.		regum Z^2ABG		
445	quos $A^vRQYGUEJ$	quo $MZAB$		quod VPW	
451	casus A^vU	casibus V		cassius rell.	
462	tempus quo noscere possent		uultusque agnoscere quaerunt		
	$A^vZRQYGVPEJ$		Z^2ABUW		
	VVLTVSQVONO S				n.l. M
471	post A^vcett.		prae ABR	comp. super p n.l. Z	
489	sed A^vQVEJ		et $MZABYUPW$		n.l. RG
493	iunxerat A^vcett. et uinxerat Z^2AB		uixerat MZW		

Readings of A^v

504	uergens A^v		uertens *rell.*	
540	isti A^vC		istis *rell.*	*d. J*
569	sic A^v		si *rell.* (sisic *R*)	*d. J*
575	confundere A^vRQVE		contundere *rell.*	*d. J*
584	regum A^vQUVEW		rerum $MZABRYGP$	*d. J*
596	procumbat A^v*cett.*		procumbunt $MZAB$	*d. J*
600	pugnacis A^vA^2BR*cett.*		pugnaces Z^2A	*d. J*
601	illo A^v*cett.*		ullo Z^2AB (ille U)	*d. J*
602	uictos A^v		uictus *rell.*	*d. J*
607	domitis A^vZA		domiti A^2BR*rell.*	*d. J*
612	stygias A^v*cett.*		patrias Z^2ABR	*d. J*
634	quod A^v*cett.*		quot $Z^2ABE(?)$	
635	ibi $A^vZMQGVPE$	ubi A^2BRYWJ	tibi Z^2A (sibi U)	
643	nunc A^v	ne hunc C	num *rell.*	
659	ait A^v*cett.*G^2		iam $ABRG(?)$	
686	fati A^v*cett.*		fatim $ZABR$	
696	erit A^vMZ		erunt *rell.*	
698	gessisse A^v		cessisse *rell.*	
701	quod A^v		quo *rell.*	
715	omnia A^v*adn.*		obuia *rell.*	
746	sic milite iusso $A^vMZQYGPJ$		nec plura locutus $Z^2ABRUVEW$	
751	ruunt $A^vMZYUPJ$		uolunt $Z^2ABRQGVEW$	
755	extulit A^vMP et extulli Z	expuit $Z^2ABR(?)$	expulit *rell.*	
757	putabunt A^v*cett.*		putabant $MZAE$	
760	capit A^v		rapit *rell.*	
770	stygiam A^v		stygia *rell.*	
807	erue A^v	eruge Z^2A	erige A^2BR*rell.*	
815	uocauit A^vC et uocabit $MZYGUVPEJ$	uocabat Q	locabit Z^2ABRW	
816	sunt $A^vMZRQYGVEJ$		eunt Z^2ABUPW	
	ibis $A^vMZRYGUPWJ$		ibit Z^2ABQVE	
817	iacebis $A^vMZGUPEJ$		latebis $Z^2ABRQYVW$	
841	*om.* A, *add. in marg. inf.* A^v			
842	feras A^v*cett.*		ferus Z^2AB	
845	nimbusque A^v		nimbique *rell.*	

Appendix VII

850	immemos A^v	immemor *rell.*	
851	infecta $A^v Z^2$*cett.*	infrácta *AB* (infata *Z*)	
852	romanus $A^v Z^2 A$	romanos $A^2 BR$*rell.*	
868	belli A^v*cett.*	bellis *MZAB*	
871	pachyni *uel* pacini A^v*cett.*	phacini *MZAB*	

Book 8

3	negantem A^v*cett. et* negante $Z^{2a}R(?)$	neganti $Z^{2b}ABM$	*u.o. Z, n.l. Q*
64	tacitus A^v	tacitos *rell.*	
	fata A^v *et* fatum *rell.*	fato $A^2 RJ$ (ferro *B*)	
66	eam A^v	eram *rell.*	
76	miser erige mentem A^v*cett.*	miserere gementes $Z^2 ABR(?)$ *et* -tos *Z et* -tis *MU et* -tem *P*	
117	uictoris A^v*cett.*	uictores $A^2 BR$	
118	habet $A^v A^2 BRYGW$	habent *MZAQUVPEJ*	
119	caesar A^v*cett.*	caessar *ZA*	
120	fatum A^v*cett.*	bellum $Z^2 ABR$	
142	sit A^v*cett.*	scit *ZAB*	
153	*n.l.* A^v	populus *rell.*	
	quamuis $A^v A^2 BCQYGEWJ$	quam uix *MZARUVP*	
159	in $A^v M^v$	ad *rell.*	
160	se A^v	si *rell.*	
170	syriam A^v	libyam *rell.*	
197	secantem $A^v BR$	secante *rell.*	
222	claustra A^v*cett.*	regna $Z^2 ABRW$	
238	uolet A^v*cett. et* uolit *MZ*	ualet $Z^2 ARP$ *et* uidet *B*	
240	famulo $A^v UP$	famulos *MZ et* famulus *W*	famuli $Z^2 QYGVEJ$ *et* famulis *ABR*
	raptus $A^v GP$	ruptis *B et* raptos $ZYUVEJM^2$ *et* rapto *Q*	ruptos $Z^2 ARW$ *n.l. M*
259	syndris A^v	sinedris *ZABRW*	synedris *MYGUVPEJ* *n.l. Q*
265	nouis $A^v UM^v G^v$	meis *rell.*	nobis *P*
270	fatis $A^v WJ$	factis *MC*	fastis *rell.* *l.o. Q*

Readings of A^v

278	quemnam A^vMZJ quaenam $YGUVE$	quem non Z^2ABR	l.o. Q
	et quem*nam P	(quae non W)	
279	uobis A^vcett.	proceres Z^2ABR	l.o. Q
280	pondere A^vadn.	pondera rell.	l.o. Q
	uergant A^vcett. et uergam M^2	uersant Z^2ABRW	l.o. Q
291	educunt A^v	seducunt rell.	l.o. Q
309	reuulsus A^v	reuulsos rell.	l.o. Q
312	uulgati A^vcett.	uulgantis AB (uulgatis MZ)	l.o. Q
315	cruente A^vcett.	cruenta Z^2ABR (cruentur Z)	
322	fauet A^v faue A^2BRrell.	paui $M(?)ZA$	
327	sentit A^vMZP	sensit rell.	
339	n.l. A^v	famulus rell.	
346	mensos A^v	mensus rell.	
370	arua A^vcett.	arma Z^2ABR	
377	illis A^vcett.	illi Z^2AB	
381	n.l. A^v	melior rell.	
390	uenisse A^vUP	misisse rell.	
405	regum A^vcett. et regnum MZ	fratrum Z^2ABR	
421	si A^v	quod rell.	
425	imperii A^vcett.	imperti $M(?)ZAB$	
430	possem A^v possi A et poss B et	possit MZ	
	possim rell.		
432	infixa A^v	confixa rell.	
444	egyptos $A^vNZABRQP$	egyptus $YGUVEWJ$	
448	debita A^vcett. et debit M	dedita Z^2ABR et dedit Z	
452	nec A^v	nil rell.	
470	casio A^vcett. et cassio A	casto $MZBR$	
479	phoebes A^vZ^2cett. et phoebe	plebes ABR	
	MZW		
483	damnasse A^v	damnare rell.	
484	nocentes A^vBRcett.	nocentis Z^2A	
491	iniusta A^vM^v	inuisa rell.	
492	gladiis A^vMZUWJ	gladii $Z^2ABRCQYGVPE$	
494	uolet A^v	uult rell.	
498	neu nos A^vUP neu te Z^2ARcett. et	neu nas Z	n.l. M
	neut B		
499	propriora A^vZCW	propiora Z^2ABRrell.	

Appendix VII

506	tonet $A^vM(?)ZA$	alt. fugit A^2BRrell.	u.o. P
514	macula[A^v	maculas rell. (-s in ras. A^2)	
515	uictori A^vA^2BRcett.	uictoris MZAJ	
	cadenti A^vZ^2Acett.	cadendi MZA^2RBW	
530	thessalicos A^vcett.	thessalicas MZAB	
540	sortes A^v	syrtes rell. et syries MZ	
541	monstro A^v	monstri rell.	
546	phariosque A^v	phariusque rell.	
562	longa A^vcett. et loniga Z	longe (e in ras. A^c)	
	birimis A^v	birimi rell.	
564	celsae $A^vMZAQVEW$	celsa $A^2BRYGUPJ$	
567	aduertere A^vUP adpellere MZABRQVEWJ	expellere YG	
571	ulli A^vcett.	nulli MZABRQ	
579	remane A^vA^2Bcett.	remanet MZAR	
587	alio A^vMZQVE et alios W	alto $Z^2ABRFYGUPJ$	
600	incede A^v	in caedes rell.	
601	uacasset A^vGUP	uacaret MZABRQYVEWJ	
618	sed A^vcett.	at Z^2ABRG et ast Y	
619	consentit A^vG consensit rell.	concessit C	
628	auctoremque A^vcett.	auctoremue Z^2ABRYP	
633	meos A^v	meus rell.	
638	complent A^v	complet rell.	
642	cuius A^vMZBQE	cui ius $Z^2ARYUVPWJ$ et cui uis G	
	sceleri A^v	sceleris rell.	
647	culpam A^v et culpa cett.	culta MZABR	
648	libera A^vcett.	ubera MZABR	
653	reges A^vMZ	regis rell.	
655	aptare A^vYUVPW artare MZABRQEJ	aptate G	
658	imputent A^v	imputet rell.	
670	semianimis A^vcett.	semianimus MZAR (semianimi W)	
682	pulsat A^v	pulsant rell.	
693	sororis $A^vZ^2AQYGVEJ$	sorori $MZFA^2BRUW$ et soleri P	
716	cypri A^vcett.	ponti ZABRW	
724	nunc $A^vFQYGPEJ$	tunc MZABRUVW	
733	proferat A^v	praeferat rell.	
734	ignes A^vcett.	ignis Z^2AB	

Readings of A^v

744	cremantis A^vcett.	cremantes Z^2AB
754	si mouit A^v	dimouit rell.
757	premit A^v	premunt rell.
763	aduerte A^vMZF	auerte Z^2ABRrell.
802	magno $A^vWM^2Erl.\ 304$	magni rell.
803	in ullo A^vZ^2AM et in nullo Z	si nullo A^2BRrell. (si in nullo W)
809	sertori A^vQGUW sertorii $YVPEJ$	sertoris Z^2ABRMF (sertor Z)
817	ullis A^vcett.	nullis $MZABRF$
824	inmerito $A^vZ^2ACYUVPEJ$	merito $MZFA^2BRQGW$
	carmine A^vcett.	carmina $MZABRFC$
832	deos A^vP^2 (u.o. P)	canes rell.
	iuuentia A^v	iubentia rell.
833	plangens A^vcett. et planges FPE	plangis $M(?)ZABRW$
838	uictores A^v	uictoris rell.
845	ausoniae $A^vU(?)VP$	ausoniam rell.
852	imbriferas A^vARMC	imbrifera Z^2A^2Brell.F et umbrifera ZP
858	casto A^v	casio rell.
864	fulmen A^vcett.	flumen $MZABRF$
865	futuris A^vcett.F	sepulchri Z^2ABRW

Book 9

4	tonanti A^v	tonantis rell.	
5	aether A^vC	aer rell.	
29	ipse A^vMYGJ illa Z^2AB	ille $ZRFQUVPEW$	
	sua A^vCQGEW	suae $MZABYUVPJ$	u.o. R
39	classi classis MZ	clausis Z^2ABR	
	$A^vFQYGUVPEWJ$		
46	sociosque A^v	sociosne rell.	
71	pompei A^v	pompeium rell.	
74	litore A^vcett.	limite $MZABRW$	
79	terens $A^vMZQGUVPE$	tenens Z^2A^2BRYWJ (ternens A)	
81	hunc A^vcett.	nunc $MZABRW$	
104	potuit A^vZ^2ABYGJ	potui $MZRFQUVPEW$	
111	artim A^v	arte rell.	

Appendix VII

133	patres A^v et patris *rell.*		matris Z^2ABR	
138	sublimia A^v*cett.*		deformia Z^2RW et deforma AB	
155	euulsus A^v*cett.*		euulsas Z^2ABR	
158	inuoluam A^v*adn.*		euoluam *rell.*	
204	fides A^v*cett.*		fide ZA	
211	uiris absque est A^v	uiri est sed Z^2ABR et uiris sed $MZQVPEW$		uiris et $YGUJ$
213	iuiram A^v		iubam *rell.*	
224	redit $A^v MQUP$		redis $ZABRYGVEWJ$	
228	fauores A^v	fauore Z^2ABR*rell.* et fauorem Z		fauori MPW et fauoris E
234	mos A^v		mors *rell.*	
237	armenium A^v*cett.*		]rmenium A	
251	romanus $A^v ZQYGUVEWJ$	romanis Z^2ABR	romana MP	
264	non $A^v M^2$		nunc *rell.*	
268	generes A^v*cett.*		degeneris Z^2ABR	
269	sternite $A^v YG$		spernite *rell.*	
286	fauis A^v		faui *rell.*	
293	incalcata A^v		inculcata *rell.*	
	iuste A^v		iusti *rell.*	
295	laborem $A^v B$		laborum *rell.*	
297	sed A^v		et *rell.*	
299	catoni $A^v Z^2 AQW$	catonis $ZA^2 BRYGE$	catonem $MUVPW$	
300	Mauri A^v		mauris *rell.* et maurus B et auris M	
329	auertitur A^v*cett.*		auerritur Z^2ABR	
331	iactata A^v*cett.*		iactato $A^2 B$	
332	frementem A^v*cett.*		prementem Z^2ABR	
338	impactum $A^v MQYGUVPJ$ et infactum C		impactis $ZABREW$	
343	terra A^v		terrae *rell.*	
355	lethon A^v*cett.* et letho P		lethes Z^2ABRW	
398	bibentem A^v*cett.*		bibentem (-em *in ras.*) A^2	*n.l.* A
401	discrimine $A^v ZQYGV$		sub crimine $MZ^2 ABRUPEWJ$	
407	incendit uirtute A^v*cett.*	incedit u. B	incendit u. *in ras.* A^3	*n.l.* A
413	par A^v		pars *rell.*	

Readings of A^v

414	absit A^v		absunt *rell.*	
421	nec A^vB^2		non *rell.*	
425	cura A^vW	pura *ZQYGEJ et* pyra Z^2AR	dira *MB et* diues *UV et* diu *P*	
426	sic $A^vM^2B^2E^2$		et *rell.*	
427	moueret A^v		nouerat *rell.*	
428	umbra A^vZQVE	umbris $Z^2ABRYGUWJ$	austro *MP*	
463	uiolentius A^vMYGJ		uiolentior *ZBRQUVPEW* (uilentior *A*)	
478	quae A^v*cett.*		qua A^2B	
488	stantis A^v*cett.*		stantes *ZA*	l.o. *BW*, l. eras. *R*
499	incensusque dies A^v*cett.*		in nothon omnis abit Z^2ABRW	
513	flumine A^v		fulmina *rell.*	
524	n.l. A^v	leptum *ZABR et* lepto *W*	lepti *rell.*	
531	polum A^vQYVEJ		locum *MZABRGUPW*	
536	ardens $A^vMZQYUVPEW$	arens Z^2A^2BRGJ	urens *A*	
541	summo A^vUVW		semper *rell.*	
548	tam A^v*cett.*		tam *in ras.* A^2	n.l. *A*
549	hortator $A^vQYGUVEJ et$ orator *Z et* ortator Z^2A *et* hortatos A^2B		hortatur *MP et* hortatu *RW*	
557	sequerisque A^v*cett.*		superisque Z^2ABR	
562	reple A^v*cett.*		replent Z^2ABR	
576	ne elegit A^vYVWJ	nec legit *MGUPE*	neglegit *ZABRQ*	
580	quocumque uides A^vV		quodcumque uides *rell.*	
581	futuri A^v		futuris *rell.*	
592	spoliare A^v	potare *ZARCYVJ et* petare *BW et* portare *GE*	certare *McQP*	n.l. *U*
602	pudebit A^v*cett.*		puderet Z^2ABR	
603	steteres A^v		steteris *rell.* (sisteris *B*)	
614	admisso A^v*adn.*		admixto *rell.*	
641	riguere sub A^v*cett.*		riguerunt *ZABR*	
652	uisum $A^vMY et$ uisum est *J*	uisu *P et* uisu est *G*	uisus *ZABRQYUVEW*	

Appendix VII

658	pallados A^vcett.		palladis Z^2A^2BR et pallades A		
659	partuque A^v		partu rell.		
661	archados A^vcett.		archades $ZABR$		
662	praepes A^vcett. et prepe Z		praeceps Z^2ABRC		
664	fuso A^vG	fuluo $Z^2ABRYWJ$		l.o. $MZQUVPE$	
668	euersae A^v et auersae C		auerso rell.		
679	spirare A^vMUVPW		spirasse $ZABRQYGEJ$		
680	oculis A^vZ		oculos Z^2ABRrell.		
686	aethera A^v		aera rell.		
	scinderit A^v et	ascenderet R et	scinderet rell.		
	scenderit ZA	ascenderit A^2B	(scanderet W)		
688	tanto A^vcett.		tantum $ZABR$		
689	ales A^vcett.		alas ABR		
690	atque A^vM		itque rell. et idque ZP		
692	solum $A^vZRQYGVEWJ$		polum Z^2ABMUP		
694	sic A^vCadn.		si rell.		
706	modus A^vM^v		pudor rell.		
707	merces A^vM^v		mercem rell. et merce MP		
708	at A^vZGEWJ et ad	aut Z^2ABR	an C	n.l. UV	
	MQP et ast Y				
711	tractuque A^v		tractique rell.		
716	coras A^v		cerastae rell.		
718	torrida A^vrell.		horrida ZAB		
721	paryas A^vM^2 et	paroeas Z^2ABRW	carias MP		
	parias $ZCQYGUVEJ$				
722	spirantia A^v	fumantia $MQUVPEW$	spumantia $ZABRYGJ$		
743	circa A^v		circum rell.		
744	linguam tergere A^v	lingua torrere $ZABRP^2$	linguam torrere rell.		
752	bibens A^vcett.		uidens Z^2ABR	l.o. E	
753	fatique A^vZ^2Acett.		fatisque ZA^2BRW		
763	mors erat A^vcett.		merserat $ZABR$		
770	rapit A^vM^v		natant rell. et natat B		
	sanies A^v		sanie rell. et saniem M et saniam P		
785	discedent A^v		discedunt rell. et discendunt P		
795	pollente $A^vQGUVEJ$ et pallente		tollente $Z^2ABRMPW$		
	ZY				
796	nexus A^vM^v		mersus rell.		

Readings of A^v

798	exundat A^vcett.	exultat Z^2ABR (ebullet W)		
799	tantum A^v	tantos rell.		
803	feres A^v	feris rell.		
804	liquere A^vM^2	fugere rell. et fulgere M et fulgure P		
810	emisere A^vcett.	emiscere $ZABR$		
811	mouit A^vZUE	nouit rell.		
820	stipite quae A^vcett.	stipitem $ZABR$		
821	saitae A^vC et satae Z^2A et satei BR et site P	sabei $ZA^2QGUVEJ$ et subei Y	sagei W	n.l. M
822	de A^vV robora A^vZA	e $MGUP$ robore A^2BRrell.	se $ZABRQYEWJ$	
824	transitaque A^v et transictaque M^2	transactaque rell.	transactaeque MP	
826	uolarent A^vA^2BRcett. et uolaret P	uolare Z^2A		
845	torpente A^vcett.	torrente Z^2ABR et torrentes Z		
848	di clamant A^vQGEJ et dii clamant $RYUVPW$	dii clamabant M	declamant ZAB	
858	uenenis A^vcett.	ueneno $ZABREW$		
862	abrumpes A^v	abrumpens rell.		
865	petit $A^vG^vM^2$	ferit rell.		
867	ista A^vcett. et iste P	istinc $ZABR$		
869	iubae A^v uibe in A legens			
874	-nunc A^vcett. regebat A^vG	-num $ZABR$ rigebat rell.		
875	exiguane A^vcett.	exiguamne $ZABR$		
886	letum A^vcett.	lentum $ZABR$		
889	docet A^vcett.	iuuet $ZABR$		
895	potes A^v	potest $ZABRQYGEWJ$	potens $MUVP$	
915	medicatus A^vcett.	medicatos $ABRP$		
935	petens A^vUM^2	potens $MQYGPEJ$	tenens $ZABRW$	n.l. V
936	angues A^v	anguis rell.		
937	uenenum A^vMYW	ueneni rell.		
943	reuerti A^v	redire rell. et rediret Z		
944	uide p. 71			
950	clade A^vcett.	caede $ZABRWJ$		

Appendix VII

955	terras A^vM^v		turres *rell.*	
960	ferens A^v*cett.*		ferans ZA	
963	multum A^v*cett.*		multa $ZABRW$	
970	latentis A^vQGVE	iacentes $MYPJ$	patentis $ZABRW$ et petentis U	
971	sederit A^v*cett.*		sedit in $ZABRW$	
979	herceas A^v*cett.*		hectoreas $ZA^2BRQYEJ$	*l.o.* A
980	leto $A^vM^vB^2W^2$		fato *rell.*	
985	nostra A^v*cett.*		nostrae ZA et nostra est BR	
986	damnabitur $A^vQYGUEJ$		damnabimur $MZABRVW$ (damnauit nur P)	
994	templi A^v		templo *rell.*	
996	priores A^v	priore MVP	priori *rell.*	
1009	regnis A^v*cett.*		muris $ZABR$	
1028	parenti A^vMUVP		parente $ZABRQYGEWJ$	
1029	nomina $A^vMQYUVPEWJ$ et nomine CG		numina $ZABR$	
1030	famae A^vM		famam *rell.*	
1040	putans A^vYGWJ et putas R	potens $MZABQUE$	potest VG^v	*l.o* P
1044	calcabat A^vM		calcarat *rell.*	
1049	generes A^v		generis *rell.*	
1061	perfide A^v*cett.*		perfida $ZABR$	
1075	romana A^v*cett.*		romane $ZABR$	
1078	caesari[A^v	caesari ZA	caesar A^2BR*rell.*	
1080	ne A^v*cett.*		nec Z^2ABRW	

Book 10

14	tibi A^v		sibi *rell.*	
29	patri A^v*cett.* et patro M		pari A^2BR (apatri C)	
30	populus A^v*cett.*		populis $ZABR$	
38	syrticus A^v*cett.*		siticus A	
50	ad A^v		in *rell.*	
56	biremi A^v*cett.*	biremus Z et biremis Z^2ABY	triremi J	
61	facie $A^vQYVEWJ$		facies $MZABRGUP$	

Readings of A^v

64	imbelli A^vcett.		imbellis ZABRE	
73	habitatas A^v	habitatam ZABR	habitata rell. (habita Q)	
76	partos A^v		partus rell.	
92	ferre A^vcett.		terrae ZABR	
94	thalami A^vMQPE		thalamos ZABRYGUVWJ	
95	sit A^vcett.		sed ZABR	
97	inire peto	ni repeto A^vBR	habere peto YGJ	
	$A^v Z^2 AQUVPEW$		(intrepedo Z)	
101	minantur A^v		minatur rell.	
108	tantarum A^vcett.		positarum ZABR	post 107d. P
110	luxu A^v		luxus rell.	
114	cristate $A^v M^v$		crustate rell. (scrutata M)	
	sectisue A^v		sectisque rell.	
123	hic torus assyrio	strata micant tyrio	strata micant tyrio	d. R
	cuius A^vQYGVEJ	cuius ZABW	quarum MU	
128	hos A^vcett.		hoc Z^2ABR	
144	silua A^vcett.		siluas ZABR	
153	abductos A^v		abductus rell.	
160	crystallos A^vMZAYG		crystallus A^2BRQUVEWJ	
177	neglecta $A^v Z$		neglecte Z^2ABRrell.	
208	ad A^v		at rell.	
210	hunc A^vcett.		nunc ZAB	
212	mutator A^vQYUVEJ		mutatur MZABRGW	
235	adit $A^v M$		adest rell.	
252	padusque A^vcett.		palusque ZABR (pauusque V)	
263	peracti A^vcett.		peracta ZABR	
268	romane A^vcett.		romana ZABR	
281	deflectus A^v		defectus rell.	
304	comes $A^v M$		comis rell.	
312	populos A^vZQYGUVEJ		populis Z^2ABRW	
318	exciperet suos A^v		excepere tuos rell.	
322	canescit A^vcett.		albescit ZABR	
323	monstra A^v et nonstra A		nostra rell.	
324	sentit A^vcett.		sensit ZABR	
325	scopulis A^vCG		scopuli rell.	
	fluuio nos A^v		fluuii quos rell.	
329	it $A^v MV$ et id ZABR	in QUE		et YGCWJ

Appendix VII

329	iacens $A^v ZCQYGVEJ$		tacens $Z^2ABRMUW$	
339	uocat A^v		parat *rell.*	
341	fata A^v*cett.*		fama Z^2ABR	
344	fati $A^v M^2$		fatis *rell.*	
346	lacesses A^v		lacessit *rell.*	
352	retentum A^v		retento *rell.*	
356	pharos A^v*cett.*		foras AB	
357	nūsit A^v	nupsit $A^2 BRW$ et nubsit E		nubit *rell.*
361	quem A^v*cett.*		quam $ZABRU$	
365	donabit A^v*cett.*		donabat $ZABR$	
372	molire A^v*cett.*		mollire $ZABR$	
385	in A^v		en *rell.*	
	uenit A^v*cett.*		nobis $Z^2 ABRW$	
389	nomina A^v*cett.*		numina $ZABR$	
413	recepto A^v*cett.*		recepit $ZABR$	
427	belli $A^v M^v$		ferri *rell.*	
430	demittere A^v	permittere G		dimittere *rell.*
431	daturos A^v		daturus *rell.*	
435	calentem A^v*cett.*		cadentem $Z^2 ABR$	
442	compressa $A^v MU$		compresso *rell.*	
455	fixo A^v*cett.*		fixa ZAB	
468	fatis A^v		pacis *rell.*	
	praestare A^v		temptare *rell.*	
471	nec A^v*cett.*		neque $ZABR$	
		post 475 *deficit* A		

Appendix VIII
Readings Originating in B

Book 1

13	placuit *B*		potuit *rell.*		d. QY
88	quis *B*	quos *RB*²	quid *rell.*		d. QY
99	ducum non sponte *BR*		non sponte ducum *rell.*		d. QY
103	sic ubi mare *BR*		mare sic ubi *rell.*		d. QY
111	non *B*		nam *rell.*		d. QY
154	perstringens *BRGPWJ*		praestringens *MZAUVE*		d. QY
156	magnam *B*		magnamque *rell.*		
217	undis *BR*		undas *rell.*		
223	in *B*		ut *rell.*		
225	iure *B*		iura *rell.*		
253	errantesque *BRMYGUEWJ*		errantisque *ZAQVP*		
261	solueret *B*		soluerat *rell.*		
276	inde *B*		in te *rell.*		
310	agit *B*		agat *rell.*		
324	lapsum *B* Erl. 304, Bern. 601		lassum *rell.*		
346	fierit *BR*		fient *rell.*		
359	scilicet *BRMYUEWJ*		si licet *ZAQGVP*		
374	dextris *BR*		castris *rell.*		
472	uires *BR*		linguas *rell.*		
474	uires *BR*		turmas *rell.*		
490	petunt *BPM*²		petant *rell.*		
530	fulgura *BRCYGUVEWJ*		fulgora *MZAP*		
600	cybelen *BRQYGUVEWJ*		cybeben *MZAP*		

Appendix VIII

606	fluminis *B*		fulminis *rell.*	
607	colligit *BRcett.*		collegit *MZA*	
608	admonet *BRPW*		admouet *rell.*	
644	urbe *BV(?)E*		urbi *rell.*	
660	grande *B*	grauide *M(?)ZAP*		gradiue *A²Rrell.*
660	parans *B*		paras *rell.*	
668	erat *BRE*		erit *rell.*	
671	continua *B*		continuam *rell.*	
	claudem *B et* cla*dem *M*		cladem *rell.*	
679	constituus *BR*		constituis *rell.*	

Book 2

6	omnia *BZUW*		omina *rell.*	
185	effundit *BRQE*		effudit *rell.*	
202	immensa *BR*		immissa *rell.*	
345	mutari et *B et* mutari *ZAAᵛ et* mutarin *A²R*		mutarim *rell.*	
361	flumina *B et* flamina *Z²A²M et* flammina *A*		flammea *rell.Aᵛ*	*n.l. Z*
417	libicias... harenias *B*	libycis... harenis *MZAUVPE*	libycas... harenas *A²RCQYGWJ*	
433	plaudite *B*		claudite *rell.*	
434	palmas *BR*		rupes *rell.*	
448	quemquam *B*		quamquam *rell.*	
515	ac *MBZ*		hac *rell.*	
517	quantum *BRUPWJ*		quanto *MZAQYGVE*	
528	uisurus *BR*		iussurus *rell.*	
529	morituri *BRY*		moturi *rell.*	
560	docet *B et* ducet *R*		uocet *rell.*	
567	omnia *BRcett.*		omina *Z²A*	
570	animas *B*		animos *rell.*	
712	in litore ad litora *B*	ad litora *Z²ARWJ*	in litora *QGVPE et in* litore *MZYUAᵛ*	
715	phasidios *BR*	phasidis *MZA*	phasidos *A²rell.*	
716	cyalias *B*		cyaneas *Z²ARrell. et* cyneas *MZ*	

Readings Originating in B

721	erigit BA^v	eripit rell.	
722	habet BRZ	hebet Z^2Arell.	

Book 3

35	timori B	mariti rell.	
65	urbis B	aruis rell.	
101	omnia BRYWJ	omina rell.	
102	factas B	fictas rell.	
131	populumque BR	populi quae rell.	
133	magnum BU	magnam rell.	
160	regni B(?)MP	regi rell.	
195	prima B	primaque rell.	
199	bellum BU	nilum rell.	l.o. R
203	tellus gelido BR	gelido tellus rell.	
242	repletis BR	repletos rell.	
301	phocis BR	phocais rell.	
342	dies B	fides rell.	
362	denso BM	densae rell. (dentur Z)	
374	om. B		
398	ager BM	agger rell.	
421	amplexus BMZ	amplexos rell.	
471	ad B	adiuta rell.	
510	temptari BRP	temptare rell.	
550	hunc BR	huc rell.	
616	aequore BW	aequora rell.	
620	regens B	tegens Z^2ARrell.	ferens MZ
658	eiectat BQYGUVEWJ	electat MZARP	

Book 4

6	tutelasque B	tutelaque rell.	
21	fluxus B	fluctus rell.	
23	aufert ibi BP	aufert tibi rell.	
34	tortorque BR	terrorque rell.	
100	ad B et at MZA	et QV	ac YGUPEWJ u.o. R

Appendix VIII

114	habent *BR*	habeant *rell.*
119	apludes *B et* pludes *A*	paludes *rell.*
142	niues *B*	riuis *rell.*
146	indomitus *B*	indomitos *rell.*
182	quod *BUP*	quid *rell.*
282	numina *B*	lumina *rell.*
288	adduxerunt *B*	adduxere *rell.*
289	manu *B*	manus *rell.*
299	sonauerunt *BR*	sonuerunt *rell.*
300	miscuere *BJM^2*	micuere *rell.*
311	haustis *BMZ*	haustus *rell.*
334	garamantas *BM*	garamantes *rell.*
335	sicorum *BRMZP*	sicorim *Z^{2}rell.*
352	asprimus *B et* asperrimus *MZA*	aperimus *rell.A^v*
426	feret *BR*	ferat *rell.*
436	ingressas *BPW*	ingressos *rell.*
452	illam *BRMZ*	illa *Z^{2}rell.*
470	capta *BR*	captae *rell.*
481	uita *BRQ*	uitae *rell.*
492	socii *BR*	sociis *rell.*
515	lucet *BR et* lucent *Z*	licet *rell. et* licent *Z^{2}AM*
546	collodat *BE(?)*	conlaudat *rell.*
551	omnem *BRY*	omen *rell.*
557	nimiumque *BRY*	minimumque *rell.*
562	consorte *BRW et* cum sorte *rell.*	cum forte *P* sic sorte *G*
568	dispectant *BRYU*	despectam *rell.*
625	urguere *BRMZ*	urgueri *Z^{2}rell.*
659	uallo *B*	uallis *M(?)ZA* ualli *rell.*
686	operare *B*	operire *rell.*
688	priuata ... ira *BR*	priuatae ... irae *rell.*
706	galea *BWM^2*	galeae *rell.*
727	comprendet *B*	comprendit *rell.C*
749	patiere *BR*	petiere *rell. et* periere *MZP*
752	auras *B*	aures *rell.*
753	monstrare *B*	non stare *rell.* non stante *G(?)*
761	illi *BMZ*	ulli *rell.*

Readings Originating in B

763	aures *BR*	hostes $A^2QYVEWJ$ et hostis *MZ*	hostem Z^2AGUP
781	constricxit *B*	constrixit *AYU*	constrinxit *rell.*

Book 5

22	non *BP*	nos *rell.* et uos *V*		
29	numquam *B*	umquam *rell.*		
58	et ubi *B*	et tibi *rell.*		
59	ptolomee *BRcett.*	ptolemee *MZAP*		
72	parnasus *BRQYUVEWJ*	parnassos *MZAGP*		
74	fatidici *B* et fatidicae A^v	thebanae *rell.* et thebani *C*		
117	recepte *B*	recepti *rell.*		
159	fingit *BP*	fingis Z^2*rell.* et finges *MZ*	fugis *U*	
196	tenebris *BMPW*	tenebis *rell.*		
210	locuta est *BYUVE*	locutae *MZAGPW*	cuncta est *J*	n.l. *RQ*
217	borea *B*	boreae *rell.*		
223	redigere *BR*	rediere *rell.*		
233	annis *BQY* et rannis A^2R	rhamnus Z^2AGVEJ	ramnos *UP* (ramnum $M(?)Z$)	
293	sciet *BR*	scias *MZ*	sciat *rell.*	
311	os *BJ*	hos *rell.*	hoc *C*	
321	bella *B*	belli *rell.* et bellis *P*		
333	senes *BRcett.*	senex *MZAC*		
399	fastos *BMYUVPEW*	fastus ZQA^v et faustus Z^2AR	fastis *GJ*	
430	crimen *BR*	primum *rell.*		
435	immotus *BM*	immotis *rell.*		
453	excutiet *BR*	excutiat *rell.*		
517	stereli *BRMZP*	sterili (*A*)*rell.*		
573	speries *B* et peries *P* et hesperies *ZA*	hesperias *rell.*		
588	nec *BVPEJ* manus *BYW*	ne *rell.* manum *rell.*		
617	illa *B*	illo *MZACPJ*	ullo *RQYGUVEW*	
621	flumen *BR*	fulmen *rell.*		

Appendix VIII

630	ne *BC*	nec *rell.*	
672	factum *B*	fatum *rell.*	*d. M*
	dictum *BP*	dictu *rell.*	*d. M*
708	consortes *B et* consortis *ZA²* et consorti *A*	consertis *rell.*	
719	temptatu *B*	temptati *rell. et* temptanti *MZ*	
736	peti *BR*	petit *rell.*	
765	dimissa *BRGUVPJ*	demissa *MZAQYEW*	
770	fluminibus *B*	fulminibus *rell.*	

Book 6

8	mensura *B*		mersura *rell.*	
11	exire *BR*		exciri *rell.*	
35	domus *BMUVPE*		domos *ZAQYGWJ*	*l.o. R*
41	tescita *B et* tescua *Z²ARrell.*	testa *MZ*	pascua *S*	
46	reuiset *BR*	riuisat *rell.*	recusant *P*	
66	sicanes *B*		sicaniae *rell. et* sicanium *M*	
87	medios *om. BR*		habent *rell.*	
88	gerit *B*		digerit *rell. et* degerit *Q*	
111	cedisse *BR*		cecidisse *rell.*	
126	quam *BQUPEJ*		qua *MZARYGVW*	
159	fortunae *BRP*		fortuna *rell.*	
199	pondere *B et* ponderet *R*		pondera *rell.*	
212	confisae *BR*		confixae *rell.*	
232	egit *BW*		eget *rell. et* egeo *V*	
244	putatis *BRcett.*		putastis *Z²AE*	
245	pompei★ *B*	pompei *rell.*	pompeium *C*	
256	hac *BR*		ac *rell.*	
276	aperti sibi *B et* aperto ibi *Z et* aperi sibi *A*		aperit sibi *Z²A²Rrell.*	
286	tremente *BRQVJ et* premente *MZE*		trementi *Z²AGUPW*	
301	tendit *BR*		tenuit *rell.*	
302	romana *BM*		roma *rell.*	
346	undis *BGᵛ*		unum *rell.*	

Readings Originating in B

367	spergeos *BR*	spercheos *MZAGE et*		sperchius *YVW*	
		sperchios *QUPJ*			
417	degeneres *BRcett. et* degener est *Z* degentes (*A*)				
425	pinthia *BW et* pythia		cynthia *Z²(A)RUPE et* cythia *Z n.l. M*		
	QYGVJM²				
440	ubi *BVW*		ibi *rell. et* sibi *P*		
506	proprior *BRMZPW*		propior *rell.*		
518	atra *BW*		atrae *rell.*		
524	ne *BR*		nec *rell.*		
548	saniemque *BRE(?)*		saniem *rell.*		
557	funere *BP*	funereae *rell. et*		FVNEREOAS *N n.l. U*	
		funerea *M(?)ZA*			
560	hac *BRP*		ac *rell.*		
561	manus *BM*		manes *rell.*		
563	morientem *BR*		morienti *rell.*		
673	medulla *BRW*		medullae *rell.*		
678	conca *B*		conchae *rell.*		
691	cantibus *B*		cautibus *rell.*		
702	laxa *B*		laxae *rell. et* laxas *MZ*		
717	milites *BMZ*		militis *rell.*		
725	mori non posse *BR*		non posse mori *rell.*		
727	immoto uiuo serpenti *BR*		immotum uiuo serpente *rell.*		
732	animas *B*		animam *rell.*		
746	nox *BMZ*		non *rell.*		
767	magnos *BZ*		magos *rell.*		
775	umbra *BZP*		umbram *rell.*		
783	diuersa *BR*		diuersi *rell.*		
785	patrumque *BYU(?)P*		patremque *rell.*		
786	belli *BR*		bellis *rell.*		
	flentem *BR*		flentemque *rell.*		
790	facta *BR*		facta *rell.*		
793	minas *BR(?)*		minax *rell.*		
805	pompei *BRW et*	pompeio *Z²A²YGVEJ*		pompeius *MZP et*	
	pompeii *Q*			pompeiis *U l.o. A*	
807	mori ... duci *B*		duces ... mori *rell.*		
819	tota *BR*		toto *rell.*		
828	id *BR*	it *Z²Arell.*		et *MZW*	

Appendix VIII
Book 7

3	cursumque *BMZQUVPW*		currumque *Z²ARYGEJ*		
7	magnum *B*	magni *QVE*	magno *rell.*		*n.l. R*
	uita *B*		uitae *rell.*		
16	fuga ex *BR et* fugax *A²UJ et* fugas *MZ*		fuga *Z²AQYGVPEW*		
21	uisus *BR*		uisis *rell.*		
67	causa *B*		causae *rell.*		
94	uiolata *BM et* uiolatae *rell.*		romane *QYER²*		*n.l. R*
95	a *BR*		o *rell.*		
96	genturi *BR*		gesturi *rell.*		
100	malet *BRP*		mallet *rell.*		
136	solo *BR*		sole *rell.*		
137	illos *B*		ullos *rell. et* ullus *VJ*		
147	erubuit *B*		et rubuit *rell.*		
	neptuna *BR*		neptunia *rell.*		
165	aram *BR*		ara *rell.*		
173	crediderunt *BP*		crediderint *rell. et* crediderim *U*		
178	noctes *BR*		noctem *rell.*		
183	tumultu *BCUA^v et* tumultum *QYGVPE*		tumultus *Z²ARWM² et* tumultis *Z*		*n.l. MJ*
184	omne *B et* omens *MZP*		omen *rell.*		*n.l. R*
220	aduersa *B*		aduerso *rell.*		
225	habenis *BRWJA^v*		habenae *rell. et* habena *QE*		
255	eminit *B et* mini *R et* meminit *A*		memini *rell.A^v*		
261	petitis *BZ*		petistis *rell.*		
262	u.o. *BR*				
274	pauca *BP*		paucae *rell. et* pauces *M*		
281	armeniusne *B*		armeniosne *rell.*		
302	horae *BRYVJ*		orae *rell.*		
342	deuectus *B*		praeuectus *rell. et* praeuictus *MZ*		
388	annis *BRcett.A^v*		annus *Z²A*		
395	quod *BRQYUVPE*		quo *MZAGWJ*		
475	illa *B*		ulla *rell.*		
477	clausae *B*	causae *MZ*		ausae *rell.*	
482	aigit *BR*	ait *ZP*		agit *rell.*	

Readings Originating in B

505	terrore *B*	torrentes *Z*	torrente *rell.*	d. R
530	equus *B*	eques *rell.*		
532	inde domum *B*	in domum *MZ*	inde modum *rell.*	
548	hic *B*	illic *rell.*		
	regnum *MBZY*	regum *rell.*		d. R
554	ciuibus *B*	ciuilibus *rell.*		
555	ac *BVW et* hac *G et* ae *P*	a *MZARQYEJ et* ā *U*		
562	pressa *B*	presso *rell.*	prenso *W* (presam *Z*)	
614	gracus *B*	graues (-is) *MZARQYGE*	duci *UVP*	
712	larissa *BQYUVWJ*	larisa *rell.*		
749	caecos *BR*	caesos *rell.*		
761	caecumque *B et* caesumque *ZQYGE*	uacuumque *RWJ*	stratumque *UPM²V²*	n.l. *MAV*
769	infectaque *B*	confectumque *QVE*	infectumque *rell.*	
814	est superest *B*	superest *rell.*		
831	castra ciuilia *B*	ciuilia castra *rell.*		
834	se tanto *B*	tanto se *rell.*		
857	effudere *BRZ²cett. et* effundere *A*	effure *MZ*		

Book 8

3	similiique *B*	stimulique *Z*	stimulisque *rell.*
33	litera *BCP(?)*	litora *rell.*	
59	dolor *om. BMZ*	habent *rell.*	
61	depressa *B Bern. 601*	decepta *rell.*	
63	priores *B*	propius *rell.*	
64	ferro *B*	fata *Aᵛ et* fato *A²RJ*	fatum *rell.*
66	seminimem *B*	semanimem *GV*	semianimem *rell.*
85	deflet *B*	defles *rell. et* deflens *Z*	
108	thessalicae *BRJ* labos *B et* lambos *J*	thessaliae *rell. et* thessalia *V* lesbos *rell.*	
118	quicquid *BRQGEW*	quid quod *MZAYUVPJ*	
129	orbem *BMZ*	orbe *rell.*	
132	crarique *B et* carisque *Z et* carique *rell.*	sacrique *G²U²*	

Appendix VIII

133	puppim *BYGUJ et* puppi *P*		puppem *rell.*	
140	docens *B*		doces *rell. et* duces *MZ*	
141	quaestum est *B*	quaerere certum est *A²Rrell.*	quaerere certum *MZ*	
155	deuixit *BW*		deuinxit *rell. et* deiunxit *P*	
170	plastro *B*		plaustro *rell. et* plausto *Z*	
	digerat *B*	dirigit *MZVW*	dirigat *Z²ARYGUPJ et* derigat *QE*	
184	aequora *BR*		aequore *rell.*	
195	*u.o. B*	chios *A²rell.*	chius *MZAU*	
196	pronam *B*		proram *rell.* (pro*ra *P*)	
197	secantem *BRAᵛ*		secante *rell.*	
204	ad litora *B et* ad litore *R*	ab litore *QYEJ*	a litore *MZAGUVPW*	
219	ducata *B*		iurata *rell. et* iura *M*	
224	decurre *BZUJ et* decurrere *rell.*		discurrere *PRW*	
238	uidet *B*	ualet *Z²ARP*	uolet *QYGUVEWJAᵛ et* uolit *MZ*	
240	ruptis *B et* ruptos *Z²ARW*		raptos *ZYUVEJM² et* rapto *Q et* raptus *GPAᵛ*	*n.l. M*
244	efferumque *B*	ephesumque *RQVEW*	ephesonque *MZAYGUPJ*	
249	medios *B*	media *UP*	medio *rell.*	
254	rursus *BRcett.*		rusus *MZA*	
260	recipitque *Bcett.*		recepitque *MZARP*	
275	qua *BMZ*		quas *rell.*	*l.o. Q*
300	assyrios *BZ*		assyrias *rell.*	*l.o. Q*
390	par est *B*		parum est *rell. et* paratum *Z*	
415	scilicet *B*	scient *M et* sciant *Z*	sciet *rell.*	
470	casto *BRMZ et* cassio *A*		casio *rell.Aᵛ*	
475	pelle *BRMP*		pellaeae *rell.*	
480	fidem *BM*		fidemque *rell.*	
484	nocentes *Bcett.Aᵛ*		nocentis *Z²A*	
498	neut *B et* neu te *Z²ARQYGVEWJ*		neu nos *UPAᵛ et* neu nas *Z*	*n.l. M*
499	nilonque *BYGPJ*		nilumque *rell.*	
514	armaque *B*		aruaque *rell.*	

Readings Originating in B

569	uicina *BMZ*		uicinia *rell.*	
573	actori *BP*		auctori *rell. et* autori *MZ*	
597	septimus *BRQYUPEJ*		septimius *MZAGVW*	
609	septimum *BMQYPJ*		septimium *ZARGUVEW*	
624	non *BJ*	ne *MZ*	nunc *rell.*	
642	cuius *BMZQEA*ᵛ *et* cui uis *G*		cui ius *Z²ARYUVPWJ*	
645	prosperas *BR*		properas *rell.*	
656	ense *BC*		ensem *rell.*	
668	septimus *BRMYPWJ*		septimius *ZAQGUVE*	
670	semianimis *Bcett.Aᵛ et* semianimi *W*		semianimus *MZAR*	
704	dies *BFQYGPE*		die *MZARUVWJ*	
733	ferialis *BF*		feralis *rell.*	
771	litore *BMZ*		litora *rell.*	
779	aurora *BV*		aura *rell.*	
791	religato fune remoneret *BQ*	religato fune moueret *Z²Acett.*	funere ligato remoueret *MZFW*	
801	uagant *BMZF*		uacant *rell.*	
830	saluaria *BU*		soluaris *rell.*	
843	omniumque *BRMZ*		o nimiumque *rell.*	
844	reuulsus *BQG*		reuulsos *rell.*	

Book 9

9	animum *B*		animam *rell.*
104	*u.o. B*	funera *MUVP*	uulnera *ZARFQYGEWJ*
115	sollicitus *BW*		sollicitis *rell.*
145	seruate *B*		seruata *rell.*
153	rectumque *B*		retectum *rell.*
156	natabant *BZ*		natabunt *rell.*
175	magna *BMZQ*		magni *rell.*
177	uelamine *BR*		uelamina *rell.*
204	fides scylla *B et* fide sulla *ZAR*		fides sulla *rell.Aᵛ*
215	sanarent *BP*		sonarent *rell.*
278	manus *BP*		munus *rell.*
285	examine *BU*		examina *rell. et* examinas *M*

Appendix VIII

303	primum *BM*		primam *rell.*	
317	superni *BMPE*		superne *rell.*	
358	spoliatus *BC*		spoliatis *rell.*	
373	terram *B*		terra *rell.*	
379	secutas *B*	secutos *MPJ*	secutis *rell.*	
383	frontibus *BRY*		fontibus *rell.*	
399	uiderat *BZ*		uiderit *rell.*	
414	primus *BQW*		primis *rell.*	
418	effundunt *B*		effundant *rell.*	
421	frontibus *B*		fontibus *rell.*	
425	dira *BM et* diues *UV et* diu *P*	pura *ZQYGEJ et* pyra *Z²AR*	cura *WAᵛ*	
434	et necat *B*	enegat *MAP*	enecat *rell.*	
477	demassa *B*	dimissa *RYGVJ*	demissa *Z²AMQUEW*	*l.o. ZP*
482	constringit *B*	constrinxit *MZARQGVPEJ*	constrixit *Y et* construxit *UW*	
488	*om. BW*	habent *rell.*		*in ras. R*
492	domus *BP*	domos *rell.*		
550	frons *B*	fors *Z²AYG*	sors *rell.*	
575	dixit *B*	dixitque *rell. et* dixique *M*		
583	cauendum *BRMPW*	cadendum *rell.*		
592	petare *BW et* potare *ZARCYVJ et* portare *GE*	spoliare *Aᵛ*	certare *McQP*	*n.l. U*
633	gaudentes *BRZ*	gaudentis *rell.*		
653	uitabunt *B*	uitabant *rell. et* uitabat *Z*		
678	amata *B*	amati *MZARCG et* hamati *PEWJ*	limati *QYU(?)J*	
690	consultat *B*	consistat *Z²A*	consita *rell.*	
713	notam *B*	notis *rell. et* notus *P*		
726	basilicus *BGJ*	basiliscus *rell.*		
741	uirtus *BG*	uirus *rell.*		
748	nec *BP*	ne *MZARQYGEWJ*	quin *UV*	
751	panumque *BP*	pauidumque *A et* padumque *A²Rrell.*	pacumque *M*	
761	discernere *BQE*	discere *rell.*		

Readings Originating in B

766	non nulla *BMQ*		non ulla *rell.*	
770	natat *B et* natant *rell.*		rapit *A*ᵛ*M*ᵛ	
821	satei *BR et* saitae *CA*ᵛ *et* satae site *P*	subei *Y et* sabei *Z*²*A et ZA*²*QGUVEJ*	sagei *W*	n.l. *M*
823	uagat *B*		vocat *rell.*	
852	inustis *B et* iniustus *A*		inustus *rell.*	
878	fata *B*	fati *ZARQYGVWJ*	fatis *MUPE*	
887	more *BMP*		mori *rell.*	
914	expugnant *B et* expugant *R*	expurgat *Z*²*AMYVW*	expurgant *ZGUEJA*ᵛ (expugnat *P*)	
985	nostra est *BR*	nostrae *ZA*	nostra *rell.A*ᵛ	
1013	crimine *BR*		crimina *rell.*	
1022	accipere regna *BZ*		accipe regna *rell.*	
1062	ne is non *B*	nec his non *ZAR*	nec non his *rell.*	
1100	ad te *BR*	a te *A*²*Mrell. et* ata *Z et* sate *Z*²*A*	abs te *QVE*	
	ueteras *B*	ueteris *UP*	ueteres *Z*²*ARrell.* (uetares *Z*)	

Book 10

20	uesania *BU*		uaesana *rell.*	
29	harenas *BZ*		Athenas *rell.*	
40	populos *BZP*		polos *rell.*	
43	qui *B*	que *Z*	qua *Z*²*ARrell.*	
84	quam *BRcett.*	qua *MZAP*		
	post 177 desinit P			
181	patronem *BQYEWJ*	platonem *ZARGV*	platona *MU*	
210	qui *B*	quam *MZ*	qua *Z*²*ARYGVEWJU*²	n.l. *U*
229	tumat *B*		tumet *rell.*	
237	meroe *BRMQYGVEWJ*		meroes *ZAU*	
264	percussit *B*	concussit *ZARY*	concussis *MQGUVEWJ*	
282	nilo *BR*		nile *rell.*	
344	instruit *BRC*		struit *ZAcrell.*	n.l. *M*
370	castra *BZ*		casta *rell.*	

Appendix VIII

387	hesperies *BM et* hesperie *Z*	hesperias *rell.*	
	post 475 desinit A		
481	non illa *B*	nulla *U*	non ulla *rell.*
487	audantia *B*	audatiam *Z*[1]	audacie *R et* audaci *rell.*
491	tantas *BR*	tinctas *rell.*	tictas *Z*
502	sole *BZ*	solet *rell.*	
506	carinas *B*	carinis *rell.*	
540	acerui *BR*	aceruis *MZQYUW et* acerbis *E*	aceruo *GVJ*

Appendix IX
Readings Originating in R

Book 1

24	quod *RMZUVPEW*	quot *Z²AB*	quae *GJ*	d. *QY*
31	discendere *RM*	descendere *ZP*	discindere *Z²ABrell.*	d. *QY*
40	munda *Rcett.*		mundo *Z²ABM*	d. *QY*
50	iuuat *RVPEWM²*		iuuet *MZABGUJ*	d. *QY*
76	nolet *Rcett.*		nollet *ZAB*	d. *QY*
88	quos *R et* quis *B*		quid *rell. et* qui *P*	d. *QY*
94	ne *R*		nec *rell.*	d. *QY*
129	coiere *RGUVW*	cogere *MZPE*	coire *ABJ*	d. *QY*
166	arcersitur *RWJ*	arcessitur *CA^v*	accersitur *rell.* *et* accessitur *M*	d. *QY*
198	iuppiter *Rcett.A^v*		ippiter *AB*	d. *Y*
199	nominis *R(?)P*		numinis *rell.*	d. *Y*
206	libyes *Rcett.*		libyae *A²B*	d. *Y*
225	sic *RJG²*		hic *rell.*	d. *Y*
250	populos *Rcett.*	populis *A²B*	populo *A^v*	
253	latii *Rcett.*		latia *MZAB*	
264–309	*folium 22 ll. recto uerso continens, om. R*			
313	catonum *RE*	catonis *Z²ABCGWJ*	catones *MZQYUVPA^v*	
317	dimittet *Rcett.*		dimittit *AZABE*	

Appendix IX

349	deerunt *RQEUVW et* derunt *MZABE*	desunt *YPJ*
359	scilicet *RMYUEWJ*	si licet *ZABQGVP*
408	monocci *R*	menoeci *rell.*
419	lates tunc *RYGUVEWJ*	late tunc Z^2MQP *et* latunc *A et* latet tunc A^2B *et* laete tunc *Z*
424	remisque *RQGVEWJ*	remusque *MZABYU et* romusque *P*
442	tonse *Rcett.A^v*	tonsa Z^2AB *et* tonsas *Z*
446	et taranis *Rcett, et* et caranis *G* et tarani *AB*	et terranis *P*
483	a gentibus *Rcett. et* gentibus A^v	agitantibus *MZAB*
490	relinquant *Rcett. et* reliquant *Q*	reliquent *ZAB*
600	referunt *RG²*	reuocant *rell.*
652	accenderet *Rcett.*	accenderat *MZAB*
667	manus *RYW*	manu *rell.*
670	dux *RMW*	duc *rell.*
679	terra *Rcett.*	terram *ABME*
684	lagaei *Rcett.*	laegei Z^2AB *et* laege★★ *Z et* laege★ *M et* lege *P*

Book 2

5	uisum *Rcett.*	uisu Z^2AB
30	pectora *Rcett.*	pectore *MZAB*
31	lumine RZ^2W	limine *rell.*
45	sortes *R*	sortis *rell.*
51	sueuos *Rcett.*	suebos *ZAB*
71	laxaeque *Rcett.*	laxere *AB*
106	limine *Rcett.*	lumine *MZABW*
117	nedum *RMQGUVPJ*	necdum *ZABEW* (dum *Y*)
120	carpentis *Rcett.*	carpentes Z^2AB
133	pararent *RV et* parerent *MZ*	paterent *rell.*
135	quod *RMZCPA^v*	quot Z^2ABrell.
151	fratres *Rcett.*	fratris *ABY*
189	informes *Rcett.*	informis *MZAB*
192	ut *Rcett.*	aut *ZAB et* at *M*

Readings Originating in R

221	his sulla *Rcett.* et sulla A^v	his illa *ZAB*		
253	fames *Rcett.*	famis Z^2ABM		
264	si *RM*	se *rell.*		
289	ualet *R(?)U*	uelit *rell.*		
312	luatur *Rcett.*	leuatur *MZAB*		
321	nunc *RP*	hunc *rell.*		
336	cineresque *Rcett.*	cinerisque *MZAB*		
349	proprior *RMZAA^v*	propior A^2*Brell.*		
361	flammea *Rcett.*A^v	flamina Z^2A^2M et flammina *A* et flumina *B*		n.l. *Z*
364	suppara *Rcett.*A^v	suppera *ZAB*		
370	cogere *R*	colere Z^2AM et colore	coiere A^2*Brell.* *Z*	
395	partes *RQGUVEWJ*	partis *MZABYP*		
398	propriusque *RMZCW*	propiusque *rell.*		
401	aequora *Rcett.*	aequore *MZAB*		
419	casuros *Rcett.*	casurus *MZAB*		
431	pinniferus *R*	piniferus *rell.*	penniferis *M(?)ZAB*	
	omnis *Rcett.* et omnes A^v et hominis *M*	omnem Z^2AB		
445	populetur *Rcett.* et populitur *M*	populentur *ZABW*		
468	archte *R* et arce *rell.*	arca *AB*		
476	uacaret *RYUVPW*	uocaret *MZABQGEJ*		
503	uacantem *Rcett.*A^v	uacante Z^2AB	uocante *MZ*	
511	timeri *Rcett.*	timere *MZAB*	tenere *G*	
525	munus *Rcett.*A^v et manus *P*	minas *MZAB*		
537	priores *Rcett.*	prioris *MZABG*		
560	ducet *R* et docet *B*	uocet *rell.*		
561	duxerit *R*	dux sit *MQGUVEWJ*	duxit *ZABYP*	
576	tuli *Rcett.*	tulit *MZABE(?)*		
585	phasidos *Rcett.*	phasidis *MZAB*		
587	flectente syene *Rcett.*A^v	flectentis yenen *MZAB*		
588	tethynque *Rcett.*	tetimque *MZABEWJ*		
589	hesperius *Rcett.*	hesperium *MZAB*		
613	hanc	hac Z^2AB	hinc *UVE RMZCQYGPWJ*	
614	producit *Rcett.*	producet *MZAB*		

Appendix IX

624	epidamnus *RYE*	epidamnos *MZABCPW*	epidaurus *GVJ et* epidaunos *QU*	
637	relinquas *Rcett*.	relinquis *ZAB*		
638	uagantis *Rcett*.	uacantis *MZABY*		
655	habent *Rcett.A*ᵛ	om. *AB*		
672	tales *RQYVWJ*	talis *MZABGUPE*		
673	ausus *Rcett*.	ausis *MZABPW*		
677	differret *RYUPW* et differet *MZA*ᵛ	deferret *QGVEJ*	defert *Z²AB*	
682	reseret *RCYGUVPEJA*ᵛ et referet *Z²AB*	referret *Q*	referat *Z et* reserat *M*	*n.l. W*

Book 3

8	cesserunt *Rcett*.	cessarunt *AB*		
23	en nupsit *RQGVJ*	innupsit *MZABYUPEW*		
33	pignora *Rcett*.	pignera *Z²AB*		
50	nec *RUVPJ*	neque *MZABQYGEW*		
68	superat *Rcett*.	superant *Z²ABM(?)Y*		
96	tam *Rcett*.	iam *MZAB* (non *G*)	*n.l. Q*	
108	uocis *Rcett*.	uoces *Z²ABP*		
113	possent *RUPJ*	possint *Z²ABQGVE*	possit *MZY*	*n.l. W*
135	polluit *RMZE*	polluet *Z²ABrell.*		
158	philippi *Rcett.A*ᵛ	philippo *ZAB*		
173	parnasusque *RQYGUVWJ*	parnasosque *MZABPE*		
174	coire *RPA*ᵛ	coluere *MZAB*	coiere *rell.*	
185	gnosasque *RMYGUW*	gnososque *ZABQVPEJ*		
186	corna *R*	coturna *M(?)ZAY*	cortina *A²Brell.*	
203	moesaque *R*	moesaeque *MZAB*	moesiaque *rell.* et misiaque *V*	
212	hominibus *RPJ et* nominibus *W* et ominibus *YGUV*	omnibus *M(?)ZABQE*		
234	est *om. RU*	habent *rell.*		
251	mergi *Rcett*.	mergit *MZABE*	*u.o. Y*	
244	ante 254 rep. *Z²AB*			
263	undas *RMZYEW*	undis *Z²ABQGUVPJ*		

Readings Originating in R

286	perses *RMQGUVWJ et* perse *P*	persis *ZABYE*	
308	fata *Rcett.*	fama *Z²AB*	
320	tonantem *Rcett.Aᵛ*	sonantem *ZAB*	
328	ullis *RMZYGP*	illis *Z²ABQUVEWJ*	
355	gratia *RM*	graia *rell.* (fata *G*)	
366	bellant *R et* bellantes *MZ*	rebellant *Z²ABQYGUPEWJ et* rebellent *V*	
382	diuerso uastos *RC(?)QYUVPEWJ*	diuersos uasto *MZG*	diuersos uastos *Z²AB*
417	fama *Rcett.*	fame *AB*	
421	dracones *Rcett.*	draconis *MZAB*	
456	aequantes *RQYWJ*	aequantis *Z²ABrell. et* aequatis *MZ*	
	turbes *R*	turres *ABMYGUVEWJ*	turris *MZQP*
479	laborem *RZP*	labor est *rell.*	
503	ne *RC et* n̄ *Y*	et *A²B et* set *M*	nec *rell.*
532	robur *Rcett.*	robor *MZABU*	
550	abeunt *Rcett.*	habeunt *MZAB*	
584	diducto *Rcett.*	deducto *MZAB*	
593	pelagus *R(?)Y*	pelagi *MZP*	pelago *Z²ABrell.*
607	dolorem *Rcett.Aᵛ et* dolorum *G*	dolore *MZAB*	
609	pectore *RQYVWAᵛ*	pectine *MZABGUPEJ*	
613	diriguitque *RGUVE et* dirigitque *J*	deriguitque *MZABQYPW*	
617	abscisa *Rcett.*	abscissa *ZABYP*	
620	perstat *Rcett.*	perstant *MZAB*	
629	sed *RYGUVPJ*	at *QW*	et *MZABE*
639	cadit *Rcett.*	cadet *MZAB*	
663	concurrit *Rcett.*	cucurrit *MZAB*	
664	pressarent *RQ*	prenserent *rell.*	
674	sidentia *Rcett.Aᵛ*	sedentia *MZAB*	
678	dum *Rcett.Aᵛ*	cum *MZAB*	
683	faciles *Rcett.*	facilis *MZABU*	
707	multus *Rcett.*	multos *MZAB*	
731	cadens *Rcett.Aᵛ*	cadis *MZAB*	
735	oculos *Rcett.Aᵛ*	oculis *M(?)ZAB*	
749	polluerat *RQVW*	polluerit *MZABYGUPEJ*	

Appendix IX
Book 4

9	uectonesque *RUEW*		uettonesque *rell.*	
39	in tergum *Rcett.A*ᵛ		integrum *ZABPW*	
45	gyro *Rcett.A*ᵛ		cyro *ZAB*	
172	est *Rcett.*		est *om. Z²ABE*	
178	admonet *Rcett.*		admouet *ZAB*	
202	iactant *Rcett.A*ᵛ	iectant *Z²AB*		luctant *MZ*
228	nefando *Rcett.A*ᵛ		nefandus *MZAB*	
246	complexu *Rcett.*		complexus *AB*	
265	nec *Rcett.*		ne *ZAB*	
276	en sibi uilis *Rcett.A*ᵛ		ensibilis *MZG et* ensiuilis *Z²AB*	
317	quos *Rcett.A*ᵛ		quis *ABM(?)*	
318	medullae *RQE(?)*		medulla *rell.*	
342	nouos *Rcett.*		nouus *MZAB*	
	gerit *Rcett.*		geret *MZAB*	
349	nos *Rcett.*		non *AB*	
352	aperimus *Rcett.A*ᵛ		asperrimus *MZA* (asprimus *B*)	
452	illa *Rcett.*		illam *MZABP*	
486	ciuis *RMZ*		ciues *rell.*	
502	obsessis *Rcett.*		obsessu *AB*	
520	sic *Rcett.*		si *ZABE*	
565	egere *R et* ex *A*	exegere *A²Brell.*		exegre (g *in ras. Z²*)*Z* u. *in ras. M²*
577	manu *Rcett.A*ᵛ		manus *MZABQ*	
579	nec *RM*		ne *rell.*	
593	gigantes *RUVPEWJ*		gigantas *MZABQYG*	
610	terras *Rcett.A*ᵛ		terram *Z²AB*	
612	proiecit *RZ²cett. et* prolegit *MZ*	proieiecit *A²B et* proleiecit *A*		
613	libyci *RMZAGVPJ*	libyco *A²BQYEW*		libyae *U*
634	aruis *RMZA*ᵛ*C(?)*		undis *rell.*	
636	conflixere *Rcett.*	conflexere *AB*		confixere *M*
645	tactae factae *R*	factae *MZAB*		tactae *YUVPEWJA*ᵛ *et* tacitae *QG*
662	geret *R et* gerat *cett.*		regat *GUP*	
672	gladibus *RMZ*		gadibus *Z²ABrell.* (gradibus *EW*)	
679	mixta *R et* mixte *MZ*		mixti *rell.*	

Readings Originating in R

700	muna *R*	munia *QUWJ*	munera *MZABYGVPE(?)*
705	pugnae *RZ²AY*		pugna *A²Brell.*
745	deiecit *Rcett.A*ᵛ		proiecit *Z²AB*
781	constrinxit *Rcett.*		constrixit *AYU et* constricxit *B*
805	urbi *Rcett.A*ᵛ		urbis *Z²AB et* urbes *MZ*
811	silere *Rcett.*		sileri *Z²AB*

Book 5

26	sequetur *Rcett. et* sequatur *P*	sequentur *Z²ABG*	
37	en *Rcett.NA*ᵛ	et *M(?)ZABY(?)*	
86	nomen *RMZ*	numen *rell.*	
89	mundique *RQYUVWJ*	mundoque *MZABGE*	n.l. *P*
93	sit *RG*	fit *rell.*	
94	qui *R(?)MZ*	quae *rell.*	
96	conexa *Rcett.A*ᵛ	conuexa *MZABW*	
	tonantis *R(?)MZ*	tonanti *rell.*	
100	uaporat *Rcett.*	uaporant *AB*	
111	non ullo *RQYGUVWJ et* non nullo *Z²AB*	non nulla *MZ et* non ulla *E*	n.l. *P*
112	maiore *Rcett.*	maiora *MZABP*	
115	uates *Rcett.*	uatis *MZAB*	
118	quippe *Rcett.A*ᵛ	quique *MZAB*	
121	immotas *RUEW et* immotus *P*	immotos *rell.*	
130	parat *Rcett.*	paret *Z²AB*	
131	trahit *Rcett.*	tradit *MZAB*	l.o. *Q*
	parnasus *RYGUVEWJ et* parnasas *MZ*	parnasos *Z²ABP*	
133	in deuia *Rcett.A*ᵛ	in debita *Z²ABM et* indubita *Z*	
141	confusae *Rcett. et* confussae *AB*	confessae *MZ*	
157	prodiderat *RQGENA*ᵛ	prodiderant *rell.*	
	tripidas *Rcett. et* tripidas *AB*	trepidos *MZ*	
170	uittasque *RQYGVEJ*	uitasque *MZABUPW*	
180	mittitur *R*	nititur *rell.*	
194	ingentes *Rcett.*	ingentis *MZAB*	
219	uidit *Rcett.A*ᵛ	uadit *MZAB*	

Appendix IX

250	non e *Rcett.*	nonne Z^2AB (non *MZ*)	
259	ipsa *Rcett.*	ipse *MZAB*	
261	effudere *Rcett.*	effundere *AB*	
279	anima *Rcett.*	animam *MZAB*	
284	ignaros *Rcett.*	ignaras *AB*	
	ad quae *Rcett.*	atque *MZAB*	
312	omne *Rcett.*	omnem *ABJ*	
313	disce sine *Rcett.*	disces in *MZAB*	
317	uultu *RCcett.*	uultum *MZAB*	
329	uictoria *Rcett.*	uictoriam *MZABJ*	
333	senes *Rcett.*	senex *MZAB*	
350	non *RMZQYUVPJ*	nec Z^2ABGEW	
355	dextra *R et* dextras *rell.A*^{v}	dextris *AB*	
379	delmatico *RMZQYUPW*	dalmatico $Z^2ABGVEJ$	
383	summum ... summo ... honori summo ... honore honorem *MZP* $Z^2ABQGVE$ *RYUWJN*		
390	imperii *Rcett.NA*^{v}	imperio *MZAB*	
407	brundisii *Rcett.*	brundisi *AB*	
420	ne *Rcett.*	nec A^2BMZP	l.o. *A*
421	iactatis *RYUVWJA*$^v U^2$	iactantes $Z^2ABQGPE$ *et* ictantis *MZ*	n.l. *U*
436	bosphoros *R(?)MZU*	bosphorus *rell.*	
449	hic *RMZQGPJ*	hinc $Z^2ABYUVEW$	
489	percussi *Rcett.*	percussit *Z(A)B*	
501	iussi *Rcett.*	iussit *Z(A)B*	
512	transsiluit *Rcett.*	tam siluit *MZ(A)B*	
	quod *Rcett.*	quo *MZ(A)B*	
519	quassantia *Rcett.*	causantia *(A)B*	
531	caesarea *Rcett.*	caesaream *(A)B*	
534	hesperiam *Rcett.* hisperiam *MZ*	speriam *(A)B*	
541	rutilas *Rcett. et* rutilans *G*	rutilos $Z^2(A)B$	
549	nota *RCcett.*	notam *MZAB*	
552	qui *Rcett. et* quid *MZ* qua Z^2AB	quod *Q*	
561	ad *Rcett.*	at *ZAB*	
573	hesperias *Rcett.*	hesperies *ZA et* speries *B*	
617	ullo *RQYGUVEW*	illo *MZACPJ* (illa *B*)	

Readings Originating in R

633	motaque *Rcett.*		mutaque Z^2AB *et* mataque Z	
647	puppim *RGEJ*		puppem *rell.*	d. M
649	erigit *Rcett.*		eregit ZAB	d. M
670	desinit *R et* desint $A^2Bcett.$		desit MZA	
677	tacta *Rcett.*		iacta Z^2AB	d. M
682	quo *Rcett.A^v*		quod ZAB	d. M
697	quod *RQUPWJ*	quae *V*	quo $ZABYGE$	d. M
708	consertis *Rcett.*		consorti A *et* consortis A^2Z *et* consortes B	d. M
751	quaterent *RVPA^{v}W^2*	quatient *MZAB*	quatiunt *QYGUEJ*	n.l. W
759	uelim *Rcett.A^v*		uelint *MZAB*	
779	euentus *Rcett.*		uentus A^2B	
782	belli *RPWErl. 304A^v*		bella *rell.*	n.l. Q
801	carinae *RQYGVEWJ*		carina *MZABUP*	

Book 6

7	casum *RQGUVPEWJ*	casus *MZ*	cassum Z^2ABCY	
11	uidet *Rcett.*		uidit *MZAB*	
48	attollat *Rcett.SA^v*		attollit *AB*	
57	latis *Rcett.SA^v*		latus *MZAB*	
62	libycaeque *Rcett.*		libyaeque *AB*	
65	medium *RM*	medio *ZAB*	mediae *YGUPEWJA^v et* medies *Q et* mediis *V*	
68	unda *Rcett.*		unde *ABM*	
76	moenia *Rcett.*		ad moenia Z^2AB	
80	ducis *RMZQYVJ*		duces $Z^2ABGUPEW$	
81	gramina *Rcett.A^v*		pabula Z^2AB	
90	nessis *RCQYGUE et* nesis *MZABYW*		nessus *VJ* (nephas *W*)	
94	pati *RZ^{2}QGUVPEJA^v*		patens *MZA^{2}BYW et* patiens *A*	
109	surgentibus *RQYVE*		turgentibus *MZABGUPWJ*	
118	claustris *Rcett.A^v*		castris *MZABYW* (caustris *P*)	
134	peribat *Rcett.*		peribant *AB*	

Appendix IX

136	quassae *Rcett.*		quase *MZAB*	
141	auferret *Rcett. et* auferre *MZ*		aut ferret Z^2AB	
144	in plebe *Rcett.*		implere Z^2AB	
157	nos *Rcett.*A^v		non *MZABC*	
159	negauit *Rcett.*		negabit *MZABP*	
178	crinesque *Rcett.*		crinemque Z^2AB	
256	nudo *RUP*(?)		nudum *rell.*	
279	elatus *Rcett.*		elatos *ZAB*	
281	ut *RZCVWA*^{v}		et $Z^2A^2BMQYGUPEJ$ (ut et *A*)	
293	aetnaeis *Rcett.*		hennaeis *MZABE*	
294	notum *RYP*		noto *rell.*	
321	dimisso *RQGUVPJ*		demisso *MZABYEW*	
329	putet *Rcett.*		putat *MZABCE*	
	fatus *Rcett.*		factus *ZAB*	
330	conduxit *RYUEW*	condixit *MZABPN*	conuertit *QGVJ*	
337	ad *RGP*		at *rell.*	
350	emathis *Rcett.*A^v		emathiis *ZABE et* ematheis *Y*	
366	euuenos *RMZYGU et* ehuuenos *A*^{v}	euhenus *V et* euenus *P*	euenos Z^2ABEW *et* euneos *QJ*	
367	malliacas *RYGUW*		maliacas *rell.*	
374	melasque *RMYGUW*	malasque *ZABCE*	melaxque *QVPJ*	
389	oetaeo *Rcett.*		oeta (*A*)*B*	
393	sidere *Rcett.*		silide (*A*)*B*	
406	populos *Rcett. et* populo *P*		populus *MZAB*	
410	inmis *R*		inmisit *rell.*	
412	incumbena *RYW*		incurrens *rell.*	
413	locarunt *Rcett.*		locauerunt (*A*)*B*	
450	l.o. (*A*)*B*			
450	magnorum *RMZ*		magorum *rell.*	
451	abducit *RMZQYEWJ*	abducet *GUVP*	obducit (*A*)*B*	
	alienis *Rcett.*		alienus (*A*)*B*	
465	nunc *Rcett.*		tunc Z^2(*A*)*B*	
481	axis *RMZ*	axes Z^2(*A*)*BGEWJ*	axem *YUVP* (agger *Q*)	
508	erichtho *RYGUVWJ*		erecto *MZABCQPE*	

Readings Originating in R

522	auras *Rcett.*		aures *MZAB*	
532	loetum *RYJ*	lectum *Z²rell.V²*	lecto *MZ*	*n.l. V*
543	nocentis *R*		nocentes *rell.* (iacentis *MZ*)	
553	raptura *Rcett.*		rapture *ZABQP*	*n.l. MG*
557	funereae *Rcett.*		funerea *ZA et* (funere *B*)	*n.l. MU*
558	si *R*	sin *N*	sic *rell.*	
565	fingens *RGUEWJ*		figens *MZABQYVP*	
568	infudit *Rcett.*		infundit *MZAB*	
629	leto *Rcett. et* leta *Z*		letos *Z²AB et* lit★s *Aᵛ*	
683	herbas *RMZYGVJ*		herbis *Z²ABQUPEWN*	
711	parete precanti *Rcett.*		arepte praecanti *Z²AB et* parate peccanti *Z*	
719	leuauit *Rcett.*		leuabit *MZAB*	
725	ericto *RYGVWJ*		erecto *Z²ABQUPE et* electo *MZ*	
747	erynen *Rcett.*		erynae *Z²AB*	
748	tenet *Rcett.*		tenent *MZAB*	
772	duraeque *Rcett.Aᵛ*		duraque *ZABQ*	
775	quo *Rcett.*		quod *MZAB*	
776	fletu *Rcett.Aᵛ et* flectu *M*		flactu *Z et* flatu *Z²AB*	
799	inertis *Rcett.*		inertes *MZAB*	
826	ericto *RYGVWJ*		erecto *Z²ABQUE et* erec★to *Z*	
				n.l. MP

Book 7

43	edere *RQYGVEJ et* ede *W et* odere *U*	sedere *MZABP*
57	trahi *Rcett.*	trahit *MZAB*
80	campo *Rcett.*	campos *MZAB*
100	sterni *Rcett. et* sternit *MZ*	streni *Z²AB*
115	quot *Rcett.Aᵛ*	quod *MZABP*
120	populis *Rcett.*	populus *AB*
139	cautibus *Rcett.*	cotibus *Z²ABW*
152	thessala *Rcett.*	thessela *MZAB*
160	sulphure *Rcett.*	sulpore *MZAB*
161	exanime *RU*	examine *rell.*

Appendix IX

192	euganeo *Rcett.A*ᵛ	euganeos *MZAB*	*d. J*
199	lumen *RUVP*	numen *rell.*	
205	summos *Rcett. et* sumnos *A*ᵛ	summus *MZAB*	
206	uacauit uacabit *Z²AB et* *RYGUVPM²* uocabit *Z*	uacabat *QEW*	*n.l. MJ*
211	mouebunt *Rcett.A*ᵛ *et* uouebunt *Y*	monebunt *Z²AB et* manebunt *U*	
234	fuso *Rcett.*	fusa *MZAB*	
240	regni *RZcett.A*ᵛ *et* regnum *M*	mundi *Z²AB*	
255	promissam *Rcett.A*ᵛ	promissa *MZAB*	
	mini *R et* eminit *B et* meminit *A*	memini *rell.A*ᵛ	
260	est *om. RMZ*	habent *rell.*	
263	mutato *Rcett.*	motato *MZAB*	
272	aut *Rcett.A*ᵛ	et *Z²ABWJ*	
273	barbaries *Rcett.A*ᵛ *et* barbarie *Q*	barbaria *MZAB*	
280	gentes *RMZQYUPEWJ*	gentis *Z²ABGV*	
	triumphum *RQYGEWA*ᵛ	triumphi *MZABUVPJ*	
286	quorum *RMZYGVWJ*	quarum *Z²ABCQUPE*	
297	haud *Rcett. et* haut *EW*	aut *MZA²B*	
310	respexerit *Rcett.*	respexerat *Z²ABM et* resperat *Z*	
	hoste *RYGPEJ*	hostem *MZABQUVW*	
319	ciuis *Rcett.*	ciues *MZAB*	
349	iubet *Rcett.A*ᵛ	iuuet *AB*	
367	exigit at *Rcett.*	exegit ad *MZAB*	
387	haeae *RA*ᵛ *et* hae *GUVEJ et* ne *P*	haec *MZABQYW*	
402	uincto *RQYGPEJ et* uicto *MZ*	iuncto *ABUVW*	
419	qua *RM et* quo *Z*	quae *rell.*	
421	armis *RZQUEWA*ᵛ	annis *Z²ABMYGVPJ*	
440	legum *Rcett.A*ᵛ	regum *Z²ABG*	
445	quos *RQYGUEJA*ᵛ quo *MZAB*		quod *VPW*
451	fieri et *R et* firet *C* feriet *MZABQYE*		feriat *GUVPWJ*
462	tempus quo noscere possent *RZQYGVPEJA*ᵛ	uultusque agnoscere quaerunt *Z²ABUW*	
	VVLTVSQVONO *S*		*n.l. M*
471	crastine *RYUVPJ*	crastine *MZABQGEWS*	
536	fundunt *RQGVEWSM²*	fundent *Z²ABYUP et* fundet *Z*	
			n.l. M, d. J
538	totos *Rcett.*	totus *MZAB*	*d. J*

Readings Originating in R

569	sisic *R et sic A*ᵛ	si *rell.*	d. *J*
571	est *Rcett.*	et *Z²AB*	d. *J*
575	confundere *RQVEA*ᵛ	contundere *rell.*	d. *J*
579	sit *Rcett.*	scit *ZAB*	d. *J*
596	procumbat *Rcett.A*ᵛ	procumbant *MZAB*	d. *J*
601	illo *Rcett.A*ᵛ *et ille U*	ullo *Z²AB*	d. *J*
611	generoque *Rcett.*	generique *Z²AB*	d. *J*
615	morior *RZYE*	moriar *rell.*	d. *J*
623	qui p. *RMZcett.*	quis p. *Z²ABQE*	d. *J*
634	quod *Rcett.A*ᵛ	quot *Z²ABE(?)*	
643	pauidi *RUW*	pauide *rell. et* prouide *P*	
670	duci *Rcett. et* ducis *P*	ducti *AB*	
690	perstat *RMZYGPW et* praestat *AB*	perstet *QUVEJ*	
722	tumulo *RQGW*	cumulo *rell.*	
732	reuocent *Rcett.*	reuocet *A²B*	
	pauorem *Rcett. et* fauorem *P*	pauore *ZAB*	
761	uacuumque *RWJ* caesumque *ZQYGE et* stratumque *UPM²V²*		
	caecumque *B*		n.l. *MAV*
773	terroris *Rcett.*	erroris *MZ et* cerroris *B et* orroris *A*	
812	hoc *RZ*	hos *cett.*	
816	sunt *RMZQYGVEJA*ᵛ	eunt *Z²ABUPW*	
	ibis *RMZYGUPWJA*ᵛ	ibit *Z²ABQVE*	
828	domosque *Rcett.*	domusque *ZABP*	
842	feras *Rcett.A*ᵛ	ferus *Z²AB*	
847	tantum *Rcett.*	tanto *Z²ABCQE*	
861	arator *RMZYGUJ*	aratro *Z²ABQVPEW*	
868	belli *Rcett.A*ᵛ	bellis *MZAB*	
871	pachyni *Rcett.A*ᵛ	pachini *MZAB*	

Book 8

3	negante *R(?)Z²ᵃ* negantem *YGUVPEWJA*ᵛ	negenti *Z²ᵇABM*	u.o. *Z*, n.l. *Q*
23	factisque *RCV*	fatisque *rell.*	
59	clausit *RQYGVEWJ*	clusit *MZABUP*	
84	bello *Rcett.*	bella *MZAB*	

Appendix IX

108	confudit *Rcett*.		confundit *Z²ABPJ*	
141	nam *Rcett*.		nunc *Z²AB*	
142	sit *Rcett.A*ᵛ		scit *ZAB*	
154	dimittere *RYGUVPWJ*		demittere *MZABQE*	
177	surgit *RQYGPEJ*		surget *MZABUVW*	
179	descendit *RQYGUVPJ*		descendet *MZABEW*	
181	tendit *RMQYGVPJ*		tendet *Z²ABUEW et* tendat *Z*	
192	portum *Rcett*.		portus *Z²AB*	
195	asinae *Rcett*.		sasinae *A²BGP*	
203	procella *Rcett*.		procellas *ZAB*	
204	ad litore *R et* ad litora *B*	ab litore *QYEJ*	a litore *MZAGUVPW*	
224	discurrere *RPW*		decurrere *Z²AMQYGVE et* decurre *ZBUJ*	
244	ephesumque *RQVEW et* efferumque *B*		ephesonque *MZAYGUPJ*	
268	nequeam *Rcett.A*ᵛ		nequem *MZB* (nequam *A*)	
298	pellaeas *Rcett*.		pelaeas *AB et* palaeas *MZ*	*l.o. Q*
312	uulgati *Rcett.A*ᵛ		uulgantis *AB et* uulgatis *MZ*	*l.o. Q*
326	concurrent *Rcett*.		concurrunt *MZAB*	
351	quam *Rcett*.		qua *Z²AB*	
354	tantis *RMZ*		tanti *rell*.	
360	lacesset *Rcett*.		lacessit *Z²ABCWJ*	
365	tempore *RC*		teporem *rell*. (temporum *P*)	
377	illis *Rcett..A*ᵛ		illi *Z²AB*	
385	uirorum est *RQGUVPEW*		uirorum *MZABYJ*	
412	non nulli *RM*		non ulli *rell*.	
424	arctoum *Rcett*.		arcto uel *ZAB*	
425	imperii *Rcett.A*ᵛ		imperti *M*(?)*ZAB*	
429	eat *Rcett*.		ea *Z²AB*	
430	possim *RZ²cett*.	possi *A et* poss *B et* possit *MZ*	possem *A*ᵛ	
431	araxen *RZ²AQUVPEW*		araxem *A²BYGJ et* araxe *MZ*	
463	casium *RP et* cassum *GUPJ*		gratum *MZABQYVEW*	
475	acoreus *Rcett*.		acoreos *A²B et* acureos *MZAP*	
525	ait *RZ*		agit *rell*.	
539	exultat *RQVE*		excurrit *MZABYGUPWJ*	

Readings Originating in R

567	uetat *RGPW et* uetas *Y*		uetct *MZABQUVEJ*	
	externas *Rcett.*		externis *ABJ*	
576	letumque *Rcett.*		letum *MZABW*	
629	spargant *Rcett.*		spargunt *AB*	
660	arcessere *RFQYPEW* arcersere *MZAB*		accersere *GUVJ*	
681	manu est *Rcett.*		manu *ZAB*	
696	seriemque *Rcett.*		sertemque *M(?)ZAB*	
734	ignes *Rcett.A*ᵛ	ignis *Z²AB*	ignem *FE*	*l.o. Q*
744	cremantis *Rcett.A*ᵛ		cremantes *Z²AB*	
772	busti	busto *FQE*	buste *AB*	
	RMZYGUVPWJ			
779	praemissa *RQYGUJ*		promissa *MZABFVPEW*	
784	in *RZF et* im *P*	sis *U*	i *Z²ABMQYGVEWJ*	
788	restinguit *RMZcett.*		restringuit *ABF*	
792	semiusto *RCQGPE*		semusto *MZABYUVWJ*	
848	mouenti *Rcett. et* mouentis *P*		mouente *MZABF*	
861	angustis *R et* angustus *AB*		angustius *rell.*	
870	quam sit *R*	qua sit *rell. et* quassit *U*	quas et *MZF*	

Book 9

3	semiustaque *RMZF*		semustaque *rell.*	
12	miratus *RMZAFVEWJ et*		miratur *A²BQYGU*	
	miratos *P*			
29	ille *RZFQUVPEW*	illa *Z²AB*	ipse *MYGJA*ᵛ	
	u.o. R	suae *MZABYUVPJ*	sua *CQGEWA*ᵛ	
104	potui *RMZFQUVPEW*		potuit *Z²ABYGJA*ᵛ	
120	timore *RMZcett.*		timori *Z²AB*	
138	deformia *RZ²W et* deforma *AB*		sublimia *Zrell.A*ᵛ	
261	uaganti *RJ*	uacanti *rell.*	uacante *QG*	
269	putet *Rcett.*		putat *ZAB*	
271	philippis *Rcett.*		philippos *Z²AB*	
288	phrygii *RMQYGUVPEW et*		tum si *Z²ABJ*	
	phygii *Z*			
295	serieque *RMYUVPEW*		seriemque *ZABQGJ*	
369	attigit *Rcett.*		attingit *AB*	
386	ueniant *RQYGUVEWJ*		uenient *Z²ABMP*	*l.o. Z*

Appendix IX

394	meliore *Rcett*.		meliora *AB*	
405	turbam *RGUVW et* tubam *MP*		turba *ZABQYEJ*	
406	pauentes *RZQU*		calentes *Z²ABMYGVPEWJ*	
412	at *Rcett*.		aut *ABE*	
419	descendit *RVW*		discedit *rell*.	
421	sed et *Rcett*.		sed *ZAB*	
424	non *RMQGPWJ*		neque *ZABY et* nec *UPE*	
440	rura *Rcett*.		rara *Z²AB*	
456	flexum *Rcett*.		flexus *ZAB*	
457	pendet *Rcett*.		pendit *ZAB*	
471	quia *Rcett*.		qui *Z²AB*	
477	dimissa *RYGVJ*		demissa *Z²AMQUEW et* demassa *B* *l.o. ZP*	
549	hortatu *RW et* hortatur *MP*		orator *Z et* ortator *Z²A et* hortatos *A²B et* hortator *QYGUVEJAᵛ*	
550	sors *Rcett*.		fors *Z²AYG et* frons *B*	
575	egit *RZ*		eget *Z²ABrell*.	
605	quam *RYGVWJ*		qua *MZABQUPE*	
617	haut si *RP*		hausit *rell*.	
686	ascenderet *R et* ascenderit *A²B*	scenderit *ZA et* scinderit *Aᵛ*	scinderet *rell. et* scanderet *W*	
692	solum *RZQYGVEWJAᵛ*		polum *Z²ABMUP*	
718	torrida *Rcett.Aᵛ*		horrida *ZAB*	
774	quantum *RZYGWJ*		quantus *Z²ABMQUVPE*	
775	terras *RQYGUVEWJ*		terra *MZABP*	
818	descendis *Rcett. et* discendis *ZAB*		descendit *GP*	
833	tutus *Rcett*.		cuius *AB*	
848	dii clamant *RYUVPW et* di clamant *QGEJAᵛ*	declamant *ZAB*	dii clamabant *M*	
914	expugant *R et* expugnant *B*	expurgat *Z²AMYVW et* expugnat *P*	expurgant *ZGUEJAᵛ*	
982	non *RQGJ*		ne *rell. et* nec *P*	
1040	putas *R et* putans *YGWJAᵛ*	potens *MZABQUE*	potest *VGᵛ*	*l.o. P*
1083	hospitium est *RW et* hospitium et *A²B*		hospitium *rell*.	

Readings Originating in R
Book 10

47	proprius *RZ*	propeus *M et* propeius *P*	propius *Z²ABrell.*	
56	biremi *Rcett.A*ᵛ	biremis *Z²ABY et* biremus *Z*	triremi *J*	
75	curas *RG*	curis *rell.*		
99	iube *Rcett.*	iubet *ZAB*		
		post 107 *desinit P*		
126	licia *Rcett.*	licea *MZAB*		
210	hunc *Rcett.A*ᵛ	nunc *ZAB*		
297	ammonuitque *R*	ammouitque *M et* admouitque *G*	amouitque *rell.*	
316	moturum *Rcett. et* moturam *Z*	moturus *Z²AB*		l.o. *M*
320	aquas *R et* aquae *Z*	aquis *rell.*		
337	ultricesque *Rcett.*	uictricesque *ZAB*		
356	pharos *Rcett.A*ᵛ	foras *AB*		
426	manus *RZQGVW*	manu *Z²ABMYUEJ*		
448	aetnam *Rcett.*	aetnae *ZABM(?)*		
455	fixo *Rcett.A*ᵛ	fixa *ZAB*		
459	lumine *RM* clauso *Rcett.*	limine *rell.* cluso *ZAB*		
469	saeuus *R(?)M*	saeuos *rell.*		
		post 475 *desinit A*		
487	audacie *R*	audantia *B et* audatiam *Z*	audaci *rell.*	